D1583888

SPORT:
A STAGE FOR LIFE

SPORT:
A STAGE FOR LIFE

HOW TO CONNECT WITH THE TOUCHSTONES OF
ELITE PERFORMANCE AND PERSONAL FULFILLMENT

**Cristiana Pinciroli
in collaboration with
Pedro Pinciroli Júnior**

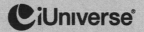

SPORT: A STAGE FOR LIFE
HOW TO CONNECT WITH THE TOUCHSTONES OF ELITE
PERFORMANCE AND PERSONAL FULFILLMENT

Copyright © 2022 Cristiana Pinciroli.

All rights reserved. No part of this book may be used or reproduced by any means, graphic, electronic, or mechanical, including photocopying, recording, taping or by any information storage retrieval system without the written permission of the author except in the case of brief quotations embodied in critical articles and reviews.

iUniverse books may be ordered through booksellers or by contacting:

iUniverse
1663 Liberty Drive
Bloomington, IN 47403
www.iuniverse.com
844-349-9409

Because of the dynamic nature of the Internet, any web addresses or links contained in this book may have changed since publication and may no longer be valid. The views expressed in this work are solely those of the author and do not necessarily reflect the views of the publisher, and the publisher hereby disclaims any responsibility for them.

Any people depicted in stock imagery provided by Getty Images are models, and such images are being used for illustrative purposes only.
Certain stock imagery © Getty Images.

ISBN: 978-1-6632-3367-7 (sc)
ISBN: 978-1-6632-3368-4 (hc)
ISBN: 978-1-6632-3366-0 (e)

Library of Congress Control Number: 2021925215

Print information available on the last page.

iUniverse rev. date: 06/03/2022

For my daughters,
Alissa, Giorgia, and Olivia,
with all my love.

For all those pursuing
their dreams. May you nurture
your seeds of greatness along
every step of life's journey.

TESTIMONIALS

___

Ashleigh Johnson

Cristiana combines her personal story of life lessons and experiences with a genuine and dedicated interest in understanding the role and impact of sport on athletes throughout their lives. In this book, Cristiana recounts all of our stories as athletes at every level—from finding meaning and guidance to gathering the strength to push past boundaries both in sport and in life.

When she points to the importance of shared values and the role of family and an effective support system in a young athlete's life, I'm immediately drawn to reflect on the extensive support I myself received as a young athlete and am reminded of how that support emanates through my successes and sustains me when I fail.

This book is not only about the positive psychology of sport and how it has impacted Cristiana's life in and out of the water; it is also a guide to how we learn and can lead the next generation to make the same discoveries.

> —Ashleigh Johnson is an American two-time Olympic gold medalist in water polo (Rio 2016 and Tokyo 2020). She is considered by many to be the best goalkeeper in the world. In 2016, she became the first African American woman to make the US Olympic water polo team.

Kahena Kunze

In a way that is natural, honest, and straightforward, Cris and Pedro have managed to capture, in incredible detail, the inspiring journey of the high-performance athlete—sports lovers like us.

Thank you for including so many details that, in the end, make all the difference—not only in our professional lives but also in our relationships around the world.

Sport: A Stage for Life is a book I will always enjoy consulting, reading, and rereading—a sports bible.

—Kahena Kunze is a two-time Olympic gold medalist in sailing (Rio 2016 and Tokyo 2020). She has won her main tournaments with longtime companion Martine Grael. In 2021, they are ranked number one in the world in the 49er FX class by the International Sailing Federation.

Marcelo Huertas

In reading, you are taken on a virtual journey, immersed in the experiences of the authors and of other elite athletes as they describe the events that occurred in their lives and careers. The wealth of details enrich an approach that covers every aspect of training, behavioral and mental preparation, performance, family structure, and all the pillars that are key to the lives and careers of athletes, including the obstacles along the path that can often lead people to quit or lose focus.

It is, without doubt, a must-read for all those who aspire to live a fulfilling life and bring out the very best in themselves, as it illustrates how, behind every success story, there is a long path filled with setbacks, challenges, and moments of pain and glory. But if we pursue our goal with appreciation for everything we do, savoring every step of the daily routine, at the end of the journey lies a wonderful reward that will be worth every drop of sweat and dedication!

—Marcelo "Marcelinho" Tieppo Huertas is captain of the Brazilian national team, recognized as the best professional basketball player in Spain in 2021. He is a two-time Olympian and a former NBA player with the LA Lakers. He plays for Iberostar Tenerife in the Spanish Liga ACB.

FOREWORD

The authors of this book, Cristiana Pinciroli and her father, Pedro Pinciroli Júnior, are both well known for their accomplishments within the international water polo community. Pedro was a member of the Brazilian national team for fourteen years and competed at two Olympic Games. Cristiana followed in her father's wake, and she was acknowledged as one of the world's best water polo players before women's water polo became an Olympic sport. They were not highly paid professionals. They played for the love of the game and for the honor of their country. Less well known is how they used their athletic experiences to achieve success in their postathletic lives.

According to the Pincirolis, if those who participate in athletics view sport as a means and not an end, they have a wonderful chance to build a foundation for success and happiness in life. Sport provides a means to acquire physical development at a time when it is most needed; the opportunity to acquire instruction and training from knowledgeable and qualified men and women; a means to learn the importance of perseverance, persistence, and willpower; a means to acquire self-confidence and courage gained from training and competition; a means to learn firsthand how collaborating and cooperating with teammates can achieve greater goals than one can achieve alone; and a means to learn the importance of time management and many other skills.

In reading their story, I was reminded of an article written by US president John F. Kennedy for *Sports Illustrated* magazine back in 1960. Kennedy wrote, "The relationship between the soundness of the body and the activity of the mind is subtle and complex. Much is not yet understood. But we do know what the Greeks knew; that intelligence and skill can only function at the peak of their capacity when the body is healthy and strong; for physical fitness is not only one of the most important keys to a healthy body … it is the basis of dynamic and creative intellectual activity."

No idiot was ever a champion, but if the skills learned through sport are not used as a foundation for achieving excellence and happiness in life, then the athletic experience has been wasted. Unfortunately, many champions of sport have suffered while transitioning from being an active athlete to being a retired one. Like the NFL and NBA, the International Swimming Hall of Fame is filled with cautionary tales, but the oldest and perhaps most tragic story belongs to the sport of wrestling and Milo of Croton. Milo was a Greek wrestler whose career spanned from 536 to 520 BCE. He was a six-time Olympic champion, and he also won titles at every other major Greek games in between. His strength was legendary. It was said that as a young teenager, he wanted to become stronger, so his parents bought him a baby calf to lift and carry on his shoulders. The thought behind it was as the bull grew bigger and heavier, Milo would get used to the weight and become stronger over time. When the calf was fully grown, it was said Milo carried the bull to the slaughterhouse on his shoulders and allegedly ate all the meat from the bull in one day. It was also said that when the athletes were ritually paraded into the Olympic stadium, Milo would intimidate his opponents by carrying a full-grown bull around the track on his shoulders, slaughtering it, and eating the meat raw. He was a character right out of the WWF. But when Milo was finally defeated by a younger opponent, he fell into depression. One day, while walking through the woods, he came upon a withered tree into which wedges had been driven in order to split the trunk. He put his hands into the cleft and tried to finish the job, but his arms no longer possessed the strength of his younger self. As he tried to break the trunk, the wedges slipped out, and the tree trunk sprang back together, trapping his hands in an unbreakable grip. That night, he was devoured by wolves, which roamed the area in great numbers.

"What cry can be more contemptible than that of Milo of Croton?" wrote Cicero. "When he had grown old, he saw some athletes training on the track, looked at his own arms, wept and said, 'And these, indeed, are now dead.' Not so, you idiot. It is you who are dead, for your nobility came not from yourself but from your trunk and your arms."

While Milo was admired as a wrestler, he was also condemned as being contrary to Aristotle's *Nicomachean Ethics*, which sought a "golden mean" between two extremes, and the Greek ideal of *kalos kagathos*, of having both a noble mind and a healthy body.

In reading this book, I visualized Cristiana and her father, Pedro, as Circe, the goddess who guided Homer's Odysseus and his ship through the hazardous Strait of Messina, with its twin dangers of Scylla on the left and Charybdis on the right. On the port side of the ship in our example is the danger of focusing too much on academics and being physically weak. The hazard on the starboard is focusing too much on physical training and ignoring the academic. Depending upon physical gifts and opportunities at different ages, the Pincirolis provide sound advice to coaches, parents, executives, and athletes for veering their ship from side to side, without being consumed by either extreme, as the means of ensuring a successful, happy, and rewarding life.

—Bruce Wigo, JD
Member of International Society of Olympic Historians
Executive director of USA Water Polo, 1991–2003
International Swimming Hall of Fame president, 2005–2017

ACKNOWLEDGMENTS

I have long craved the opportunity to write this book with my father. From the outset I sensed it was destined to be a collaboration. It has been more work than I was expecting and more rewarding than I imagined.

None of this would have been possible without the expert contributions of a group that came together to share the stories and knowledge that went into creating this book.

I am grateful to Dr. Tal Ben-Sahar, my teacher and inspiration in the study of positive psychology and the science of happiness, who has contributed so much in helping me to refine my sense of purpose with my current career.

Special thanks to the Olympic and world champions, and other outstanding professionals from the world of sport, for sharing their personal experiences. You are all shining inspirations of those who have performed in life as you have in the sporting arena.

I would like to thank the coaches, mentors, and educators who have shared with me their beliefs and strategies for developing the best in each person, be it mental strength or technical ability: Sandy Nitta, Adam Krikorian, Ratko Rudic, and Frank Steel.

My thanks to Priscila Covre and Daniel Waismann, who have proved to be both resourceful researchers and great partners and who made our meetings a strategic moment in identifying the best way to voice our ideas. Thanks also to my friends who have devoted their time to offering new perspectives, information, and knowledge: Alexandra Araújo, Camila Pedrosa, Cristiana Conti, Giuseppe LaDelfa, Gisele Durazzo, Gustavo Sette da Rocha, Maria Eugenia Sosa Taborda, Marcelo Orticelli, Mariza Tieppo de Andrade, Montserrat Napolitano, Myriam Ortolan, Patricia Alessandri, and Wilma Gonçalves.

I would like to thank Roberta Landmann and Helena Brant Carvalho for creating sparks of inspiration through storytelling. Thanks as well to Giles, who went beyond translation, bringing suggestions and ideas duly adapted from the native language for English, while always retaining the meaning and interpretation of the original text.

I wish to extend my thanks to the iUniverse team for being my window to the readers and for offering their vast experience in editing, publishing, and communication.

I want to express my gratitude for the encouragement I have received from my family. My husband, Luis Carlos Pascual, has supported me in this endeavor through his bold ideas and challenges. My daughters—Alissa, Giorgia, and Olivia—have accompanied me every step of the way and are my greatest sources of learning, love, and evolution. My brothers, Guilherme and Filipe, always support us in realizing purposeful projects.

Endless gratitude from both me and my father goes to our inspiring muse, mother and wife, Olga Pinciroli, who has been always present, keeping our ideas grounded, helping us relive our experiences, and inspiring each word. She is always there for us. In this project she was our trusty advisor. Her suggestions helped shape this book.

Dad, you are my great companion in bringing the best version of myself to life. From my first strokes in the sea, to my achievements in national and international sport, to my corporate experiences and the creation of WeTeam to develop the human potential, and finally, to the writing of this book. You have always given me your full support, encouraging me to push beyond my inner limits.

And to you all: I feel blessed, grateful, and happy today for having completed this book, which represents a new beginning in unravelling the challenges of human science through sport and in creating a system that supports the development of each person who aspires to lead a fulfilling life.

Thank you, reader, for being my inspiration and my purpose in this detailed recounting of memories, research, and findings. We hope you feel motivated to make the choices that will guide you to a life that offers many moments of happiness and well-being in a fulfilling journey.

CONTENTS

———

DIMENSION 3: COURAGE AND COLLABORATION

INTRODUCTION

─────

Sport has the power to change the world. It has the power to
inspire, it has the power to unite people in a way that little
else does. It speaks to youth in a language they understand.
Sport can create hope, where once there was only despair.
—Nelson Mandela

He sought approval from the lifeguards. We entered the water slowly,
sensing the temperature, the current, and the rhythm of the waves. We
waited awhile, as if asking the sea for permission to begin our adventure.
Then we set off toward the horizon. We swam and swam, and then
he said, "Look, Cris, we're out past the surfers." I felt butterflies in my
stomach, a sensation colder even than the early morning waters. I clung
to my father's shoulders, wide-eyed. I could feel his warmth, his energy.
He was calm, confident, and brimming with pride at our daring, while I
was gripped by fear but also a sense of power. I was six years old. This is
my first memory of pushing beyond my limits.

Experiences like this one were becoming ever more common. We
did a lap around the island and jumped from the rocky ridge into the sea.
At first, it was just me and my dad, but as they grew, my two younger
brothers joined in. These adrenaline-soaked sunrise excursions ended
with a family breakfast that was awash with a sense of well-being, along
with pride and satisfaction at what we had achieved.

With each new experience, I felt I was going one step beyond,
overcoming my fears, perfecting my skills, and learning more about
myself. The bonds between us grew ever stronger, and my trust in my

father grew ever greater, as did his trust in the three of us. Despite the audacity of our challenges, we never suffered an accident, and this was not mere luck. My father taught us to observe the sea; to communicate with nature; and, above all, to respect its grandeur. "The force of nature is much greater than that of man," he said. Thus, we learned that the point of these adventures was not just to push ourselves but also to adapt and be able to quickly find the right response to the changing environment.

"I am preparing you for war," my father used to gibe. It was a joke that lived on among us. The truth is, he was pursuing his instinct to prepare his children for the slings and arrows that life would throw our way. His chosen way of doing this had something in common with all our family's exploits: the presence of physical or sporting activity. My father has always believed in the power of sport in acting as a laboratory for learning about life, and it was through sport that we picked up our main lessons.

Sport was an everyday part of our lives and our conversations. It was our main pastime and a key way for us to connect. When I raised my own family, I sought to create a similar environment with my husband, Luis, and my three daughters, Alissa, Giorgia, and Olivia. It brings me enormous pride and joy to see them share with us the same passion for sport and the same sense of purpose.

From parents to daughter and from daughter to grandchildren, we have become a sporting dynasty. Many people ask me what the family secret is. The main point is to cultivate an enabling environment, with no pressure, wherein things happen naturally. Children learn much more by example than from any speech by their parents.

Examples can be inspiring and generate deep insights for adults too. In sharing aspects of my life story, I invite you, dear reader, to reflect on your own journey.

The Sporting Dynasty

My father, Pedro Pinciroli Júnior, was a leading water polo player. He captained the Brazilian national team for nine years and competed at two Olympics—in Tokyo in 1964 and Mexico City in 1968—in which he was one of the top scorers. Among other achievements, at the Universiade[1] in 1963, he won the bronze medal and was chosen for the all-star team. In 1967, he was named as one of the top ten in the sport worldwide.

A few years after I was born, he interrupted his sporting career while still at his peak. I never got to see many of his games, but I do remember one. It was a friendly match against the Hungarians, who were—and are—a water polo powerhouse. Just before the game, the Hungarian players threw some balls up into the stands to fire up the crowd. "I want one, Dad!" I cried out. As I was very small, I had no idea what it might mean to a sportsman, who was about to go into combat, to have to ask one of the opposing players for a ball to give to his daughter. But he did so all the same. When he tossed the ball up to me in the stands, I celebrated wildly. Then, paradoxically, I cheered on my father while clutching my Hungarian ball.

My mother, Olga Pinciroli, was a tennis player who took part in the Brazilian championships in her youth. She was always highly supportive of my father and, later, of me and my brothers. As the director of women's water polo in Brazil, she fought hard to develop the sport in the country and for gender equality in the sport worldwide.

From a very young age, I danced ballet and swam. My father always encouraged me to take part in physical activities of all kinds. "One supports the other. What matters is gaining contact and experience with sport," he would say. I took part in some swimming championships. I did not stand out from the crowd, but I loved the competitive environment. At fifteen, I came across a sport to call my own. In water polo, I found my calling.

Water polo involves speed, endurance, strength, agility, a high level of skill, and physical prowess. According to Bleacher Report, it is considered the toughest sport, ahead of Australian football (Aussie rules), boxing, and rugby.[1] For a long time, the sport was exclusively male—so much so that even though it was the first team sport to be welcomed into the Olympics, in 1900, women were not allowed to compete until the Sydney games one hundred years later. I am honored to say that my mother played a

---

[1] The Universiade is an international multisport event for students that takes its name from the words *university* and *olympiad*. It is organized by the International University Sports Federation (FISU).

major role in bringing this about. As a result, in 2014, she received the Paragon Award from the Swimming Hall of Fame in the USA. This honor is awarded to people who have made exceptional contributions to the development of water sports worldwide.

In Brazil, women began playing water polo in 1986. The two main centers were the Paulistano club in São Paulo and Flamengo in Rio de Janeiro. As soon as I heard of the team in São Paulo, I tried to join. I felt as if the game were in my DNA, and everything just seemed to flow naturally with me. That does not mean I did not need to train—quite the contrary. I poured myself into practicing and learning all about the sport, and I started to reap the rewards with victories and recognition, but there were also losses, errors, and frustrations. At that stage, my focus was on continual learning, and the further I went in the sport, the more I wanted to progress and evolve.

I was captain of the Brazilian national team for thirteen years and played professionally for four years in Italy—two years with Visnova in Rome and two with Orizzonte Catania in Sicily, when we won the Champions Cup in Europe, which represented a first, as no Italian team had won the tournament before. Having dual nationality, I came to represent the Italian national team for eighteen months, but then I returned to Brazil. The Italian team went on to win gold at the Athens Olympics in 2004. For Brazil, I participated in the South American Games, Pan American Games, world cups, and three world championships. At the last of these, in Perth, Australia, I was the second-highest scorer in the tournament and was voted one of the seven best players in the world—the only player from the Americas in the group.

However, one of the most significant achievements for me took place at a venue where my father also shone. In 1967, the Brazilian men's water polo team took the silver medal at the Pan American Games in Winnipeg, Canada. My father was the team captain. He finished the tournament as top scorer and ended up being selected for the all-star team. Thirty-two years later, he was back in the same city, not as a player this time but as a fervent supporter of his daughter.

Women's water polo had only just been included as an Olympic event when it came to Sydney in 2000, so the 1999 Pan American Games in Winnipeg decided qualification for the Olympics. There was only one spot up for grabs. We beat the tournament favorites, the United States, in the first phase, only to face them again in the semifinal. With both sides giving their all, there proved nothing between us; the game finished in a tie at the end of normal time. Then, in extra time, we lost to a golden goal.[2] We had gotten a taste of what it was like to compete as equals with the United States, who went on to take the silver medal at the Sydney Olympics the following year.

The Brazilian team had just turned ten years old and was no longer in its infancy. We had matured a lot in that time. We had a dream team, united, at the peak of our powers, both physically and mentally. We had two excellent coaches, Sandy Nitta and Rodney Bell, while my mother was also doing a great job on the board for the women's game. We proudly took home our bronze medals after an unforgettable victory over Cuba.

Tradition plays an important role in building a winning team. Experience is passed down from generation to generation. Possible mistakes, difficulties, and moments of psychological pressure can be anticipated. The younger players coming into the team get a leg up. They begin their careers more mature, starting from a higher level. This phenomenon gained a lot of traction over time with the national team, and I saw something similar with my family. I had a built-in advantage because of my father. He trained with me, passed on his experience, and offered tips from things he had seen before.

I have done the same with my daughters. I started by creating an atmosphere in which sporting activities were ever present, as they were during my own childhood. Luis, my husband, like me, has a deep connection with the sea. When I first met him, he used to windsurf. Today he kitesurfs, and he has always enjoyed free diving without equipment. The girls join him on some of his adventures. Their version of going out beyond the surfers is to get closer to the fish, which are often not small. Together they have discovered caves on the sea floor, and they often have returned home carrying octopuses, clams, squid, delicious fish, or urchins.

---

[2] Water polo games have four seven-minute periods with a two-minute break. In the event extra time is required, there is a five-minute rest period, followed by two periods of three minutes each. If the score remains tied, there is a third period of play that ends as soon as the first goal is scored —the so-called golden goal.

I gave them the freedom to choose the sport they wanted to play. At first, perhaps because we are close to the sea, everyone got interested in swimming, which is also important for safety and survival. Alissa, the eldest, started playing soccer and did well, winning an award in elementary school. Giorgia, my middle daughter, took up ballet and also excelled. Later, the two discovered water polo.

Giorgia stands out for her perseverance. She has made great strides. Alissa, meanwhile, has already represented Brazil at the under-seventeen world championship and has just been accepted at Stanford University as a student athlete in the sport. Olivia is younger and not yet participating in competitions. She loves to swim, sing, and dance. She has already been given a polo ball from her sister and had her first moments of guided entertainment in the pool.

Has our family's history with water polo influenced the girls' interest in the sport? Absolutely! But it is not something we have forced upon them. For me, it did not matter which sport they preferred. I believe in the power of sport as an arena for learning about all areas of life.

What We Learn in Sport Applies to Life

Having gathered the most recent and important scientific evidence, a group of researchers reflected on how the educational system could be improved. The school of the future, in their opinion, should consider the physiological aspects of learning, with the aim of optimizing the benefits of sleep, nutrition, and physical exercise, so students are well prepared to deal with life in the future.[2]

Regular exercise not only benefits the body but also helps the development of cognitive skills in children and adolescents. This is not news. More striking in the study were the characteristics that the physical activities should have in order to be effective in helping the development of the prefrontal cortex, the region of the brain associated with the cognitive processes involved in controlling behavior. The study showed a strong correlation between academic and professional success.

According to the researchers, physical activities should be enjoyable; enhance cardiorespiratory capacity; develop motor coordination and visuospatial attention; provide physical and cognitive challenges, with a gradual, appropriate, and continual increase in the level of difficulty; offer opportunities for social interaction and teamwork; and transmit moral values and respect for the rules. In other words, physical activity set in the context of sport promotes the development of the prefrontal cortex.

The benefits from sport span beyond health and motor or cognitive development. Sport helps develop focus, determination, and responsibility while also stimulating creativity, risk-taking, and independence. It strikes a balance between developing team spirit, strengthening communication skills and collaboration, and fostering healthy competition, which leads the individual to strive to do his or her best.

Just as with life, sport provides the opportunity to experience the well-being and satisfaction of success, along with the pain of failure, disappointment, and adversity. The advantage is that the cycles are shorter and more frequent and occur in a safe and controlled environment. There are countless opportunities to tone the resilience muscle.

Knowledge, skills, and attitudes learned in practicing sport can be applied to every other area of life, whether academic, professional, or related to maintaining harmony at home. I see influences from my experience with sport in practically everything I do.

My parents encouraged me to be a good student, while I wanted to prove to myself that it was possible to devote myself to both physical and intellectual pursuits. In parallel to my sports career, I was a dedicated student. I have a bachelor's degree in economics, completed a postgraduate program in the subject in Italy, and earned a professional master's in business administration (MPA) at São Paulo's FGV-EAESP, which included an extension program at the University of North Carolina, Kenan-Flagler.

As a sportswoman, I was driven by passion and a strong sense of purpose, which energized me and gave me the strength to exceed my limits in the search of excellence. I was worried I would not find something I enjoyed as much when I entered the job market. But I soon realized it is possible to discover other goals and passions, and moreover, it is up to us to find meaning in what we do.

I pursued a career at Unibanco, which later merged with Itaú, creating the largest private bank in Brazil. I began in the finance department before spending periods in human resources, quality, customer excellence, and sales. I was highly motivated to work at the company, as its values matched my own. I saw value in what I was doing and an opportunity to learn and develop in each of the areas in which I worked. Focus, adaptability, and a strategic view were the main skills I took from sport and incorporated into my daily life. Team spirit guided my relationships with my team, superiors, and colleagues. My years as captain of the national team taught me a lot about communication, surpassing limits, and leadership. Sport prepared me to start my corporate life at another level.

Shortly afterward, I moved to the United States and took on the role of chief executive of human resources at Itaú. I was responsible for the human resources area for the business units in the United States and the Bahamas, plus a private bank in Chile. On my corporate journey, I applied a lot of the dedication and courage to act that I had practiced in water polo. In Brazil, we implemented and encouraged excellence in client services through the introduction of a client forum, and we set up programs for perfecting the quality of services, with the name All for the Client. In addition, our team introduced remote working at the business units in the United States (long before the COVID-19 pandemic made this practice necessary) and was a great supporter of gender equality and cultural diversity, developing a culture of inclusion, respect, and integration.

In the same way, my father always used sports metaphors to explain to me how he dealt with work situations. He had a successful career in reaching the position of CEO at Grupo Folha, one of the main communication companies in Brazil.

As a sportsman, he stood out for his leadership, creativity, and strategy. He was often the game's top scorer. He was always sniffing out opportunities, waiting to pounce, trying something innovative, and building team spirit—these were his trademarks at work. He was hungry, dedicated, and self-confident. He also scored several goals in his corporate career. One of them was coming up with the idea for UOL and making it happen. Today UOL is the largest Brazilian content, products, and services company on the internet.

When he came up with the idea to create an online news portal, he went to the owners of two large databases: Grupo Folha and Editora Abril. In 1996, he headed off to Silicon Valley in search of an IT partner to help build the business. In his meetings with the IT companies, typically around ten people came to hear his pitch. Even though, on the other side, my father's team was small—a publisher, journalist, and software engineer—they were united and organized, as he was always quick to point out.

When I think about those meetings, I imagine a friendly tournament between Brazil and Hungary in water polo. On one side was an experienced team recognized as an international powerhouse; on the other was a team whose members were full of talent, united, and engaged but with less tradition. For the smaller team, some mental preparation was needed, including gathering self-confidence and knowing the team's strengths, weaknesses, and limitations, as well as those of the adversary, in order to give a good account of the team. The idea in Silicon Valley was not to compete but to seek a partnership. However, in both contexts, business and athletics, it is necessary to earn the respect of the other side. The strategy was to highlight to future partners their most valuable asset: the most complete database of the Southern Hemisphere. A short while later, the biggest news portal in Latin America was born.

In 1999, as a senior manager with Folha, my father pitched the idea for a new vehicle focused on the economy, business, and finance to João Roberto Marinho.[3] From this conversation came the partnership between the groups Folha and Globo, which gave rise to the newspaper *Valor Econômico*. He knew it would take a strong team to create this complex product with the highest level of quality, something that was missing in the market, and this would only be possible by bringing together the two giants of Brazilian journalism. The first edition came out in May 2000. Fifteen years later, Folha sold its shares in the newspaper to Globo, but the publication remains the most important in the sector in the country.

Excellence and Happiness

While my sporting experiences taught me how to persevere no matter how hard things got, they also taught me that sometimes we need to take a step back and bring the team off the field. When I was out on the high seas, having adventures with my father, we respected these two extremes, finding the courage to push ourselves to our own limits while

---

[3] João Roberto Marinho serves as president of Grupo Globo's board of directors and editorial board.

also recognizing that we had limits when faced with the forces of nature. Grit and adaptability are equally important on the quest for excellence and happiness. Often, circumstances change, and our needs, desires, and goals change with them. Self-awareness is key to identifying the right moment to pursue new goals and targets to achieve a greater sense of self-fulfillment in life.

Many people associate happiness with the absence of suffering or the acquisition of material goods. However, according to philosophy and science, the concept is much broader and more complex. For the Greek thinker Aristotle, happiness was the goal of human existence and had nothing to do with a life of pleasure, acclaim, or riches; rather, it had to do with the practice of virtue.[3] For Tal Ben-Shahar, PhD, founder of the Happiness Studies Academy and professor of two of the most subscribed courses in the history of Harvard University, happiness is linked to a sense of completeness, or "being at one." Ben-Shahar uses a neologism to define it: *wholebeing*, a cross between *whole* and *well-being*. He proposes that to cultivate this state, we should strive to develop our potential across five dimensions: the spiritual, the physical, the intellectual, the relational, and the emotional.[4]

Thus, individuals who are whole have a sense of purpose in life, take care of their mind and body (as the two are interconnected), and are open to new experiences, seeking to learn from them, building constructive relationships with both themselves and others, and coming to terms with their emotions, positive or negative, equitably. The goal does not need to be something grandiose or heroic; rather, it is related to finding meaning in the small things they do each day.

According to Viktor Frankl, Austrian neuropsychiatrist and creator of logotherapy, the search for meaning in life is a primary motivation for humans.[5] He demonstrated that it is possible to find meaning even under the most miserable or cruel circumstances. In sharing his painful experience as a survivor of a concentration camp, he corroborated the celebrated maxim of German philosopher Friedrich Nietzsche: "He who has a *why* to live can bear almost any *how*." When you have something you believe in, you will find a way.

This lesson also holds true in less tragic circumstances. Having meaning in life allows us to contextualize pain and deal differently with obstacles and adversity. In the continual search for excellence on my journey, I have come to realize that high performance can be sustained only if there is purpose attached, and this is not a static concept but a dynamic one. As Frankl said, there is no sense to life in general. What matters is the specific meaning we give our lives at any given time.

I worked in the corporate world for more than twenty-five years, and when I left, I realized I had a great opportunity to rethink my goals in life and chart a new course. I decided to help others by sharing what I had learned as an athlete, executive, and mother.

From this experience, I developed a theory regarding ways to achieve a life that is successful and fulfilling. I called it the WeTeam method. It has enabled me to structure, in a didactic way, the knowledge I have gained. Over the last few years, I have obtained a certificate in the science of happiness from the Happiness Studies Academy and immersed myself in the study of philosophy, positive psychology, and neuroscience so I might establish a theoretical and scientific basis for the elements proposed in my theory.

I founded WeTeam: Chasing Excellence and Happiness, a training and mentoring company whose main objective is to help people and teams to fulfill their potential and become the best versions of themselves for the moments they are facing. Why the name WeTeam? Because we develop not on our own but through the communities we are part of; the people we choose to join us on our journeys; and the search for diverse thoughts and ideas. I believe in teamwork, from childhood to adulthood. At different points and stages of our development, we meet people who leave a profound mark upon us and who help us to evolve.

I have worked with athletes who seek to hone their skills and sustain high performance; with executives and educators who seek excellence and happiness both at work and in life; and with parents who see in sport an opportunity to guide their children to success and happiness. With each job done and each client who prospers, I feel more connected with my goal of contributing to a better world through helping people to become happier and more fulfilled.

I have long held dear the chance to write this book with my father. Our hope is that it will bring inspiration and knowledge to you, the reader, and help you to reach your full potential and support those around you to seek lives of success and happiness. In illustrating the main concepts, I share practical real-world examples based on theory and science, recalling both my father's career and my own experiences in sport, in the corporate world, as a mother, and as an entrepreneur.

In addition, I present examples from other top athletes, sports medalists, and authorities in the areas of education, neuroscience, psychology, health, and business. These carefully chosen professionals agreed to share their experiences and knowledge in order to further enrich this content. As we learn from the stories of people in different walks of life, we are inspired not to achieve something every day but, rather, to carefully make decisions and small, incremental changes that ultimately become powerful enough to make a big difference in our lives and the lives of others.

The WeTeam Method

To achieve excellence and happiness in sport and in life, we need to (1) establish a strong foundation that provides us the freedom to choose; (2) connect with our inner energy to deal with the challenges and obstacles in our path; (3) cultivate the courage to act and a spirit of collaboration; and (4) seek a sense of meaning that inspires, guides, and sustains our choices. Together these four elements form the dimensions that comprise the WeTeam method.

We typically use the images and metaphors of water polo in explaining our method, but the concepts and their applicability clearly transcend just this sport. I consider it a useful tool for any sport or, indeed, any area of life, one that serves as a guide to help individuals and teams reach their full potential.

The image of a water polo player ready to make a pass or shoot at goal (see the image below) symbolizes an effort that goes beyond the physical to incorporate equally the spiritual, intellectual, relational, and emotional aspects.

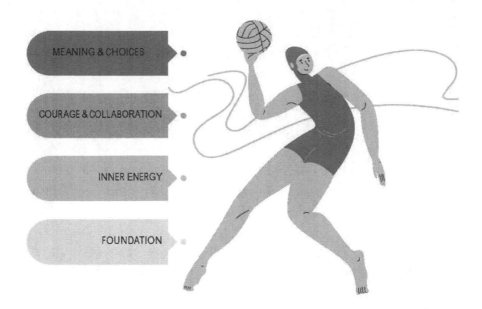

To sustain the position that leads to action, all parts of this athlete's body are in harmony. In the same way, the four dimensions of the WeTeam method should be thought of as interconnected elements coordinating with one another, as shown in more detail below.

The Foundation

Water polo is played in a pool that is at least two meters deep, so for support, the body depends on intense movement of the legs, known as the eggbeater. The better the player's legwork, the better the leverage and the more choices the player has in the game. Those outside the pool can barely see players' legs, but that doesn't make them any less crucial in providing a platform. In the WeTeam method, the platform is about bringing together the aspects that ensure a foundation for action, enabling the balance and strength necessary to act in a flexible and decisive manner. The elements that make up this dimension are not always visible but, as with the legwork in water polo, need to be practiced and cultivated in a consistent manner. They are as follows: the connections and relationships that form our support network; in-depth learning and practice; and a healthy lifestyle.

Inner Energy

The central region of our body is called the core. The strengthening of the deep-lying muscles in this region stabilizes the spine and provides a second layer of support for action. A well-honed core provides the player with a repository of energy, which he or she accesses when contracting these muscles and concentrating to make a play. Accessing the core is about more than just connecting with the present moment; it is about summoning the energy necessary for true engagement in the game of life. In the WeTeam method, I associate the idea of the core with an inner strength, which we should learn to access to ensure the necessary engagement in each action and which we should nurture so our reserves of energy are topped up regularly. The elements that make up this dimension are those that prepare us to deal with challenges, using our strengths to overcome obstacles and unexpected situations. They are as follows: learning from adversity; self-confidence; and the routines for reenergizing.

Courage and Collaboration

A consistent game played well with a sustained level of performance requires presence, the ability to read the game, creativity, and, above all, teamwork. You need to know, trust, and communicate with your team if you want to make a special play or precise pass or create a good chance to take a shot at goal. In the WeTeam method, I have summarized these behaviors in the dimension of courage to act and spirit of collaboration. The skills and attitudes involved here are those that enable us to act, create, work as a team, and collaborate. They are as follows: courage and willingness to experiment, reflect, learn, and deal with failure; teamwork; and communication skills.

Meaning and Choices

Behind every action in the game, such as deciding whether to pass or shoot or deciding to throw the ball at that exact moment or seconds later, there is intent and a decision-making process. With the ball in her hand, the player chooses where to make her play. In the WeTeam method, I discuss the importance of meaning in inspiring, channeling, and sustaining our choices. The elements that make up this dimension are those that motivate us, move us, and enable us to act intentionally. They are as follows: self-knowledge; purpose and values; and happiness.

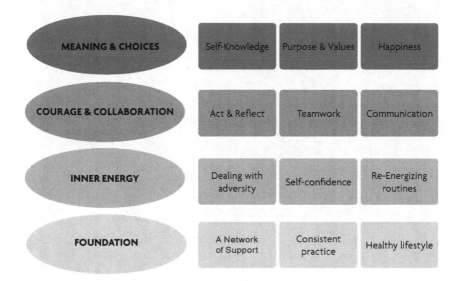

I have divided this book into four parts, with each corresponding to a dimension of the WeTeam method. In each chapter, I explore the key elements needed for a fuller and more successful life. The book is an invitation to reflect on your own journey and how you can fulfill your potential and positively influence those around you.

Just as in preparing for an important competition, each stage prepares the reader to fully assimilate the one that follows, until all parties share a deep understanding. The idea is to illustrate ways you can think, feel, and act like a champion in achieving your own dreams and goals in order to lead a full life aligned with your sense of purpose, savoring and learning from each moment of the here and now.

The intention is for you, the reader, to reflect on the importance of the choices in your life and to visualize how implementing the suggestions in this book can help you achieve your goals and dreams.

DIMENSION 1

THE FOUNDATION

CHAPTER 1

———

A **NETWORK OF SUPPORT** AND SECURITY IN THE STANDS

Call it a clan, call it a network, call it a tribe, call it a family.
Whatever you call it, whoever you are, you need one.
—Jane Howard

Those who have a strong sense of love and belonging
have the courage to be imperfect.
—Brené Brown

The air was fresh and cool at that time of morning. My father and I loved being the first to say good morning to everyone we met on the way to the club, from the security guard to the lifeguard. We walked up and eyed the length of the pool, as if to be sure we would be the first to enter and make the first laps of the day. "Lower your voice, as we don't want to wake your opponents," my father joked. As well as water polo training in the afternoons after school, I practiced with him at least once a week at sunrise in the pool at the club. I can still close my eyes and imagine the hectic schedule as I left the pool, took a shower, enjoyed breakfast, and went to school with my brothers. As we came out of the water, we met some acquaintances, who smiled at the sight of father and daughter training intensely in front of the goal. There in that pool, I learned about the Hungarian water polo school of ball handling, about how hard the Yugoslavs shot at goal, and about the creativity of the Italian team called il Settebello[4] and, without realizing, took my first steps toward my dream of playing with the best in the world.

My father always challenged me to give my all in everything. He did so not by pressuring me but through examples—his own and those of the champions of different sports. He made it clear that he was there to support me as I started out on the long climb to sporting achievement.

In a world that is increasingly sedentary, with children and adolescents spending an average of seven and a half hours per day in front of televisions, computers, video games, and cell phones,[1] what can make a teenager wake up before sunrise of her own accord and work on her sports technique? The answer lies in how the sport is introduced to her in the beginning.

A study by the Performance Lab for the Advancement of Youth in Sport (PLAYS) at Queen's University, Canada, found that the way elite athletes relate to playing sports in their lives passes through three stages: experimentation, specialization, and investment.[2] In the early years, they try out different sports to experiment with different forms: sports played individually and in groups, with and without a ball, at school and in clubs, and during the week and on weekends with the family. The focus is on stimulating fun and experimentation.

Over time, young athletes gradually reduce their involvement in multiple activities and focus on the sport that gives them the greatest enjoyment, sense of belonging, and development. Specialization occurs. Through practice and repetition, they start to develop specific skills and perform better, and this creates a virtuous cycle, as they gain greater satisfaction, continue to play even better, and develop a desire to train more. In the third phase, there is investment in growth and improvement, and the intensity of the practice increases greatly in the search for excellence.

I recognize these same phases in my own relationship with water polo leading up to the time I turned professional. As a child, I was exploring my own interests and naturally selecting the activities that most appealed to me, such as swimming and catching waves in the sea. As my skills and

---

[4] The Italian men's national water polo team is known as il Settebello.

knowledge developed, I plunged headfirst into water polo and entered a virtuous cycle, wherein I felt driven to invest ever more time into perfecting my craft.

How can we help young people create this virtuous cycle of improvement? The key is to understand the specific challenges involved with each of these stages of development and to identify how best to support each person.

Early Years: Experimentation and Fun

Children are little explorers, curious scientists who want to experiment on the world around them. Their repertoire of tastes and skills is still forming, and thus, the greater the contact they have with different experiences in a fun, playful, and recreational context the better.

The family plays an important role in creating an environment supportive of experimentation. In my case, sporting activities were prominent in our leisure time on weekends and vacations, moments in which the family connects. Parents do not need to be sports aficionados to provide these opportunities. The main thing is to show an interest and become engaged in the children's sporting activities. This gives them the platform they need to continue. This logic applies equally to the development of other talents, such as music and art.

My paternal grandmother was a pianist, while my grandfather was a jeweler. Neither was especially sports-minded, but they both valued the practice of sport for its numerous benefits, such as staying healthy physically and emotionally. My grandfather was one of the founders of Clube de Regatas Tietê in São Paulo, and in that pool, his children took their first swimming strokes. It is something my father still remembers today, just as I remember our first experiences in the sea. These are experiences that live long in the memory and that we tend to repeat with our families, as they come to be part of our values.

During my childhood, we often went to the coast, and the sand and sea were witness to many family adventures. We were also members of clubs in São Paulo, which offered different sports in addition to providing a place to socialize and network.

The onus of creating this environment does not necessarily fall specifically to parents or grandparents. Often, other family members are part of this equation. Marcelinho Huertas has been the point guard for the Brazilian national basketball team since 2005 and has been captain for the past ten years. He played at a high level in Spain, at DKV Joventut and Barcelona, which led to his being signed by the Los Angeles Lakers in the NBA. Marcelinho currently plays for Iberostar Tenerife, where he continues to shine. He told me his brother, who is four years older, was the one who sparked his interest in playing sports. He said, "When I was a kid, I saw my brother playing basketball, and I wanted to be like him. We had a ball at home, and I spent a lot of time playing on the court."

The focus during this experimentation phase is on having a range of experiences and, especially, having fun. Playing sport with family and friends becomes part of a child's daily life, in activities outside, in nature, in public spaces, at the club, or at school. This is not the time to force choices upon the child or to up the intensity. With the right support, greater intensity and practice will evolve naturally in the years that follow.

Researchers at George Washington University, alarmed by the statistic that roughly 70 percent of children in the United States stop playing sports by age thirteen, carried out a study to explore what drives young athletes to play a sport. The main reason they found was that the athletes enjoyed it and had fun playing or competing. The researchers went further and investigated what made practicing fun and enjoyable. They unearthed no fewer than eighty-one factors.[3] The main ones were giving the best of yourself, having positive experiences with a coach, getting playing time, and building relationships with teammates. It might seem intuitive to think that the feeling of victory would be the main factor to be celebrated, but in fact, winning the game ranked only forty-eighth in the children's opinion.

The researchers also investigated what it meant to the children to be treated with respect by the coach: for him or her to be encouraging, be a role model, communicate clearly and consistently, be knowledgeable about the sport, and listen to them. It should be noted that these characteristics are important not just for coaches but also for educators and leaders in an organization.

Growth Mentality

Renowned Stanford University psychologist Carol Dweck demonstrated in a series of studies that valuing the process, the journey, and the effort—rather than the victory, the end result, or the natural talent—leads us to develop a positive relationship with learning.[4] Children who are praised and recognized for their involvement, dedication, engagement, or perseverance develop a growth mindset. They believe they can improve their skills through effort and, therefore, have greater self-confidence and more willingness to learn and to accept challenges. This enables constant evolution and development.

On the other hand, praising children for their intelligence or natural talent by saying, for example, "You are an excellent player," instead of "I could see how hard you worked in this game," can make them believe that their skills are a fixed and immutable trait and that if they have the talent, they don't need to put in the effort. They develop what Dweck calls a fixed mindset, which can lead them to reject more challenging learning situations, as they will tend to hide from their mistakes instead of correcting them and learning from them.

Competitiveness flows naturally in a sports environment, but it should not be the deciding factor during this experimentation phase. At Gulliver Schools, to which I enrolled my daughters when we moved to Florida, children are only permitted to participate in official competitions from middle school, with the competitive environment taking on greater significance only once they join high school.

The system for evaluating academic performance follows the same logic. Initially, children are assessed with respect to the proficiency acquired in each skill and are only awarded grades from middle school. Frank Steel, head of schools at Gulliver, argues that children develop at different rates, be it physically, emotionally, or intellectually. For example, a seven-year-old who is the fastest in his class will win any race simply because he has developed this skill ahead of his peers. Rewarding him for this ability may lead to the development of a fixed mindset rather than encouraging him to further improve himself.

Practices developed for youth sports programs based on scientific evidence suggest that at this stage, the selection of players for matches and for each position should not be based on talent. Instead, all children should have a chance to participate, experiment, and have fun, learning along the way.[5]

Specialization: Preferences and Choices

Introducing sport early on in a way that is low pressure and fun does not mean every child will want to become a professional athlete, but it can be key in helping children to choose a healthy lifestyle by practicing sport throughout their lives. Physical activity is necessary for all, due to the many health benefits it brings, but that is not to say everyone should or will want to practice a high-performance sport. "Allow your children to discover for themselves why they want to play a sport. The more they understand what it is about the sport that attracts them, the more likely they will want to practice it," Frank says.

Open dialogue with young athletes is one of the best ways to support this and other decisions they may come to make. This is a basic premise for identifying how best to support them on their life path. Ask them what their goals are in the sport or in any other activity they wish to pursue. This will help them to reflect on their choices. In addition to broadening the connection and deepening the bond, this attitude will make the children feel they are listened to and respected.

At the stage of specialization, in which the young athlete begins to identify his preferences and starts to narrow his options to dedicate himself to the sports with which he most identifies, the family's role in providing emotional support and guidance is key. Showing interest in the sport chosen, attending games and occasional training sessions, and celebrating a child's progress are ways to do this.

How Would You Like Me to Cheer for You?

Encouragement and vocal support are welcome, but care should be taken not to be overbearing. We should be in tune with the level of skill the young athlete possesses. It is also a challenge for parents not to burden young athletes with the weight of their own expectations regarding which path they should follow. Doing so can backfire, often pushing them in the opposite direction.

I once took my daughters to a competition in California and came across a sign at the entrance to the pool that read, "Reminders from your son: I am a child; it's just a game; my coach is a volunteer; the referees are human; no scholarships will be awarded today. Thank you, and have fun." I thought it was a wonderful way to connect parents with reality and the true reason they are there: to support their children and enjoy the opportunity to see them in action.

The impact of parents' behavior also depends on how their actions are interpreted by their children. Researchers from North Carolina State University demonstrated, in the *Journal of Sport Behavior*, that there is often a disconnect in the way parents and children view the support being offered.[6] Parents often believe they are encouraging their children to do their best, whereas the children feel pressured and burdened by expectation. Again, dialogue is essential. I loved a video I watched on YouTube called "The Truth about Sports Parents..." (from the channel Ilovetowatchyouplay.com), which is dedicated to parents who support their children in playing sport. In it, children are asked how they feel about the way their parents behave when watching them play.[7] Inspired by the research and the clip, I decided to ask my daughters how they felt when I watched them compete and how I could best support them. They knew my interest was genuine, as I was, and continue to be, deeply interested in this field of study.

Alissa, the eldest, likes it when I help her focus before a game, and she loves to see me cheering her on, but she gets distracted when I shake my head at her mistake if a play does not work out. Until she pointed it out, I hardly knew I was doing that, but I started to notice how I automatically tended to shake my head and put a hand on my forehead at such times. Giorgia, on the other hand, loves when I talk to her from the stands. She says it motivates her and gives her confidence. She loves to see my excitement when she scores or makes a play. However, she does not like it when I want to go over things right after the game. For me, it was important to understand that my reactions had different effects on each of my daughters. It was also a chance to remind them that my only goal is to be there for them, come what may.

Olivia, my youngest, who does not compete in tournaments, mentioned that she likes it when I watch her at swimming practice and point out something she can improve, but she does not feel comfortable when I just watch her stone-faced. When I asked if my being there made her nervous, she said, "A little," but she was not sure why. Given her reaction, I reflected on the importance of such conversations even with younger children.

The sporting environment, on its own, drives everyone to seek his or her best, and thus, even when there is no external pressure, the child has to deal with the internal pressure to perform well. Talking about it can be a way to help children deal with their own emotions.

The Different Types of Intelligence

As children dedicate themselves more to sports activities, parents might start to worry about imbalance between play and study. However, research shows the benefits of sport in enhancing the degree of focus on studies, thanks to the release of "good" hormones, such as dopamine and serotonin, which also create a sense of well-being.[8]

When my oldest daughter was in elementary school at a traditional school in Brazil, my husband and I were called in to meet her counselor, who told us to seek external support, as our daughter was very restless and had difficulty focusing. We ran some tests, which came up with nothing, but the doctor suggested a drug that would help her focus. We were opposed to the idea.

For a moment, I contemplated whether, in order to help my daughter, I should reduce the time she spent playing sport. But her psychologist suggested otherwise. She said, "If you take sport out of your daughter's daily life, she may have even more difficulty, because this is exactly what helps her to focus her attention." Indeed, I noticed that on days when she was doing some physical exercise, she was able to concentrate much better on her studies.

When my husband was in graduate school at Harvard and shared the case with one of his professors, the professor raised the study of multiple intelligences by American psychologist Howard Gardner.[9] In addition to the types of intelligence traditionally measured by IQ tests, such as logical mathematics and linguistics, he has identified six other types of intelligence: musical, kinesthetic-corporal, spatial, interpersonal, intrapersonal, and naturalistic. The challenge is to identify which types of intelligence emerge naturally, because these are the ones we should focus on in order to obtain our best results and achieve a sense of fulfillment.

The psychologist's argument and the information on Gardner's multiple intelligences changed the way we viewed the situation and the way we supported our daughters. The pieces of the puzzle fit together when we moved to the United States and enrolled our daughters in a school with an innovative teaching methodology. Soon after joining, middle school students underwent an assessment of their skills to identify the ways in which they learned best. It was a broad assessment that took into account the multiple intelligences, and Alissa's natural kinesthetic-corporal intelligence became clear. She said to me, "Mom, now I understand why you always suggest I write the main points in a notebook. That is what works well for you. But for me, I need to move." That insight not only gave us a better understanding of her strengths so that her support network—her teachers and us—could help her but also increased her self-awareness, which encouraged her to explore her own ways to learn. Alissa has learned to create a study routine that complements her skills, in which she sets alarms to move from time to time, and as a result, her performance has improved a lot.

Looking back, I am happy we have supported all her talents— sporting, musical, and artistic—and am grateful we did not discourage her from playing sport. If we had, we would not be celebrating her enrollment today as a student athlete at Stanford University, one of the most prestigious learning institutions in the world.

The Investment Phase: Time for Dedication

With the right support and greater focus on their chosen sports, adolescents can take their skills to the next level, realize their potential, and reap the rewards. Then comes the investment stage, in which they feel driven to reach an elite level in their chosen sport. The athletes increase their commitment, and practice becomes more intense, including in terms of how it relates to their physical well-being, such as nutrition, sleep, and recovery.

Oftentimes, sport occupies a central place in the life of a family, which dictates a time commitment to take the children to weekend competitions, predawn training, and specialist clinics. This often means giving up other leisure activities or family trips. It can be wearing, but the answer is to see these moments as an investment in the child. These actions, which often seem like insignificant gestures, can make an enormous difference in the lives of children. It is essential that they feel supported as they begin to reap the benefits of all their practice, expanding their range of experiences and balancing their time among competition, study, and leisure.

I remember well the presence of my parents at the edge of the pool, talking me through the precompetition routines, which I will discuss more in chapter 6. In this phase, emotional support in helping the young athlete deal effectively with injury, fatigue, pressure, and failure is critical. In one of my first competitions, a game in Mococa, a town in the interior of the state of São Paulo, a defending player on the opposing team caught me off guard with a more physical approach to the game than I was used to. At the end of the game, I was in tears, outraged. My father was at my side but made no move to intervene or protect me. He just waited for me to calm down and then said, "Cris, water polo involves a lot of physical contact. These situations are going to happen and are going to happen more often. With time, you will learn to adapt and how to position yourself. But the choice is yours. Do you want to continue playing?" Right then, I realized that to improve, I would need to learn how to position myself better during the game and how to respond to moments of frustration, error, and defeat.

We need mentors in our lives who can be honest with us and confront us with the tough questions. These are the questions that force us to look deep within and find the innermost motivations needed to excel.

Children and adolescents need space to learn how to deal with the tough times, and sport provides this in a controlled environment. Allowing this space does not mean withholding support or subjecting the young athletes to extreme suffering. However, it is important to let young people deal with these moments, create their own strategies, and grow. This will benefit them throughout the ups and downs in life. We should not make the mistake of overprotecting our children, however difficult this may be—for them and for us.

Support for Life

Rita Pierson, who was a teacher for forty years, said in her vibrant lecture on TED Talks Education that every child deserves a champion—that is, an adult who will never give up on her, connects with her, and inspires her to become the best version of herself. [10] A relationship of trust established with a child has immense power over her destiny.

With the right level of support at each stage of development, the adolescent will enter adult life with greater independence and a sense of autonomy. That is not to say the support of family and friends is no longer important. Physical proximity is not always necessary. Emotional and moral support can be conveyed through other means or even through our thoughts, through recalling past events. If a solid support network is established in childhood and adolescence, the adult will be able to connect with that inner sense of security from her past, even when the support network is no longer present.

I had the privilege of being able to count on my parents throughout my childhood, and this fortified me for dealing with situations when my parents were not on hand, such as when I did an exchange program at the age of fifteen and lived in the United States for a year or when I turned professional and joined a team in Italy in early adulthood. The experience of living in another culture, away from family and friends, teaches you a lot about adapting and being flexible. On both occasions above, my parents and I maintained frequent contact by phone, and I got the sense that they were following my progress from afar and celebrating my successes, which gave me great peace of mind.

A Beautiful Enemy

Whether from up in the stands or in life, the relationship with those who support us and celebrate our achievements while offering us a shoulder during the hard times can be the greatest catalyst for happiness.

I like the definition used by nineteenth-century philosopher Ralph Waldo Emerson in describing the quality of the people we choose to accompany us through life. It combines the idea of beauty, which represents love, care, empathy, and goodwill, with that of an enemy, who would be our antagonist. We are not talking about a hostile enemy but a friend who is transparent and often difficult to face because he or she drives to become better. He called these people, who represent a gift in our lives, beautiful enemies.

A genuine, authentic relationship can lead us to intellectual and spiritual enlightenment, but to achieve this, we need someone who challenges us and tells us the truth, no matter how hard it is to hear. This inconvenient truth, rather than constant praise and accommodation, forces us to evolve and become the best version of ourselves. Our friend should be autonomous, assertive, free, and independent for this relationship to work. Emerson suggests, "May he be for you a kind of beautiful, indomitable enemy, revered with devotion, and not a trivial convenience to be soon overcome and put aside."[11] When I read, interpreted, and analyzed this concept, I immediately thought of my father. As our relationship matured, he became my beautiful enemy—and he still is today. I have established real and authentic relationships with many people, but my relationship with him is one of those that has most led me to grow and push back my boundaries.

In sport, he cheered me on and celebrated the progress I was making, while his tongue was sharp whenever he saw a drop in my level of performance. When he watched my games, I quickly located him in the stands—he was alone, up on high—and we communicated during the game. From his eyes, gestures, or signs, I got the message. When I was tired, my intensity would drop, and I would pass the ball more in order to take a breather, but I would soon hear my father shouting from afar, "Get back in the game!" He knew I could give more, and through his urging, I found a way to connect with my inner energy and give my all.

My teammates often asked, "Cris, how do you cope with the pressure from your father?" It was not always easy. There were times when I got frustrated and angry. But I wanted to grow and fulfill my dream of being a top international, so I sought his feedback after each game, as I knew the value of it, no matter how hard it was to hear. I learned how to deal with the pressure and was encouraged to do my best. I trusted my father, and he trusted me and my potential. In order to have a beautiful-enemy relationship, there must be mutual trust. This type of relationship is not established overnight. It takes time to build.

Other athletes relate similar experiences. Rafael Nadal, considered one of the greatest tennis players of this century, talks in his biography about his relationship with an uncle who was extremely demanding and gave him harsh feedback, even when he thought he had played well.[12] When I interviewed Marcelinho Huertas, captain of the Brazilian basketball team, he described his relationship with Coach Jesús Vidorreta Gómez as follows: "We have a very good connection, on and off the court. Having a good relationship does not mean that he pampers me. We have a deep understanding. He trusts me, but he pushes me to the limit. He is very demanding of me. When it comes to chewing someone out, I am the first one to get it."

The beautiful enemy can also be a teammate who drives other players to their physical and mental limit, as was the case with Kobe Bryant, who starred in the NBA between 1996 and 2016. "His commitment, focus, and seriousness were impressive. He would do anything to win the game, and he demanded the same from the other players," Huertas told me, having played with him while he was in the NBA. Later, the North American star created the Mamba mentality, which he set as the definitive mantra for the competitive spirit: "a constant quest to try to be better today than you were yesterday."

It is not possible to achieve and maintain excellence without exceeding your own limits. The support network provides a safe platform to enable full development, embraces us at times of vulnerability, and knows how to give us the push we need to leave our comfort zone.

Coach and Mentor

Emeric Imre Szasz was a prisoner in a concentration camp during World War II, after his homeland, Hungary, was invaded by the Nazis. In an attempt to escape, he lost an eye. Perhaps because he had lived during many atrocities, he had a keen sensibility. Emeric was one of my father's greatest mentors, coaching him in both swimming and water polo.

He was educated differently. When my grandmother went to watch the training sessions, he would grab a chair and place it where she would best be able to monitor her son's performance. Back then, it was not common for parents to attend training, but my grandmother made her presence felt. My grandparents often invited the coach and the other players to get together for pizza and to socialize.

Everyone on the team had a lot of respect for Emeric. By his behavior and standards, he set an example, and he held strong opinions. One time, when the club decided to ban water polo training on weekends, he protested. As a result, the board fired him. But the team sided with the coach. They met at my grandparents' house in downtown São Paulo to decide what to do. All of them were honorary members at the Tietê Club because of the tournaments they had won with the club, but they did not hesitate to follow the coach out the door.

It is always helpful when families are on good terms with the coach. That is not to say they will always agree with one another. The basis for these relationships should be one of partnership, in aiming to support the development of the athlete. As parents, we are important role models for our children, so the way we communicate or behave toward coaches, opponents, and referees is important and should be based on respect.

Learning to deal with situations that arise from the relationship with the coach is part of a child's development. As with any relationship, there will be moments of joy and moments of conflict as the player is forced out of his or her comfort zone. Respect is essential. Parents can and should be aware of what is happening, but at the same time, they should also let the child learn how to manage the situation. As adults, the children will have to deal with people they do not always like and may not agree with. Respecting the opinions of others and knowing how to lay out an argument and communicate will make a difference to their success and well-being. Remember that there are different ways to express our thoughts, emotions, and desires, and when we are able to recognize positive intentions, we become more tolerant of one another.

When talking about his vast experience with different teams and in different countries, Marcelinho Huertas confided in me that he has always tried to extract as much as possible from his relationship with each coach, and this has helped his continual development. "I have had a lot of coaches, and they have had different styles and approaches with respect to everything, in the way they push you or chastise you or in their training methods. There is the coach who screams, the one who is more practical, the one who is more motivational. I established a good bond with all of them. You must adapt and understand the message they want to convey. The coach wants to win as badly as the player does. But there are players who do not adapt or who take it personally, which hampers both their development and that of the team," he said.

Going beyond the Support of Family and Coaches

When he was fifteen, my father was spending a quiet vacation at Copacabana Beach in Rio de Janeiro with his friends, when he bumped into a coach he knew. "Pedro, aren't you training with the water polo squad?" the coach asked, and he added that the Brazilian team was preparing for the Rome Olympics a few months later. My father did not even know about the training sessions. This coach, who had a lot of belief in my father's potential, took him to the Olympic team's training camp.

At that time, although my father still was very young, his ability was clear, physically, technically, and strategically. Training with the national team, he played well and caught the coach's eye. But once he was out of the pool, the coach pulled him to one side and broke the news: "If you had shown up earlier, you would be on the squad, but the names have already been submitted to the IOC [International Olympic Committee], and we cannot add anyone else." In other words, there was a lack of communication between my father's club and the national federation, and my father missed out on the opportunity. Breakdowns in communication can occur at all levels. To identify the best players to represent the country, it is important to have a framework for communicating between the different levels of the hierarchy.

Despite feeling the disappointment of a young man in missing out on the Olympic Games, my father was undeterred. Later that year, soon after the Olympics, he was invited to play for the national team at a tournament in Buenos Aires. He went on to compete in the Olympics in Tokyo in 1964 and Mexico in 1968. He turned his disappointment into focus, dedicating himself to the sport and improving further. This communication failure, however, could just as easily have curtailed his sporting career. Faced with this disappointment, it would have been easy to give up and look for opportunities elsewhere. How much talent has been wasted in such situations, and how many sports have been negatively impacted? Therefore, it is important to have a good infrastructure for identifying, tracking, and communicating with up-and-coming talent, involving not only the clubs but also sports, education, and government bodies.

My mother's performance as director of Brazilian women's water polo set an example for her contribution to developing sport both nationally and internationally. As a volunteer director, she did a lot to promote and develop the sport in the country. She sought to look after the players' best interests, created a water polo community in which everyone supported one other, and negotiated sponsorships specific to women's water polo. From these, she was able to set up a program of national tournaments, which were fundamental to encouraging the spread of the sport in the country, and international tournaments designed to raise the competitive level of the players. She knew how important it was for us to play against the best in the world if we wished to develop. In addition, she promoted games in the sea, watched by a sizeable crowd, to popularize the sport. Her relationships, built on credibility and partnership, with schools, companies, international sport representatives, and the media were essential.

My mother did this out of her passion—out of her love for her daughter, fellow athletes, the sport, and the country. For her dedication to this cause, in 2015, she received the Paragon Award from the Swimming Hall of Fame in the USA for her extraordinary contributions to the development of international sport. Her influence and her lobbying alongside other international leaders for women's water polo to become an Olympic sport changed forever the status of the sport and how it is viewed. Her argument was always based on respect; gender equality; and the development of a society that is healthier, more balanced, and more fair-minded.

There are many serious and competent leaders who strive to promote and develop participation in their sport and to build the structure needed to support young talent and top athletes. But it takes more than that. It is necessary to nurture a sports-friendly environment in the country, from the way it is taught in schools to the physical structure needed to train high-performance athletes: good pools, well-equipped gyms, and professional athletics tracks.

Never doubt that a small group of thoughtful, committed citizens can change the world. Small changes lead to greater changes and, ultimately, transformation. Having an effective network of individuals united around a single goal is extraordinarily powerful. One good deed leads to another, and momentum builds, until the impact is far-reaching. Good deeds and acts of kindness can release the light and bring people together to effect positive changes that can impact those around us and around the world.

Support from Schools and Universities

At many schools in the United States, sport is constantly integrated into the academic routine. One example is when an athlete represents the school for the first time or achieves something special. He or she is recognized in the morning announcement, which communicates to everyone, through the sound system, what the student has achieved and publicly congratulates him or her. Sport is part of the school's values and is positively reinforced as part of academic development.

For university students, there is a structure for competitive play between colleges and integration with the country's professional game. Many alumni continue to cheer for their university teams. For example, the University of Michigan's football games have had crowds of more than one hundred thousand since 1975, a run that has been interrupted only because of the coronavirus pandemic. Some alumni are not merely supporters but actively help to fund the university's sports facilities.

The NCAA, the agency responsible for university sports in the country, raises $1.6 billion in support from a single season. All of this provides the basic structure needed for the athlete to thrive not only in sport but also academically, an aspect that is important in establishing alternatives later in life, once the sporting career is over.

Tournaments, both for high schools and universities, attract athletes from all over the country. The best are monitored by the federations. The organization and structure of many sports creates opportunities for talent to flourish and be recognized, and the results are clear when you look at the Olympic medal table, where the Americans invariably top the list.

In the United States, sport is a means to promote social change and development. University scholarships are a way of safeguarding the futures of athletes when they stop playing. Of course, incentive models can always be improved upon, and in the United States, it is no different.

In Italy, where I played, there is a professional structure of longer championships, with weekly games in different cities. Water polo teams are divided into leagues (or series) A, A2, B, and C, with 56 women's teams and 216 men's. At the last count, in 2020 by Federazione Nazionale di Nuoto, there were 1,857 federated female players and 14,524 male players in the Italian *di pallanuoto* championship. It is another format offering incentives amid an ingrained tradition. In Europe, professional championships manage to attract the best athletes in the world due to the financial rewards on offer, the duration of the championship, the technical quality, the fantastic training facilities, and the game experience on offer—all of which promote high performance.

Engaged Companies

Many expect that careers in sport might end when athletes enter the corporate world. However, depending on their values, some companies actively encourage their employees to continue, as they see the benefits of being an athlete on a professional career. At eighteen, I joined the then Price Waterhouse trainee program. I received paid leave and all the support I needed to participate in the tournaments. They accompanied and valued my efforts to study and work while still training at night. Later, when I returned from my time in Italy, I joined Unibanco, one of the largest private financial institutions in Brazil. I was able to demonstrate my commitment to the company while also representing the national water polo team. The executive president of Unibanco when I joined was Pedro Moreira Salles. He quickly saw how my sporting activities benefitted my work and vice versa, as the body and mind are interconnected. I took part in many interviews for the corporate magazine and an internal video that went to all employees, illustrating how the psychological muscle can be trained to achieve both performance excellence and physical well-being.

My manager, Marcelo Orticelli, was also supportive of my pursuing a sports career in parallel with my profession. This support and respect were hard-earned. My bronze medal from the Pan American Games in Winnipeg was displayed in a glass dome at the entrance to the building, in the same spot where the corporate awards the bank had received were displayed. Some people might ask why a bronze medal should receive so much attention. It was simply recognition of the hard work and dedication that had gone into developing an internationally competitive team despite not receiving the same level of support available in other countries.

Many companies encourage their employees to practice sports and support sports initiatives organized by foundations. Others promote running races in the city and open events. This is good not only for employees but also for the companies themselves, who see an improvement in productivity and the engagement of their teams, in addition to gaining brand promotion, which can boost profits. In this instance, I have focused on sport, but the logic applies to achieving excellence in other areas of expertise, such as the arts or science. A support network that allows an individual to develop his or her full potential extends way beyond the family. It includes the social network, the sports and school communities, and society as a whole, in the form of companies and governments.

Main Points Covered in This Chapter

- A good platform enables freedom to choose.
- We are social beings: to love, be loved, and feel a sense of belonging are among our most basic human needs. We need a network of people we can count on during the hard times and with whom we can celebrate our successes.
- The types of support vary through different stages of life. It is important to look closely at the point of development and individual needs to ensure that each person realizes his or her potential. Dialogue and active listening are essential tools in facilitating this process.
- When providing emotional support, it is important to arm children with the strategies and tools they need to be aware of, reflect on, and manage their emotions. By having space to experience firsthand and learn from adversity, they develop the resilience muscle, which allows them to learn, gain confidence, and respond constructively when dealing with challenging situations in the future.
- To achieve excellence, people should be encouraged to push back the boundaries. Establishing a genuine and trusting relationship with a partner, close friend, or family member—someone who has our best interests at heart and will provide sincere feedback and state hard truths—is essential for us to connect with our essence and sense of purpose and, thus, grow and develop.
- The support network may extend beyond family and friends to involve the local and wider community of schools, clubs, companies, and government.

Powerful Questions to Reflect Upon

- How has your support network influenced your journey till now? How has this experience made a positive contribution to your life?
- How have you offered support to those around you? What could be improved?
- What have you done, or what could you do, to cultivate beautiful enemies in your life?
- What have you done to contribute to the children and adolescents around you to help them unlock their potential, identify purpose, and lead happy lives?

CHAPTER 2

―――

YOU ARE WHAT YOU **PRACTICE**

One is not born a genius. One becomes a genius.
—Simone de Beauvoir

Nobody told me it was impossible, so I did it.
—Jean Cocteau

He opened the book and put on the 3D glasses—the ones with blue and red lenses—and the photo showing a water polo game taking place in a crowded sports arena practically jumped off the page. For a few minutes, my father felt as if he were there, hearing the roar of the crowd. Just a rookie, he could sense this feeling move him. He imagined himself in the pool, with the crowd screaming his name at the sight of him playing.

Delighted, he closed the special edition on the 1936 Berlin Olympics that his coach Emeric Imre Szasz had shown him. It was yet another time when his Hungarian coach inspired him while challenging him to surpass his own limitations and become an Olympic athlete, something that would come to pass a few years later.

Beside the pool at the Clube de Regatas Tietê, there was a small room, a cubicle, in which Emeric kept his books. Another story he used to share with my father was that of Béla Rajki, the legendary coach who led the Hungarian team at the 1948, 1952, and 1956 Olympics, securing a gold medal each time. The book was illustrated throughout with photos of the athletes' performances. Emeric went through it page by page with my father, highlighting the position of each player. He pointed out the best player on each team and described all of their moves in detail. He then challenged my father to reproduce them. When my father entered the water, confident he was reproducing everything he had seen in the photos, Emeric was on his case, saying he had completed only 40 perfect and still had 60 percent to go. He then demonstrated the exact height that the arm should reach and the precise movement, and my father went back into the water, constantly coming and going, until he finally captured the precise movements of the player in the photo. After ten or fifteen days, he got to move on to the next page.

Another exercise he gave my father was to swim with the ball in the middle of the pool at midday on a Sunday, when it was crowded with members. The challenge was to cross the fifty meters without touching anyone. It seemed impossible, but Emeric was there egging him on. His path was fraught with people who suddenly plunged into the water beside him and children going back and forth. It was chaos, like crossing a minefield, except with the mines bobbing at random. But it was a useful challenge for both him and the team. There were few times when he managed to complete the task without hitting anyone, but there was not a single time when he left the pool without learning something from the experience. Even when he ran into a teammate along the way, he felt he was improving in several respects: in the zigzag, in drawing back the ball, and in his attention to his surroundings.

The Hard Yards: Practice and Dedication

It is common for people to attribute the success of elite athletes—or others who demonstrate expertise in their fields, such as musicians, scientists, or chess players—to an innate talent. Identifying such a talent gives us a basis for finding the right fit, but talent alone is not enough to reach excellence. Athletes need the practice element, appropriate guidance, and belief in order to achieve and sustain high performance. Many athletes and icons admired for their mastery separate themselves from the crowd not because they have a gift but because they are committed, focused, and hardworking.

And it is not enough to practice until you do it correctly just once. You need continuity and consistency, as observed by Daniel T. Willingham, professor of cognitive psychology and neuroscience at the University of Virginia.[1] The objective of practice is to improve. It requires time, repetition, effort, concentration, and constant feedback on the progress being made, as with the countless times my father got in and out of the pool, conferring with his coach on the exact positions of his Hungarian idols in the photos.

Marcelinho Huertas is a great example of how a passion for sport and dedication to training can converge to build a platform for a solid career. He told me he started playing basketball for pleasure: "When you are a child, you do what you like. I counted down on my fingers the hours before I could go onto the court. I stayed there as long as possible—the whole weekend. I didn't even stop for lunch." As a young man, he started to get noticed but was never called up for the junior teams. He said, "My career was different. I had to work extra hard. I forced my way little by little into the Brazilian team. I didn't arrive there taking my place in the team for granted. I had to earn my space." And he did it with a lot of dedication and perseverance, investing time and energy into honing his skills for his passion: basketball. In 2004, he put on a Brazil shirt for the first time, and from there, his career took off. More than fifteen years later, he continues to play at a high level in Europe. The secret? Do not stop investing in your own advancement, not even for a minute. Even after winning so many international tournaments, he is as dedicated as he was at the beginning of his career.

Great sports icons, such as Kobe Bryant, are also known for their strong commitment to practicing. Marcelinho, who was Kobe's teammate in the NBA, confided to me that he was impressed by his dedication. He said, "Kobe really was an inspiration. In one game, he missed a shot after a big play. Not satisfied, once everyone had left the gym, he went back onto the court and continued throwing the ball well into the night. He kept repeating the shot, exhaustively, so as to perfect it. It was also not uncommon to watch Kobe under the hoop with the ball in his hand but not throwing it, just working on his [trademark] footwork for hours at a time."

Deep Learning

Having been the coach of the American water polo team for many years, Sandy Nitta was also the coach of the Brazilian team when we won the bronze medal at the Pan American Games in Winnipeg in 1999. Sandy played a huge part in our getting there. Renowned and experienced, she was elected to the Water Polo Swimming Hall of Fame in 1998. When I asked her what advice she would give a young athlete, her response was emphatic: "Study, study, study! And practice! You must dedicate yourself for hours and hours. Always keep thinking of better ways for you to get there and continue excelling."

The key is to seek constant improvement. In addition to the training itself, we also need to study the theory and to read about the sport and about tactics, strategy, and especially mental preparation, nutrition, and recovery techniques. Watch every game you can—of your own team, the opposing team, and teams from different countries. It is always possible to learn something new or a different way of doing things.

Nowadays most championship games are filmed, and it is easy to get access to the videos. In my time as a player, when we participated in competitions, we tried to watch as many games live as possible right there at the venue. In addition, my mother, as director of women's water polo, invested in filming equipment and went out of her way to record the games we were not able to watch live. After dinner, the coach would bring in the VHS tapes so we could all watch them together and prepare for the next games.

On my gaining my certificate in the science of happiness from the Happiness Studies Academy, our professor, Tal Ben-Shahar, doctor of psychology, said, "To fulfill our potential as rational animals, we must engage in a process of deep learning. Although there is no connection between intelligence and happiness, there is a strong connection between how we use our intellect and how happy we are. Committing ourselves to a process of deep learning broadens our horizons and has the potential to promote our well-being." The greater our well-being, the greater our willingness to train, the better our immunity, and the more confident and able to evolve we become.

This was well illustrated by Portuguese soccer star Cristiano Ronaldo, who has been elected the best player in the world by FIFA five times. He said, "I feel an endless need to learn, to improve and to evolve, not only to please the coach or the fans, but to satisfy myself."[2]

Deep learning is about refining our skills to the maximum. An effective way to improve is through seeking questions rather than ready-made answers. Timothy Gallwey, author of the highly successful Inner Game series of books, is considered the father of modern sports psychology. He brought a lot of innovation to training methods, replacing the authoritarian style in which some coaches relate to players with the development of self-awareness regarding the athlete's body and technique. Gallwey instructed through asking questions, saying for example, "Tell me how you feel about doing this. When you turn your body in this way, what seems different to you?" These questions take the player into his own personal experience, building awareness and knowledge of his movements and variations.

Emeric deployed the same technique. "When you swim, do you carry the ball with your arms or your head?" he asked, until my father came to the conclusion that the correct answer was with his arms, since he needed to have his head raised to watch the game and the moves of his opponents. This is one of the most powerful ways to create learning. Instead of memorizing basic rules, players reflect on questions that help them find the answers from within. The knowledge that they themselves uncover ends up being more profound and flexible.

My father passed on Emeric's methods to me. At one point, he asked me, "In a quick counterattack, do you carry the ball with your arms or with your head?" Before I had time to choose the first option, he gave me a tip: "What feels wrong can actually be useful on certain occasions. When you sprint with your head down, you create a ripple in the water ahead of you, which helps you carry the ball." In this case, when the field is open before you, lowering your head enables you to counterattack more quickly, which, in that situation, is more important than being able to see the game and the opponents.

The Power of Habit

I used to awaken very early; put on my jeans, T-shirt, and sweatshirt; and go to college. I had lunch, swapped my student clothes for business attire, and went straight to work at the audit firm Price Waterhouse. I already had on my swimsuit, and after work, I went to water polo training from seven to ten at night. I came home exhausted, ate, and slept, and the next day, I started it all over again. I loved my routine, with its changing roles. I felt great satisfaction from investing in deeply learning the different skills associated with being a high-performance athlete and with putting my academic knowledge into practice at the start of my corporate career. On weekends, I practiced with my father and brothers, met up with friends, and got involved in other sports activities.

Given my grueling training schedule, even amid everything else I did each day, I was often praised for my strength of will. And it is true—I have always been disciplined and focused.

My life was a series of routines. In order to keep up with my studies and training routine, I needed a well-organized schedule. More than willpower, I focused on creating habits and routines and prioritizing my actions.

It might seem that people with great self-control are not trying hard, but this is because they have switched to automatic mode. According to Charles Duhigg, award-winning writer of the book *The Power of Habit*, willpower is the most important habit of all for individual success.[3] It acts like a muscle, and we need to exercise it every day to make it stronger, increasing the load each time. We just must be careful not to overload the willpower muscle with too many tasks requiring self-control, as we can get tired and become more likely to fail.

It is interesting to note that when we choose to develop or do something that will benefit ourselves or someone else, the activity becomes more pleasurable or at least not as tiring. When we have limited autonomy to make choices on a project and are merely following orders, our willpower muscles get tired much more quickly.

Practicing a sport from childhood is about progressively developing self-control, discipline, and perseverance or, put another way, exercising the willpower muscle. If you find meaning in a practice, if it is linked to a goal, you will have a better chance of turning it into a habit.

"Champions don't do extraordinary things. They do ordinary things, but they do them without thinking, too fast for the other team to react. They follow the habits they've learned."[4] This quote from Tony Dungy, one of the few people to win a Super Bowl both as a player (in 1979) and as a coach (in 2007), captures the importance of developing habits in achieving high performance.

But how do we form habits? Habits stem from changes in the neural pathways, which turn the behavior into a natural part of you. For the most part, we establish habits by repeating a certain sequence of actions— which can be a physical, mental, or emotional routine; thus, habits are dependent on consistent, regular practice.

Duhigg goes into more detail by dividing the habit into three stages: a cue, a routine, and a reward. For example, for the automated behavior of brushing your teeth at night, the cue could be thinking, *It's time for bed.* Just by entering your head, these words stimulate your brain to go into automatic mode and run the routine, which is the automated sequence of actions you perform, from opening the bathroom cabinet where you keep the toothbrush and toothpaste through to rinsing out with mouthwash. You do it all without thinking. The feeling of freshness and clean teeth is the reward, which is what reinforces your brain to memorize this routine and make it a habit.

To automate new behaviors, it is important to be clear about which routine you wish to automate and to identify impactful rewards, preferably linked to your goals, values, and desires. The routine should be linked to a cue, which might be a cell phone alarm, a wristband, or a phrase you repeat to yourself—anything that makes you remember and quickly access the routine. Then repeat, repeat, and repeat, practicing this cycle exhaustively.

Focus on the Present Moment

Mindfulness is a term that refers to a form of meditation or mental state. Being mindful means being present, with a focus on the here and now, aware of our experience moment by moment and of our own thoughts and emotions without judging them.

In sport, high performance generally occurs when we perform our moves and routines automatically but with all our attention and awareness focused on the present moment. The state of full attention amplifies the power of the habit.

Automating behaviors has the function of freeing cognitive and mental resources so we can focus on the strategic aspects of each move. For example, in a water polo game, movement of the arms and legs must be automatic, while thought should remain focused on the present moment so as to execute the best strategy. In the same way, to deliver an important report, typing should be automatic, so you are free to focus on the content.

When we are feeling distracted or too worried about the future, regretting something we did in the past, or letting anxiety take over, we may be able to carry out automated moves and routines, but our performance falls well below our potential.

In order to improve any skill, it is important to learn from past mistakes and have a clear vision of our future goals. However, during training and practice, we must be fully focused on the present moment. Ellen Jane Langer, professor of psychology at Harvard University, says there are two ways to act when we do something: attentive, conscious, and present (mindful) or distracted and careless, with our head anywhere other than the present moment (mindless).[5] The consequences of being in one or the other of the mental states are enormous.

The state of mindfulness allows you to enjoy life as it happens in the present moment and to learn more from each experience. If we are engaged with the present, the here and now in our lives, we learn to observe the ordinary in an extraordinary way. Maintaining this mental state is not an easy task, but it is a worthwhile effort and becomes easier as we practice the skill. Practicing mindfulness and meditation—along with other techniques in mental preparation—should be part of the high-performance training.

Amplifying the Talent

I always liked to describe myself as an all-rounder in water polo, as I learned to play in all the positions, except in goal. When I went to Italy, as a forward, I started to learn defensive techniques, a weakness of mine to that point. That not only strengthened my defensive side but also improved my attacking skills, as I learned more about how defenders thought and behaved.

Water polo is a dynamic sport that is a lot like life. There are some plays in which you may be a specialist at playing out wide but end up defending the center or in which you need to shoot from your weaker side. When the players on the team acquire systemic knowledge of the game, they can improvise when faced with unusual situations, and the chance of success increases.

I, as a forward, was rarely required to play like a center, a position in which the player has her back to the goal and is at the center of the team's formation. However, at the end of a game against Spain, with the score tied, the opposing defense was man-marking our players very well, so I took the initiative to suddenly play like a center. I received the ball and took a reverse shot, scoring the winning goal. It was the first time I had scored such a goal. My improvisation came about only because I had practiced it in training, even though I had had no intention of trying it. While practicing passing and shooting drills with me in the pool, at one point, my father had taught me the reverse shot. We'd alternated repeatedly until the movement became natural.

To enhance my overall sporting performance, I did not just learn all the positions in water polo. Back in high school, when I took part in an exchange program in Maryland, I took up many sports, including basketball, horseback riding, and lacrosse. Each taught me skills that contributed to my development as a water polo player. From basketball, I learned how to better position my body and the importance of teamwork; from horseback riding, I learned balance; and from lacrosse, I gained coordination.

My father always told me, "Play other sports as much as you wish. You will learn new techniques and strategies, other ways to shoot and serve, and different ways to position your body. After all, all these skills and experiences come together to create your own technique and view of the game and make up the building blocks to becoming a champion."

Frank Steel, director of Gulliver Schools, commented to me about the importance of cross training, saying, "When you play different sports, especially in the early stages of experimentation, you deal with distinctive physical and mental challenges. And then, when you reach a higher level in your chosen sport, you have a broader set of experiences to call upon, and you become more adaptable. When you are trying your best in a game and it is not working, you'll be able to adapt and innovate. Even if you've never faced a situation before, you'll be better equipped to figure it out."

A good coach prepares the team to be able to respond at critical points in a game, but at any given moment, it is the players in the arena who will make the decisions, based on their reading of the opportunity that presents itself, which might only last a few seconds. Therefore, in training, it is essential to prepare as much as possible for these situations that take you outside of what is expected of your position.

When Emeric coached my father and his teammates early in their development, he encouraged them all to train in different positions and even asked some players to act as referee during training. The players thus gained a different perspective and, come game time, better understood what the referee was thinking and how to deal with and adapt to his decisions.

This system of learning different skills rather than focusing purely on your area of expertise is called talent rotation. It is a process that can enhance both individual and team performance and can take people out of their comfort zone.

Staying in the comfort zone, while it offers satisfaction, safety, connection, and predictability, prevents the athlete from improving. During training, always repeating the same moves, marking the same player, or practicing the same shots is limiting. Repetition is important, as is introducing small challenges to every practice session that teach something new to the athlete. Seeking versatility can be key to achieving better performance and pushing back the boundaries.

Of course, in any sport, it is difficult to master every position. But it is necessary at least to try to learn those things you find difficult. It is important to have the courage to experiment and take risks.

To expand your arsenal of tools and techniques and learn new positions is to put aside the status quo and think beyond what you are used to. In the beginning, you might feel awkward, but over time, these new abilities start to come naturally and will make you a more complete player.

Corporate Use

Researchers Tor Eriksson and Jaime Ortega studied Danish companies to investigate the main benefits of job rotation.[6] Although many theorists point to the motivational effects, as employees may get tired of performing the same tasks repeatedly, Eriksson and Ortega demonstrated that the greatest benefits of carrying out such rotation come from the learning experience, with respect to both employees and managers. Employees accumulate more skills and knowledge, as they are exposed to a wider range of experiences, while the company gets to learn more about its employees, as it can observe how they perform in different functions. To find the corporate role in which an employee performs best, the manager needs to observe how he or she performs in different positions and with different sets of responsibilities.

When I was working at Unibanco, I passed through several areas of the company, such as finance, human resources, quality and customer excellence, and sales. When I moved between departments, I not only learned new skills but also disseminated experiences acquired in the previous area. A new role can be permanent or temporary, just to expand knowledge of related areas. It is also important to be aware of how frequently people have moved. Staying in one position for a certain period also has its benefits, as it allows the employee to master and improve the activities integral to the role being performed. Therefore, it is important to review each case on its merits.

At the bank, we established the practice of putting oneself in others' shoes, an experience in which employees spent a few days in other areas related to theirs. From this exercise, they realized how new perspectives could enhance their performance. By better understanding the different positions, employees improve the quality of the work they carry out—as they understand how the information or product impacts the related area—and are less likely to enter into conflict with people from other areas when a problem arises. They gain a more holistic view and can be protagonists in promoting efficiency and teamwork. In this sense, job rotation can be useful for broadening perspectives on how the company functions as a whole and on the business and strategy.

Through this practice, people can discover skills they did not even know they possessed and even take their careers in a new direction. The role of management, as with sports coaches, is to identify the skills any given individual has the potential to develop in a new role and the best moment to make the switch.

Programs like this must be managed responsibly and be well planned, creating a process that brings benefits to both the department that releases the employee and the one that receives him, not forgetting the employee himself. Placing someone in a role for which he does not have the right profile can cause efficiency problems. The focus is on the learning process.

Practice Taken to the Extreme

From my time playing for Orizzonte Catania in Sicily, I have fond memories of a great coach and true sporting enthusiast: Mauro Maugeri. His veins were throbbing during every game. His trademark was his booming voice as he barked commands in training or during games.

At one of the training sessions, in which we were doing a series of swimming sprints of up to ten strokes, Mauro challenged me. "I want to see your best time in the hundred-meter freestyle." He put Cristina Consoli up against me. She was one of the fastest swimmers and a member of the Italian national water polo team. I was already tired, it was the last activity, and I already felt as if I had given my all. But I accepted the challenge.

We took off, and I was racing side by side with the Italian. At the fifty-meter turn, I realized that we were in the same rhythm and that I could win. We reached the finish almost together—Cristina won by a stroke. But I had beaten my personal best by two seconds, which is a lot for a hundred-meter race. I reached the edge, and the inevitable happened: as I left the pool, exhausted, I brought everything up. But Mauro just stood there applauding with a look of pride and shouted, *"Brava*, Pinciroli! *Brava!"*

It was only part of a training session, but I faced it as if it were the Olympic final of the sport. I achieved peak performance. I am not advocating that every athlete should try to put this level of effort into every training session, but it does illustrate that it is surprising what we can achieve when we break beyond the barrier of physical tiredness.

I started to reflect. How can we enable people—in sport, at work, in science, or in the arts—to reach peak performance more frequently and consistently? Peak performance is possible when we match our level of expertise to the challenge provided.

The more we undergo extreme situations in training, the more confidence we gain in ourselves, creating anchors that enable us to summon the same level of performance later. In addition, according to Robert J. Harmison, professor of sports psychology at Argosy University in Phoenix, an athlete needs to invest in self-knowledge, become aware of the mental state that leads to high performance, and acquire the psychological skills that will allow him to return to that state.[7]

I have always felt that training should not be something robotic, just repeating the same motions, with all the excitement saved for game day. There should be extra challenges occasionally. In training, it is possible to go beyond your limits, especially when you put yourself in a game situation. It is important to simulate extreme circumstances, such as a tied championship final with the clock running down, and to find solutions as to what to do at those times—before they occur for real.

Ahead of any game, my father would always say to me, "Play like you are in a world final." I carry this idea into training. Practice like you are in a crucial game. In the pool, when I practiced shooting against our team's goalkeeper, I saw her as an opponent I had to defeat and pulled out every trick to try to score.

When I spoke to Sandy Nitta, who became a great mentor of mine and a friend for life, she recalled my determination in training, including my desire to always learn new things and carry out her instructions to the letter. "You were one of the only players I ever coached that I had to ask not to train but to go rest," she confided in me recently. It is true. She needed to remind me of the importance of taking a break and recovering so as to not only achieve excellence but also sustain it. I will talk more about this in the next chapter.

Another coach who has pushed players to the limit in training is Ratko Rudić, considered one of the most renowned coaches in the history of water polo. The Croatian became known in Brazil beyond just the water polo community when he trained the men's team at Rio in 2016. The same year, he was elected by the Brazilian Olympic Committee (COB) as Coach of the Year in Team Sports. Rudić told me that award was one of the most important he received in his entire career. He led the Brazilians in a historic campaign. They fell in the quarterfinals after three consecutive victories in the competition. In the first phase, Brazil defeated a strong Serbian team, who went on to take gold.

Rudić's curriculum is immense. He has taken part in nine Olympics for five different countries (four as a player—in 1968, '72, '76, and '80—and five as a coach) and won four gold medals. One of the secrets to his success has been putting together a training plan that considers the physical, psychological, and teamwork aspects, with general knowledge, ethics, and values thrown in. The training is considered insane by many who have been through it.

Between 2001 and 2004, Rudić coached the American team. When Rudić arrived, he subjected the players to exhausting training for eight hours a day - twice a day for four hours. His former players say Rudic was the most inspiring leader they have ever met. "He always knew he could get more from players than players can even imagine," said UCLA University water polo coach Adam Wright.[8]

The training also included tough weightlifting sessions, endless legwork, exhausting repetitions for improving technique, and tactical sessions. His philosophy is that if a player quits during practice, he will end up quitting in the game too. He spares no one. For Rudić, there are two types of players: those with talent and those who complement the team, without whom it would be impossible to build a top team. For both, practice is essential. From his perspective, the talented ones are the ones who train even harder because they know that is the only way to achieve excellence.

Ian Adamson, an adventure racing champion who has accumulated seven world titles and three Guinness World Records, posits that if you experience intense situations frequently, this can help you face difficult situations when they arise. "Dealing with adventures or extreme situations makes the everyday problems seem less problematic. You learn to see challenges, not problems, lessons, not mistakes, and over time, more things become possible."

Where Are the Limits?

Until 1954, people believed it was impossible to run a mile in under four minutes. Australian John Landy, one of the great runners at the time, called this limit "the brick wall." Experts compared the feat to climbing Everest and said that anyone who tried to achieve a time under four minutes could face serious health risks. However, a medical student at Oxford University, Roger Bannister, who also was a brilliant runner, sought to break through the barrier. He said—shocking people at the time—that this limit was not physical but mental.

He set the date for May 6, 1954, on Iffley Road, the main arterial road in Oxford. In one of the most exciting moments in the history of world athletics, he achieved the unbelievable time of 3 minutes and 59.4 seconds.

Usually, it is enough for someone to demonstrate that the seemingly impossible is possible for others to do the same. Landy beat the Iffley Road record the following month with a time of 3 minutes and 57.9 seconds, and in the three years that followed, another fifteen runners accomplished the same feat. Bannister had proven that his theory was correct. The limit had been in the minds of the runners.

Croatian Rudić used to teach, "It's all in the mind." He used to take his athletes beyond their limits, and he made them believe they could work even harder when they were at the peak of fatigue. He knew he could get more out of a player than the player himself could ever have imagined. Rudić told me he tried to set an example since his own actions and attitudes influenced the whole team. He said, "My goal was to prepare men for life and not merely to be the best in the sport."

To achieve performance peaks more often, it is necessary to develop mental toughness. This concept is central to sports psychology and refers to the ability to resist and overcome doubts, concerns, fears, and anxieties to constructively manage adverse situations.

When Sandy Nitta coached the Brazilian team and helped set up our dream team, the aspect she invested the most time in was mental preparation.

Mental toughness requires regular practice and total focus and is often taken to the extreme. Every time we anticipate game situations in training, we are not only improving our skills but also preparing to deal with H hour and better manage the emotional factors involved.

It is also possible to train and improve our mental fortitude through work focused on our thoughts and attitudes toward problems, errors, difficulties, and pressure. "Read books about mental toughness," advises Sandy. "I have read more than thirty-four books myself and have come to reread some of them," she adds.

The Most Powerful Simulator in the World

"I got hurt badly before going to the Olympics. There was no treatment for my back injury, and I was unable to train, which killed my chances of winning. Well, I trained—in my mind. I visualized every detail that would lead to my best performance. When my competition arrived, my back was rested enough to allow me to compete, and my mind compensated for what I needed physically. When I entered the Olympic stadium on the day of the competition, I felt good. During the warm-up, I felt ready. My mind was convinced that this was my day."[9] This account, which illustrates how powerful visualization can be, came from American Dana Hee, winner of the lightweight category in tae kwon do at the 1988 Olympics in Seoul.

The most powerful simulator in the world is our mind, and visualization is the most efficient way to use this simulator for important life situations. Visualization involves repeatedly imagining, in a conscious and organized way, what you want to achieve, in order to make it happen in real life. The simulation can include motor actions, planning strategy, and other sensory experiences, using all five senses.

This process activates the same areas of the brain as those we use to accomplish what we are visualizing: the motor and sensorimotor cortex. In other words, our nervous system does not know the difference between an imagined event and a real event. For our minds, it is all the same, and this is what makes this technique so powerful. However, it is not about focusing on the results, such as imagining yourself on the podium with the gold medal around your neck. It is about simulating the process and living the experience, following each step that takes you to achieving the main objective.

Russian and Eastern European athletes were the first to use this technique to improve their performance. The practice has been widely disseminated and is common among elite athletes. Pelé, the soccer legend, is known to have spent thirty minutes before each game lying down with a towel over his head, mentally rehearsing his moves amid different game scenarios. In addition to improving performance through generating greater focus and confidence, these mental images enhance our ability to control anxiety. It is as if we have already gone through the experience.

A study published in *Applied and Preventive Psychology* reviewed all the situations in which visualization has been used by athletes and found five main uses: acquiring skills; managing anxiety; boosting self-confidence; controlling pain; and acting as an adjunct or substitute for physical practice,[10] as illustrated by Dana Hee's account.

Practicing and Visualizing

I always enjoyed training, and the practice did not end when I got out of the pool. Many nights, after training, with my head resting on my pillow, I used to go through moves that needed to be improved. Like a video replay, I relived the most unusual periods of a game, training, or even my own moves. It also was not unusual for me to find my father ready to share some ideas about the game at breakfast. Together we simulated the moves that would happen later in the water.

One time, I was playing in Italy and cut my eyebrow. With the blood running, I lost my focus and let my anger get the better of me. After the match, a player from the opposing team, Napoli, taunted me. "I've already got you figured out. Once you get hurt, you lose your head, and your skills go out the window," she told me. That remark made me more upset than the cut itself. My priority became to improve my way of dealing with anger when I got hurt, and I used the visualization technique to help me with this.

A few months later, I was attending the men's water polo final at the Barcelona Olympics in 1992, when Manuel Estiarte[5] cut his eyebrow but remained unperturbed. He didn't even get out of the water. The doctor went over to him and stapled his cut to stem the bleeding, as it is not permitted to play while bleeding, and he continued playing as if nothing had happened. I incorporated that scene into my visualizations. In my imagination, I was the one who suffered the injury but remained in control and went back to the match and performed my best afterward.

One of the advantages of visualization is that it can be practiced as often as you wish, anytime, and anywhere. With just five minutes a day, it can have a huge impact, whatever the goal you wish to achieve.

Even back in the 1960s, my father often practiced visualization. He went over key events from the match in his mind—on the bus going to the pool, when the teams lined up before the game, during the breaks, and after the game. He would do this nearly every day, with visualizations that took no longer than a couple of minutes.

The first step is to breathe and try to empty your mind as best as you can. Then you learn to create and shape your reality (mentalization) in order to awaken within you a feeling that will help you put into practice everything you need to get to where you wish to go.

When imagining these scenarios, the athlete should add in the details and the sensation he would feel in a real performance. These scenarios should include as many of the five senses as possible. They can be visual (images and photos), kinesthetic (the feelings in the body), or auditory (the cries of the crowd). These sensory factors help to make the visualization more detailed and powerful.

---

[5] Manuel Estiarte was part of the golden generation of Spanish water polo. He was an Olympic runner-up in 1992 and gold medalist in Atlanta in 1996.

The practice of visualization should be similar and complementary to physical training. It is only effective if accompanied by the right real-world training. Like Olympic athletes, you still need to spend many hours physically working on your skills to get results. Visualization acts like software for the subconscious. With practice, you will build a strong platform for mental development, which is essential to the quality of your game. As a result, you will perform better in and out of swimming pools, on and off courts, in and out of sports arenas, and in life. Being a champion is not only about overcoming your opponent but also about exploiting your talents to reach the highest level.

The limits are only in our minds, and if we learn how to use the right tools to improve our training and performance, we uncover limitless possibilities.

Main Points Covered in This Chapter

- Achieving and sustaining high performance takes practice and dedication. The practice should be regular and consistent and involve deep learning.
- The repetition of behaviors and routines leads to the formation of new habits, which enable the release of cognitive and mental abilities that allow us to be more strategic in our performance and more connected with the present.
- In order to increase the frequency and consistency with which we achieve peak performance, it is important we strive to surpass our own limits not only during games but also when training.
- Limits and barriers exist in our minds. Therefore, mental preparation should be an integral part of training in order to enhance our ability to overcome doubts, concerns, fears, and anxiety.
- Visualization is a powerful technique that can be deployed as part of mental and emotional preparation and as a complement to real practice.

- Does your daily behavior reflect your objectives? How dedicated have you been to practicing and training the skills you need in order to achieve and sustain high performance?
- Have you been dedicated to deep learning in your own areas of interest? How mentally prepared are you to deal with adversity? Have you included these aspects in your training?

CHAPTER 3

HEALTHY LIFESTYLE: TAKING CARE OF THE DETAILS

If we adopted the right lifestyle, we could add at least ten good
years and suffer only a fraction of the diseases that kill us
prematurely. This could mean an extra quality decade of life.
—Dan Buettner

Your longevity in sport is dictated by how you live between fights.
—Carl Froch

From Argentina to Auckland, New Zealand, the journey took thirty-two hours. We crossed the world, stopping over in Tierra del Fuego in Patagonia and passing through Sydney, until we arrived in Perth in Western Australia. We touched down a few days before the start of the tournament. I was nineteen years old and was on my way to my first aquatic sports world championship. The best athletes in swimming, synchronized swimming, marathon swimming, diving, and water polo would all be there. The first Brazilian women's water polo team, of which I was a part, was just starting to establish itself in the sport. It was basically made up of players from São Paulo and Rio de Janeiro, which, at the time, were the only centers for the sport in Brazil.

On arrival, we held a few training sessions and acclimatized ourselves to being around all these top athletes. We knew we were too inexperienced to have any chance of winning, but we were there to learn and not let ourselves down.

The championship lasted ten days, and we found ourselves in a tough group, alongside the Hungarians, the Americans, and the Australians, the hosts. The matches were intense, and I did not leave the water for even a minute. I gave my all in the pool, playing as if each game were the last of my life—so much so that I lost six kilos while there. During the final days of the championship, when I breathed, my ribs hurt.

We soon realized the size of the gap between ourselves and the top teams. I could see that good technical and tactical preparation was not enough to be among the best in the world. Up close, I saw that the players on the best teams were not only stronger than we were but also more in tune in how they moved, in the routines they followed both before and during the matches, and how consistent they were in their style of play. The difference was not only in experience or technique. The secret was in the details.

Years later, at the Pan American women's water polo tournament in Puerto Rico, the scenario was different. We were now among the favorites in the competition. I flew directly from Rome, as I was living there at the time. It was a challenging environment, as the pool was outdoors, and we were playing in heat of 40 degrees Celsius. We drove ourselves to new heights in each game, and we won. A few days later, I was back in Italy, playing in the semifinals of the Italian championship for Visnova in Caserta, Naples. The following week, I crossed the ocean again and played in Quebec, Canada, representing Brazil in the women's world water polo tournament.

By that point, I understood the importance of the details in sustaining that sequence of games, which require intense effort of body and mind. The foundation we need to deliver and sustain high performance includes—in addition to a support network and continual practice, as discussed in previous chapters—care of the body, mind, and spirit through the adoption of a healthy lifestyle.

What Works for Each of Us

There is no one way to achieve a healthy lifestyle. It is important that we find what works best for us. There are three levels of knowledge: universal, cultural, and individual. A universal truth is something that holds true for human beings in general, such as the importance of a good diet, a good night's sleep, exercise, and connection with others. A cultural truth follows the customs, habits, and values of a given culture, such as the way in which people from different parts of the world show their affection. I realized that in Italy, as in most Latin American countries, it is common to touch one another in relationships, whether through kisses, hugs, or touches on the arm when explaining something. Individual truth relates to each of us as an individual. How much food do I need to feel satisfied? How many hours of sleep do I need each night to feel energized the next morning? What kind of exercise do I enjoy? Do I feel at ease in hugging and touching people, or am I more reserved?

Universal truths can be identified by studying both the ordinary and the extraordinary. In order to understand a behavioral or natural phenomenon, many scientific studies investigate what is expected, or common, in an average population. Abraham H. Maslow, one of the main exponents of humanistic psychology, took a different approach to unlocking the mysteries of human potential. He suggested studying a select sample of extremely talented individuals in depth in seeking to understand the extraordinary. "If we want to know how fast a human being can run, then it is no use to average out the speed of a 'good sample' of the population. It is far better to collect Olympic gold medal winners and see how well they can do," he argued.[1] Some criticized his approach as being undemocratic, but what he proposed was just the opposite. By our promoting a greater understanding of people who differentiate themselves in the most diverse of environments, the concept of excellence is democratized, and it is possible to develop strategies and actions that will enhance and improve everyone.

To find our individual truths, we should equip ourselves with universal and cultural knowledge while at the same time immersing ourselves in self-knowledge, learning from trial and error about what makes sense for us. The methodology proposed by Maslow can also be applied to exploring our own experiences. We can reflect on the times when we were extraordinary and the factors involved in reaching our peak performance. By identifying the elements that lead us to achieve our best, we can reproduce these situations more often and enhance our overall well-being over a long period of time.

The Study of the Blue Zones

Dan Buettner, author of several *New York Times* best sellers, working alongside *National Geographic*, has identified four areas in the world where people live the longest, often exceeding one hundred years old, while also enjoying their quality of life. He has named these areas Blue Zones. They are as follows: a region on the island of Sardinia, Italy; the islands of Okinawa, Japan; the Nicoya Peninsula in Costa Rica; and a Seventh-Day Adventist community in the city of Loma Linda, California.

He interviewed the people in each of these locations and identified that they not only lived longer but also enjoyed good health and a high quality of life. Buettner studied their habits, practices, and behaviors and identified the fundamental ingredients for a long and healthy life.

The inhabitants of the Blue Zones have a strong sense of purpose in life and sense of belonging to the community. In general, they are associated with a religion and have an interest in the spiritual aspects of life. Family and social connections are extremely important to them. They do not eat to excess. Their diet is rich in vegetables and plants and includes a glass of wine. In addition, they remain active. They do not frequent the gym, but they do incorporate physical activity into their daily lives, such as taking care of the garden or walking to their appointments. But they also find moments to stop to rest and replenish their energy levels.[2]

A classic study carried out using pairs of Danish twins found that genetic and hereditary aspects contribute only 25 percent to the factors determining whether someone has a long life, while lifestyle contributes the other 75 percent.[3] Thus, taking Maslow's approach, investigating the behavior of the healthiest people on the planet, who have the longest lifespan, should teach us a lot about the daily choices we make in our own lives in order to maximize health and life expectancy. Similarly, we can learn a lot from athletes who maintain high levels of performance over a long sports career.

Longevity in Sport

Not long ago, in most sports, when athletes passed age thirty, they were considered to be at the end of their career. However, in recent years, this has changed. Robert Scheidt, a champion yachtsman and the greatest Brazilian individual Olympic medalist, is an example of longevity in sport. He has spent the past twenty-five years among the best in the world. After winning his first world championship at the age of twenty-two, Scheidt won another twelve major tournaments. He also took gold at two Olympics, in addition to two silvers and a bronze. At forty-seven, in perfect physical shape, he qualified for his seventh Olympics, becoming the first Brazilian to achieve such a feat.

When I interviewed him for this book, Scheidt attributed the greater longevity of current athletes to more complete preparation, highlighting several aspects of the athletes' health. He said, "In the past, there was physical conditioning, training, and competition. Today we have 360-degree preparation, with a physiotherapist, osteopath, nutritionist, and sports psychologist. Over the years, training has become more qualitative than quantitative, and the athlete can devote more time to recovery and to the physical aspects."

Scheidt argues that you do not have to be a machine or have an extremely rigid routine to get the results he has achieved for so long. He told me, "Of course, you need discipline to stay true to the process you create. But there must be time for fun or a break or time with family and friends. You have to have this balance, because if you stretch the rope too far on one side, it will snap on the other."

The paradigm of an athlete being considered old at age thirty is changing, as illustrated by Swiss tennis star Roger Federer. Holder of a record-breaking twenty Grand Slam titles, Federer is the player who has spent the most time at the top of the world rankings, a total of 310 weeks between 2004 and 2018. At the age of thirty-five, he secured his eighteenth Grand Slam title at the Australian Open in 2017, where he beat Rafael Nadal of Spain. Nadal was five years younger and known for his superb physical condition. The match lasted more than three and a half hours and was decided in an epic fifth set. After being down three games to one, Federer turned things around in one of the most memorable moments in the history of world tennis.

René Stauffer, a biographer and Swiss compatriot, puts Federer's vitality down to long-term planning: "Roger never set short-term goals. He always wanted to maximize his time on the circuit."[4] When he was younger, starting out on his career, he played fewer tournaments than many of his peers, which preserved his condition. As he grew older, Federer adapted his style to finish points more quickly, with shorter rallies and less movement on the court.

Marcelinho Huertas says that at thirty-seven, he does not have the same physical condition as when he began his basketball career. "But my mind is much sharper. I do performance coaching, watch what I eat, rest, get a good night's sleep, and am always looking for ways to improve." For him, off-court factors are important in delivering his individual performance within the collective. The more time that passes, the more attention we need to pay to factors outside the sport. "There are few players who reach my age and continue to shine," he told me. "I take great care of myself because I want to continue playing."

Longevity in athletes has been seen in the most diverse of sports, such as surfing, in which North American eleven-time champion Kelly Slater remains active at forty-five; gymnastics, in which Uzbek Oksana Chusovitina competed at the Olympics in Rio de Janeiro at the age of forty-one; and equestrianism, in which New Zealander Julie Brougham competed in the dressage in Rio at an unbelievable sixty-two years old.

Peter Diamandis of Singularity University believes that human longevity will soon increase by forty years, thanks to advances in medicine and technology. "With Big Pharma, start-ups, and the FDA [Food and Drug Administration] starting to treat aging as a disease, we are starting to turn those answers into practical ways for extending our lifespan," he has said.[5]

All of these advances could also further extend the life of top athletes. The expectation is we will see more and more elite athletes at advanced ages. Combining physical condition and experience, they will be able to challenge younger athletes as equals.

The Secrets of Healthy Eating

When I played in that first world championship in 1991, we did not hear much about the importance of sports nutrition, but when we looked at our opponents, we realized we needed specialist help in that area. Our team could not carry on leaving the pool so exhausted and barely recovering in time for the next game. We needed nutritional guidance both for training and for games and also on the supplements we needed.

Years later, when I played for Orizzonte Catania in Sicily, there was a nutritional plan for the entire season. It was a detail that made a difference. Once a month, we had a visit from a nutritionist, who opened our refrigerators, made a note of what we were eating, and offered us some guidance. This proved decisive in improving my performance both as an individual and as a contributor to the team. We arrived mostly in good shape to face the best teams across the nation and in Europe. Healthy eating was one of the key factors in our winning the Copa dei Campioni interclub tournament, the equivalent of the UEFA Champions League in soccer.

Dan Buettner observed that nutrition had a great effect on longevity and quality of life in the Blue Zones. He reached a few conclusions. The first relates to food intake. Okinawan seniors eat from smaller dishes, with the food kept at a distance from the eating area, on a counter from which they serve themselves and bring their dish to the table. Before eating, they repeat the phrase *hara hachi bu*, which literally means "80 percent of your stomach." It serves as a reminder as to when to stop eating. Today the average daily calorie intake at the location is only 1,900 calories.

Another conclusion was to drink red wine. Of course, consumption should be done in moderation. In Sardinia, a glass of red wine with each meal is essential, especially when friends meet for dinner. "A glass of wine occasionally goes down well. I always drink some. You just can't drink a bottle," Robert Scheidt told me from Italy, where he currently lives with his family. I too learned to appreciate a glass of good wine while living in that amazing country, which has a unique fusion of food, wine, and culture.

We should also avoid processed foods, something nearly all nutritionists agree on. Most of the centenarians in Nicoya, Sardinia, and Okinawa never had a chance to develop the habit of eating processed foods, such as soda or salty snacks. In addition, they avoid meat—not least because they never used to have access to it—except on rare occasions. Grains, fruits, nuts, and garden vegetables form the basis of their meals. In other words, they have a plant-based diet.

Marcelinho Huertas told me he has made an important change to his diet in recent years. He said, "I followed the recommendation of a nutritionist and gradually cut out meat and cheese. I am almost a vegetarian. I still eat fish, but the rest of the food is plant-based. This change has brought many benefits for my health. I have lost fat and gained muscle mass. I used to feel a lot of pain in the joints and knees, with a lot of inflammation. Incredible as it may seem, this has all gone away. I don't know how I would be if I hadn't changed my diet."

The trend of many top athletes switching to a plant-based diet was discussed in the movie *The Game Changers*, directed by Oscar-winning filmmaker Louie Psihoyos. The documentary tells the story of James Wilks, winner of *The Ultimate Fighter* in the United Kingdom, as he travels the world in search of the ideal diet for maximizing performance. In his saga, he discusses the change in diet of various stars, including seven-time Formula One champion Lewis Hamilton; tennis player Novak Djokovic, a winner of nineteen Grand Slams; weightlifter Patrik Baboumian, considered the strongest man in Germany; and others.

American cyclist Dotsie Bausch earned a silver medal in the team pursuit at the 2012 Olympic Games in London. She was thirty-nine years old and became the oldest woman to win an Olympic medal in one of the most intense sports in the competition. Dotsie reveals that in her preparation, by adopting a plant-based diet, she saw a dramatic improvement in performance and recovery: "I was able to move 300 pounds (136 kilos) on the inverted leg press before going plant-based, but right before the Olympics, I had gotten up to 600 pounds (272 kilos), [doing] sixty reps [for] five sets."[6] The diet, in her opinion, was essential to achieving the ideal preparation for winning an Olympic medal.

American football star Tom Brady—who, in 2021, at the age of forty-three, became the oldest player to compete in a Super Bowl—created a more flexible diet to balance food harvested from the land with other foods. He launched the *TB12⁶ Nutrition Manual*, in which he declares that 80 percent of his diet is based on organic plants and fruits, many of them harvested from the player's own garden and eaten raw. According to Brady, this diet should not include sugar, iodized salt, caffeine, alcohol, processed foods, gluten, or even certain vegetables, such as tomatoes. The other 20 percent of the diet includes meat, fish, and chicken and allows for a little of whatever you fancy, even if it is not especially healthy. "If I am craving bacon, I have a piece. Same with pizza," he said in an interview.[7] He attributes his ability to continue to play at the highest level, even at forty-three years old, to his diet.

Robert Scheidt has never tried a plant-based diet, as he needs to gain weight and maintain a high degree of muscle mass. He has said, "I am afraid of having the opposite effect. With respect to food, I avoid excess. I eat a lot of fish, salad, and fruit, without a lot of fried food or red meat."

This balance has worked for me too. At home, with my parents, I learned to eat healthily. In Italy, I realized how food could further enhance my performance. However, I did not completely forego my personal tastes. While caffeine was not highly recommended for sport, from time to time, I drank a cup of coffee. This connected me, on some level, to Brazil. It was a way of compensating for missing my family and friends, which itself gave me more energy. Another thing I could not go without for long was savoring an Italian *vero gelato* (ice cream) or an almond granita with a touch of coffee, a dessert typical of Catania, Sicily, which gave me a moment to relax, laugh with friends, and recover after a long and demanding physical routine. The key message here is to delve into the latest nutritional trends while at the same time identifying what works best for you.

Obeying Nature in Order to Command It

When I was pregnant with my first daughter, Alissa, my pace of life was pretty frenetic. I was deeply involved with my work at the bank. I loved what I did and was committed to achieving excellence, by then as an

---

[6] *TB* stands for *Tom Brady*, and 12 is the number of his shirt.

executive. I accepted all the challenges my manager sent my way and often urged my team to go the extra mile. In my striving to achieve the targets we set, it was not uncommon for me to skip a meal or two, sleep less than I needed, or compromise my rest and leisure time.

During my sporting career, I had learned to go beyond physical pain and discomfort in pursuit of my goal to be one of the best water polo players in the world. "Great athletes never ask to get out of the water or give in to fatigue. They know that the barrier is mental, and they can always give more," my father reminded me. I took that lesson on board and carried it into my corporate career.

With pregnancy, everything changed. Suddenly, I found myself exhausted, tired, and sleepy, and I could not escape those feelings, no matter what I tried. If I did not eat during the day or decided to put in overtime at work, my body stopped me. It was as if it were saying to me, "You are going to have a baby. Take it easy!"

I realized it was time to accept my limitations and to listen to my body, interact with it, and find out what I needed with each passing month of pregnancy. Sixteenth-century English philosopher Francis Bacon said, "Nature, to be commanded, must be obeyed." This presupposes understanding it, respecting it, and keeping to what comes naturally. This lesson holds true not only for our contact with the environment but also in how we manage our own bodies and our most basic needs—that which is part of our nature, so to speak.

With pregnancy, I learned to listen to my body. At the same time as it reached its limits, it also discovered new potential. It was a wonderful phase in which I connected both with my baby in the womb and with myself.

Self-knowledge is the key to a life of excellence and happiness. It is essential to connect with nature itself and to identify the times when it makes sense to obey nature and the times when we can dare to tame it, exceed our limits, and push back the boundaries.

The case of marathon runner Derek Clayton illustrates the risks of ignoring what our bodies tell us. Ahead of each race, Clayton used to follow an exhausting training regime. Every Saturday, he ran the equivalent of a marathon and completed up to seventeen miles most other days of the week. He only slowed down on Fridays, when he ran about ten miles. The price he paid for his grueling practice regime was high. He suffered a lot of injuries, undergoing nine surgeries in the period in which he competed. In addition, his results were inconsistent.

He sustained one of these injuries during the run-up to the international race in Fukuoka in 1967. During his recovery, he was forced to rest and take a break from training. The result? He achieved a remarkable feat. He completed the twenty-six-mile route in two hours, nine minutes, and 36.4 seconds, beating the previous record by two and a half minutes. Less than eighteen months later, he broke his own record in Antwerp, Belgium.

"The mistake I made over the course of my career was that I sometimes went too far. I didn't always listen to my body. I continued training when I should have held back, and this started a chain reaction, which often led to injuries," Clayton said. "The secret to training is to push yourself without destroying your body. A lot of people thought me crazy to do all the training I did, and maybe I was."[8]

His story shows that listening to one's own body and, thus, valuing opportunities for rest and recovery is not merely a way of preserving our health and preventing injuries but indeed an essential condition for achieving excellence.

Rest and Vacation

We live in a globalized world, in which there are countless advantages: increased rights and freedoms; a growing number of women in power; medical advances and consequent improvement in the quality of life; the accessibility of art and information; greater openness of debate; and the emergence of initiatives that deal with themes related to diversity.

At the same time, the burdens we place on ourselves are often exhausting. We tend to strive to seek our best on different fronts: health, work, studies, sport, and relationships. Digital technology, once eagerly embraced, has proven not to be the ideal tool for connecting with one another and sharing experiences and feelings; rather, it has caused additional anxiety and loneliness, in which we continually compare own lives with the countless happy pictures published on social media. That is not to mention the volume of information we receive and must process each day. We therefore have an increasing need for practices that enable us to rest both physically and mentally. The phrase "I can do a year's work in nine months but not in twelve," attributed to banker and financier J. P. Morgan, sums up the importance of vacations and rest in supporting our prosperity. There is a lot to learn from watching high-performance athletes carefully alternate between periods of intense exercise and relaxation. When they are not practicing, they are deliberately resting, preparing for the next session. When we are rested, our minds focus more easily, and we are able to engage in the different activities of the day. In this state, we are more likely to practice near our peak performance or even surpass our limits. Many educators believe that trying to focus on an activity when tired is not just wasteful but actually detrimental to sustained improvement.

For rest to be truly restorative, it should not be thought of as just stopping a tiring activity or exiting from a state of fatigue. Resting goes far beyond not working, not studying, or not training. It involves taking some time out to do nothing and focus on your own well-being—physically, mentally, and spiritually. It is important to make the most of the silence and inactivity to create space in our routine and have time for introspection.

When we become introspective, we reflect on our own experiences and on what is happening within us. From this, we develop the ability and flexibility to switch our perspective on events in our lives from the macro to the micro and vice versa. It is also important that we try to free up time in our children's routines so they have time to do nothing and, thus, explore their own creativity and what gives them pleasure.

Rest needs to be part of the plan and scheduled in just the same way as we prioritize other work activities or sports practice. A good way to feel refreshed is to choose activities we enjoy doing. For me, having contact with the sea engenders a sense of renewal of mind and body. It has since my childhood, and I carry this feeling to this day. As we are social beings, it is part of our nature to become part of a community. We feel better, safer, happier, and more complete. Thus, prioritize activities that encourage connection and build your relationships.

Slowing It Down

Raffaella Monne, a resident of the village of Arzana, Sardinia, was calmly peeling an apple when Dan Buettner interviewed her. She replied laconically to his questions about her diet, level of physical activity, and relationships with her family. Frustrated by her evasive answers, he asked, "From the vantage point of your 107 years, do you have any advice for those somewhat younger than you?" She replied, "Life is very short. Don't run so fast that you don't get a chance to enjoy it."

Setting aside some time to recover from fatigue is also one of the lessons from the Blue Zones. Residents of Sardinia usually take to the streets around five in the afternoon, while those on the Nicoya Peninsula take a break in the middle of the afternoon to rest and socialize with friends. The Loma Linda Adventist community keeps Saturday for observing its religious traditions. From sunset on Friday to sunset on Saturday, they create a sanctuary in time, during which they focus on God, their families, and nature, foregoing the use of tech devices, such as cell phones. For the Adventists, it is a time when they step back from the hustle and bustle of daily life and put the rest of the week in perspective.

This slowdown brings together, to some extent, many of the other lessons gathered from the Blue Zones, such as eating mindfully and healthily, valuing friends, making family a priority, engaging in physical activity, finding time for spirituality, and living each moment in the here and now.

A Good Night's Sleep

According to John Underwood of the American Athletic Institute, "The top eight finalists in the Olympic 100-meter sprint in track and field were separated by .35 (hundredths) of one second. The top ten finishers in the Olympic men's downhill in alpine skiing were separated by .53 hundredths of one second. TIME is important—even the time we spend asleep! It has been said that little things make big things happen. The Human Performance Project advises many Olympic, NCAA and Professional Teams. The sleep recommendation for athletes training at this level is 9 hours and 15 minutes every night."[9]

Sleep is one of the most important forms of physical and mental recovery. Sleep deprivation, or poor-quality sleep, can cause a lot of harm.

Professor Marco Túlio de Mello, a prominent Brazilian researcher and professor in the field of sleep, said, "If you sleep badly overnight, the main symptom will be bad mood and irritability. In the medium term, poor sleep will lead to problems such as forgetfulness, difficulty concentrating, and a greater probability of mistakes and accidents, due to a deterioration in the reflexes. In the long run, the main area affected is the immune system. You fall sick more often and may even have difficulty responding correctly to vaccines."

Our sleep is divided into four phases, which have different restorative functions. Phases one and two characterize light sleep. In the first, we are still falling asleep, while in the second, despite our body being already asleep and relaxed, we are more likely to be awoken by something happening in the external environment, such as noise or light. Phase three is a deep sleep associated with the release of growth hormones and physical recovery. Finally, phase four, known as REM sleep (referring to the rapid eye movements that take place while we are in this stage), is associated with cognitive aspects. Sleeping well means passing through all of these phases sufficiently to feel refreshed and in a good mood the next day.

Most of the population needs seven to eight hours of sleep per night. However, there are also short and long sleepers. For short sleepers, four or five hours per night is sufficient, while long sleepers might need more than nine hours in bed.

People also vary in function of their biological rhythms. There are morning people, who prefer to sleep early and feel more active in the early hours of the day; evening people, who feel more productive at the end of the day and tend to feel sleepy in the morning; and those in between, who go to sleep around midnight and wake up at eight in the morning.

Knowing your own biological rhythm and your individual need for sleep is essential in order for you to be able to organize your routine with the right level of recovery and is a key factor in optimizing performance.

For this process of self-awareness, Professor De Mello advises using the vacation period, especially the last fifteen days, because in the first few days, you may need to sleep longer in order to compensate for sleep deprivation arising before the vacation. During this period of self-observation, try to respect your biological rhythm, sleeping when you feel sleepy and waking up without an alarm. For this, it is essential to avoid using screens—television, tablets, and cell phones—at night, as the light emitted by these devices can make this process less natural. "Our organism reacts to light and dark. There is a region of our brain that detects the arrival of night and releases hormones that help us to enter the sleep process," the professor noted.

Once you have identified what works best for you, it is important to sleep and wake up around the same time every day, as "our body is rhythmic and works better if this rhythm is respected." Of course, we can vary our routine from time to time, but we should not make a habit of it.

The Sleep of Athletes

How much sleep does an elite athlete need? Roger Federer says he needs to sleep eleven to twelve hours per day, and he is not alone in that regard.[10] Other top athletes, such as the world's fastest man, Jamaican Usain Bolt, who is a three-time Olympic champion in the hundred meters and two hundred meters, and LeBron James, one of the greatest basketball players of all time, have also said they need to sleep more than ten hours per day.

Even allowing for individual differences, sports people may need more sleep than average. The physical wear and tear of the activity requires a more intense recovery process, which is achieved during sleep. For an athlete, getting less sleep than needed can mean not only a drop in performance but also an increased risk of injuries.

This quantity of sleep is not necessarily achieved in a single session. Federer, for example, sleeps ten hours per night and takes two naps of approximately an hour each during the day. One of the most successful gymnasts in US history, Shannon Miller, who won seven Olympic medals, nine world championships, and five Pan American Games, also enjoyed a nap and recognized the importance of sleep in maintaining her high-performance levels. She said, "I learned early on that sleep was as important to my training as conditioning, stretching and technique. I needed to give my mind and body time to recover. I aimed to sleep at least eight hours or more whenever possible. I took naps. I took a nap just about every day, from the moment I started intensive training until the day I retired."[11]

Professor De Mello emphasizes how naps have a powerful effect on performance recovery, but care should be taken not to exceed sixty minutes. "A longer nap than this can delay the onset of nighttime sleep, and this negatively interferes with the individual's rhythm," he explains. Athletes usually have intense routines, making it necessary to reconcile practice, study or work, and family with travel and time-zone changes when competing. All of these factors can hinder the establishment of a regular sleep pattern. It takes a conscious effort to manage this aspect, decreasing the use of digital screens at night or increasing the number of naps during the day.

During many important games and competitions, sometimes with the Brazilian team and sometimes in Italy, I often slept in transit. I would get into a car, a plane, or any moving vehicle and fall asleep. I never had trouble sleeping. Some teammates needed to close the curtain or isolate themselves from any outside noise. I did not. Often, I would wake up on the plane while catching an imaginary ball or making a movement from the game. The people around me would be falling about themselves with laughter. This constant replacement of sleep was essential for my recovery.

Sleep in the Olympics

Professor De Mello has been working as a sleep consultant for the Brazilian Paralympic Committee since 1994 and also consulted for the Olympic Committee in 2016. He told me about the innovative work he carried out with athletes from different sports at the time. He and his team performed a thorough sleep assessment of the athletes and offered specific advice to individuals who sought him out.

"It is possible to delay or postpone sleep by using very simple devices. By using a glove to cool the hand, we can induce sleep, as it decreases the temperature of the blood reaching the central nervous system. Using special glasses, it is possible to create a bath of light that keeps the individual awake for longer and delays the onset of sleep," the researcher explained. Using these techniques, it is possible to adjust the athlete's biological clock to a competition's unusual times and facilitate adaptation to changes in time zone.

Breathe and Meditate for a Healthy Life

The pregnancies and births of my three daughters were intense in different ways and taught me a lot of lessons. I connected with my body and my nature and was swept up in unconditional love for each of them. When the eldest was born, I wanted to handle everything on my own, but I realized it takes a village to raise a child, as the African saying goes. I learned to ask for help and strengthened my conviction about the importance of having a support network.

With the birth of Giorgia, my second daughter, even with all the support I received from my family, maintaining a healthy lifestyle and balancing my time between work and family became a big challenge for me. That was when I met former equestrian Maria Eugênia Anjos, a yoga devotee for almost thirty-three years and director of Arhka Medicina Integrativa. She created therapeutic breathing, a methodology that uses meditation and yoga to promote health and prevent and treat disease.

She helped me to establish better balance in my routine, exploring new behaviors and actions during my day that contributed to small but meaningful changes, such as incorporating a break for a few deep breaths every two hours or so. When I became pregnant with my third child, Olivia, Maria Eugênia helped me find a deep sense of fulfillment at each stage of my pregnancy, preparing me for the birth and connecting me with the changes in my body, the baby, and my own feelings. We explored breathing methods that we all freely possess but rarely put into practice.

Maria Eugênia argues that breathing exercises should be included in our routine for a healthy life. "They should be taught in schools, which would help both students and staff to improve the quality of learning and general well-being. They should be used in hospitals to support the healing process along with conventional medicine. Just twenty minutes a day would suffice," she says. "To devote time to your breathing is to devote yourself to caring for your life, your health, and the nourishment of your cells with oxygen. Just as we need to strengthen the muscles in our body, we need to take care of the respiratory muscles. Learning to breathe properly is to promote the conditions needed for our bodies to reach their maximum potential. Breathing exercises also help to calm the mind, balance the emotions, and maintain a healthy energy flow."

She suggests people should pay attention to their own breathing and prioritize inhalation through the nose rather than through the mouth, as a slow and deep breath through the nostrils stimulates the production of natural tranquilizers in the body. Breathing exercises should be segregated into practicing shallow, medium, and deep breathing, which involve the abdominal muscles, rib region, and upper part of the chest, respectively.

In addition, the gateway to meditation is slow, deep breathing. After taking several deep breaths, we exit the automatic state and enter a meditative state.

The practice of meditation has gained adepts all over the world, as it promotes well-being and brings benefits to physical, cognitive, and emotional health. Meditation relieves chronic pain and anxiety, promotes a healthy heart, improves mood, and builds immunity. Scientific studies with Buddhist monks have shown that regular meditation generates lasting changes in cerebral activity, leading to improvements in attention, memory, and learning.[12]

Jon Kabat-Zinn, professor emeritus at the University of Massachusetts Medical School and founder of the Stress Reduction Clinic and the Center for Mindfulness in Medicine, Health Care, and Society, argues that the essence of the practice of mindfulness—one of the most widely researched forms of meditation—is about being aware of what we are doing while we are doing it, focusing on one thing at a time. By making this a habit, we promote periods of rest for our minds. It is the equivalent of creating islands of sanity during our hectic lives.

By decreasing the number of distractions and reducing absentmindedness while doing our daily tasks, such as eating, studying, cooking, or talking to the people we love, we stay more connected to the present moment.

Connection and Relationships

For seventy-five years, Harvard University has monitored the lives of 724 men year upon year, asking them questions about their jobs, home lives, and health.[13] This research, considered the longest study of adulthood ever carried out, is currently led by director Robert Waldinger, who has shared the findings regarding factors associated with well-being. The answer does not lie in accumulating wealth, fame, or hours on the job. The tens of thousands of pages from this investigation, generated over many years, point to a single factor: cultivating and maintaining good relationships.[14]

People who are more socially connected with family, friends, and the wider community are happier, are physically healthier, and live longer than people who have few connections. "It is not just the number of friends you have, and it's not whether or not you are in a committed relationship. It's the quality of your close relationships that matters," says Waldinger. Good, intimate relationships in which people feel they can count on one another when the need arises protect the body and mind, promoting healthy aging and preserving cognitive abilities, such as memory.

Other scientific studies also emphasize the centrality of relationships in our lives. After years of research into intimacy in interpersonal relationships, Arthur Aron, a professor of psychology at Stony Brook University, has concluded, "The single biggest predictor of human happiness is the quality of a person's relationships."[15] We are social beings "innately wired to forming strong, lasting and harmonious bonds with other people," as suggested by social psychologist Ellen Berscheid in a chapter of a book whose title I found thought-provoking: *The Human's Greatest Strength: Other Humans.*[16]

In the study of the Blue Zones, Dan Buettner noted that the healthiest and most successful centenarians were those who put their families first. They tend to get married, have children, and build their lives around this nucleus, creating family rituals or routines that encourage gatherings, such as meals with everyone around the table, celebrations of special occasions, or family vacations.

Once my brothers and I grew up, we established a family tradition wherein every two years, my parents get to choose somewhere to take their children and grandchildren on vacation. We usually identify vacation spots offering sports activities and a cultural experience, as this helps the family to bond. My parents have established a rule: if all the members of the family are present, they will take care of the travel and accommodations.

This focus on family life is also found among top athletes, such as Robert Scheidt, who, even though he is passionate about his sport, confessed, "Competitions are no longer my number-one priority, like they were ten years ago. Today I have a family, and my life has changed. I have managed to maintain a balance between the two, but if it came to choosing between them, I would choose the family."

In addition to family life, people who are part of our circle of friends can also have an influence on our health and longevity. A survey published in the *New England Journal of Medicine* showed how our immediate social network, formed of people with whom we have most contact in our daily lives, affects our lifestyle. Monitoring a community of 12,067 people over a thirty-two-year period, researchers found that people were more likely to become obese when their friends became obese. In a group of close friends, if one became obese, the chances of the others doing the same almost tripled. The same effect was observed with weight loss.[17]

The Power of Touch

In more than thirty years of research, Tiffany Field, psychologist and director of the Touch Research Institute at the University of Miami Miller School of Medicine, has proven the numerous benefits of touch. The simple act of hugging, kissing, holding hands, stroking, or massaging someone's back can reduce pain, anxiety, depression, and aggressive behavior and promote improved immune response and stress relief.

American researchers Brittany Jakubiak and Brooke Feeney published an article in the scientific journal *Personality and Social Psychology Review* in which they argued that giving and receiving caresses of affection promotes physical, psychological, and relational well-being, independent of the culture or individual preferences. That is, even people who are more reserved and prefer to maintain greater physical distance in relationships are positively affected by touch.[18]

Field concurs and states that even if touching people is not something that comes naturally, we can make a conscious effort to add more physical contact to our daily lives. "Hug your kids when they leave for school in the morning and when they come home. Hold your partner's hand when you take a walk. Pet your dog or cat. Schedule a few sessions with a professional massage therapist," she says by way of offering examples we can put into practice.[19]

As I mentioned at the beginning of the chapter, there is no one path or one truth about what represents a healthy lifestyle. But here are six key aspects: keeping active, taking care in what you eat, respecting your need to recover, getting quality sleep, being aware of your breathing, and nurturing your relationships. Now, how you go about this depends on your experience, your values, and your goals. But how do we discover those? Often, we need to go through a process of trial and error until we find what works for us. We thus need to keep our eyes open, be attentive and curious like a child, and develop our own path to growth and evolution.

- From the inhabitants of the Blue Zones and from athletes who have sustained a high performance for many years, we can learn a lot that can help us achieve a long, high-quality life.
- Healthy eating is essential to your well-being, and a plant-based diet has been a growing trend among top athletes.
- Listen to your body, promote moments of silence and recovery, respect the need for vacation, and learn to rest. Breaks are just as important as training.
- Sleep is a crucial process in restoring energy to your mind and body. Find out how much sleep you need and which times are best for you.
- Exercising your breathing muscles and meditating can be just as beneficial as exercising the muscles on your body.
- Maintaining close relationships with those you care about and who care about you is the single biggest predictor of human happiness.

- Does your current lifestyle promote well-being in the short and long term?
- What can you do to create more moments of recovery in your current lifestyle?
- What was the happiest moment or period of your life? Perhaps it was a project related to your work, a special place you have been, or a period you spent with a certain person or even alone. What did you do during that moment that made it special to you? Who was there with you?
- What are you seeing, hearing, and feeling right now? How connected are you to your present moment?
- When did you feel better physically in the past?
- What did you do then? What were your habits and routines?

CONCLUSIONS FROM DIMENSION 1:
THE FOUNDATION

———

In this first part of the book, I have presented the aspects, attitudes, and choices that we should consider in order to develop and strengthen the foundations for a life of excellence and happiness. Achieving and sustaining high performance requires a support network; consistent and continuous practice; and a healthy lifestyle that integrates the care of the mind, body, and spirit.

In applying the WeTeam method, I have acted from three perspectives: in looking back at the journey taken so far; in understanding the present moment; and in establishing a plan of action for enhancing the sustainability of peak performance in whatever areas of life we wish to improve.

DIMENSION 2

INNER ENERGY

CHAPTER 4

DEALING WITH ADVERSITY: EMBRACE THE DISCOMFORT ZONE TO SURPASS LIMITS AND DEVELOP EMOTIONAL MUSCLES

The more time you spend in your discomfort zone,
the more your comfort zone will expand.
—Robin Sharma

Between stimulus and response there is a space. In
that space is our power to choose our response. In our
response lies our growth and our freedom.
—Viktor Frankl

My uncle Ricardo, the youngest of the three brothers, was a great water polo player. He used to train with my dad every morning before school and every evening until ten thirty. On the eve of the 1968 Olympics in Mexico, the two were based between Rio de Janeiro and São Paulo. When it came to selecting the team who would represent Brazil at the games, my uncle was cut. Each team was permitted eleven players, and my uncle was one of the eleven, but for budget reasons, Brazil decided to participate with ten, and my uncle was the unlucky one. My father still remembers the coach's words after the last training session at the pool in Rio: "Pedro, you marked your forward out of the game. And I know he was competing with your brother for the spot, but I have decided to cut Ricardo—even though he showed more—because I don't think he was marked so tightly. Ricardo has a long future ahead of him."

My father was outraged by the decision. On the bus back to São Paulo, he was raging away, while my uncle remained serene and uncomplaining, as was his way. He even calmed down his older brother, who was still indignant.

From that point on, Ricardo began to devote himself fully to his engineering and math degree at one of Brazil's top universities, his talent and his passion. In the first year, he became an assistant to the professor and even produced handouts on integral calculus that were used by the faculty for several years afterward. My uncle complained of a pain in his back, but he thought it was due to the intense training he had undergone in the months prior while fighting for a place on the Brazilian water polo team.

In October 1968, exactly four months after my parents' wedding, the Brazilian delegation set off for the Olympics in Mexico, with my father as one of the water polo team members. While at the games, he communicated with my mother, Olga, and my grandparents via postcard. International calls were expensive. On returning eighteen days later, he was greeted at the airport by just my mother and grandfather, and he realized something was wrong. Where were Ricardo, my aunt, and my grandmother? It was a family tradition always to meet travelers at the airport, especially after such a special trip.

They went to my grandparents' house, where my father felt some of the deepest sorrow in his life. His brother was in a wheelchair following surgery that had detected bone marrow cancer.

After this initial shock, months of intense therapy followed. Ricardo had the support of his friend and teammate João Gonçalves Filho, an athlete who participated in Olympic Games as a swimmer (in Helsinki in 1952 and Melbourne in 1956); as a water polo player (in Rome in 1960, Tokyo in 1964, and Mexico City in 1968, at which he was a flag bearer); and, later, as a judo coach. To help Ricardo's recovery, they did rehabilitation exercises in the club pool in the morning and then more exercises, meditation, and visualization in the evening. There were some small improvements, but following a second surgery, my uncle, who had been my father's companion in sport, at study, and in life, died at the age of twenty-one.

My father felt lost afterward. His world fell apart. Ricardo was the creative brother who liked to delve deeper into their studies. My father, meanwhile, was always goal-oriented. The two complemented each other well and dreamed of forming another partnership, this time professionally. He managed to shake off his profound grief only when my grandfather told him, "Pedrinho, we need you now." He then had to find a mental strength and resilience he did not yet know he possessed. The coming together of the family was essential for transforming the pain arising from a sense of loss and incomprehension into a sense of purpose to build a life of joy and fulfillment, something that lay ahead for everyone.

Life is full of adversities that are beyond our control. They can be of varying degrees of intensity, appearing as contretemps, setbacks, or fatalities. Sport has the advantage of being a controlled environment that presents, in gradual increments, ever greater obstacles, which makes it a perfect learning environment to forge our resilience muscles. After all, it's not the difficulties we encounter in life that matter but how we choose to respond to them.

My daughter Alissa highlighted in her Stanford University admissions essay how sport has helped her through adversity. She wrote,

> The lessons I've learned from competitive sports extend way beyond the pool: they shape the way I live, make choices, judge situations, embrace new things, and treat people. In middle school, sports cushioned my landing in America when I moved from Brazil; they helped me embrace a new culture and language and build self-confidence. My high school years have been challenging—playing two varsity sports, traveling with the Brazilian Youth Water Polo Team, earning good grades, and trying to have a social life is not easy! But what I've learned in sports has helped me get through difficult times and enabled me to grow. The saying that by teaching us to embrace our "discomfort zone," competitive sports make

us more successful in the long run has been true for me, and not just in the pool. Resolving tricky situations and coping with failure; constantly setting new, higher goals; collaborating with people who I might disagree or have little in common with; being open to different perspectives—this is what athletes do and this mindset has benefited me in all areas of life.

Going beyond Resilience: Antifragility

Hydra is a creature from Greek mythology that possesses many heads. Whenever one of them is cut off, two grow back in its place. That is, the more often it is knocked down, the stronger it gets. The Hydra represents *antifragility*, a term coined by Nassim Taleb, a researcher at New York University and author of the book *Antifragile: Things That Gain from Disorder*.

This concept goes beyond resilience, which is associated with our ability to resist and recover from adverse situations. In the face of misfortune, the resilient remains the same, whereas the antifragile gets better. When I think of an example of antifragility in sport, I remember the United States women's water polo team at the 2016 Rio Olympics.

The coach of the national team, Adam Krikorian, had been in the Olympic village for two days, when he received news that his brother had suffered a massive heart attack and died. In addition to his grief, he was gripped by doubt over whether to return home or not. On the one hand, he wanted to be with his family, but on the other, he did not want to abandon the players at such an important moment in their lives. In the end, the team made the decision for him. "Go be with your family," they told him.

He spent a few days in the United States but returned to meet up with the players ahead of the games. The coach accessed his inner strength to fulfill his sense of responsibility and, surprisingly, turned his recent experience into a means to inspire the players in overcoming adversity. He told me, "The thought that was fixed in my head right then was *I can't let my team down. I can feel sadness or pain about what happened—there's nothing wrong with that—but I must be there for them.*"

An hour before the team's first game, Krikorian received more bad news: the mother of one of the players, Melissa Seidemann, had suffered a stroke and had been admitted to a hospital in Rio de Janeiro.

The coach handled these adversities by preparing the team more diligently. Seidemann excelled in the pool and played in every subsequent game, with the United States emerging victorious. In between, she could be found by her mother's bedside in the hospital.

The team had already won gold at the 2012 Olympic Games in London, and it was no different in Rio de Janeiro. "There are two options when it comes to adversity. Either it breaks you, or it makes you stronger," Krikorian told me. The team emerged from the experience as giants. Not only did they win in the face of challenging conditions, but the teammates also came together even more. After stepping down from the podium, the thirteen players placed their medals around the coach's neck as he wiped the tears from his eyes.

It is possible to develop the necessary skills to become antifragile and thus respond to traumatic situations with growth rather than paralysis. One of the ways to do this relates to the way we interpret painful, stressful, or uncomfortable situations.

As Tal Ben-Shahar said in a class on post-traumatic growth, "While I do not believe that things necessarily happen for the best, I know that some people are able to make the best of things that happen."[1]

Is Stress Harmful to Our Health?

In around the 1960s, the World Health Organization declared war on eating fat, considering it harmful to our health. However, science has demonstrated that this is not entirely true. While there are harmful fats, there are also beneficial ones, such as those found in olive oil, nuts, and avocados. Fifty years on, stress has become the new villain. Scientists, health professionals, and the media have all pointed out its devastating consequences, associating stress with a weakened immune system; an increased risk of developing heart disease, depression, or addictions; and an acceleration of the aging process. However, a new body of researchers is challenging this notion and demonstrating that we may once again be fighting the wrong enemy.

Stress is a state of mental or emotional tension resulting from adverse or demanding circumstances. But what is stressful for one person may not be for another. For example, one individual may feel anxious when faced with taking school tests but remain calm when skydiving. Another may require sedatives before traveling by plane but feel no pressure when speaking in public. Not only do the causes of stress vary for everyone, but the way people approach stress also varies. Some see it as harmful and negative—something to be avoided—while others believe that experiencing painful or challenging situations can bring a lot of benefit.

In 1998, a survey of thirty thousand adults was carried out in the United States to find out how much stress they had experienced in the previous year. They were also asked if they believed stress to be harmful to their health. Eight years later, researchers at the University of Wisconsin-Madison trawled through public records to try to identify which of the respondents had since died. They concluded that high levels of stress increased the risk of death by 43 percent, but this increased risk applied only to those who also believed stress to be harmful to their health. People who had reported high levels of stress but had not considered the stress to be harmful had not been more likely to die. In fact, this group recorded the lowest risk of death in the study, even lower than those reporting very little stress.[2] Thus, the conclusion is that the main factor to consider is not the level of stress but how it is perceived.

If you happen to belong to the group who view stress as a negative, then you will be interested to hear that simply reading about a different perspective and reflecting on it may already be helping you, as illustrated by research done by Harvard University, in which participants were trained to view their stress in a positive way. They were told that the physiological symptoms arising from a tense or nervous situation, such as sweating or a rapid heartbeat and breathing, did not suggest difficulty in dealing with pressure or anxiety; rather, their bodies were summoning strength and getting ready to deal with the challenges by sending more oxygen to the brain and muscles. Soon after this explanation, they were asked to give an oral presentation in front of examiners who had been trained to give negative and cruel feedback—a situation that would leave most participants stressed.

The participants who had been shown how to view stress more positively not only felt more confident during the presentation but also displayed a physiological change. In a typical response to stressful situations, our heart rate goes up, and our blood vessels constrict, which is one reason chronic stress is associated with cardiovascular disease. It is unhealthy to remain in this state for a prolonged period. But during the study, even though the participants' hearts did indeed pound, their blood vessels remained relaxed. This is the healthiest cardiovascular profile, as it is similar to what happens to our bodies during moments of joy or courage.[3]

These two studies impressed Kelly McGonigal, a Stanford University professor and author of *The Upside of Stress*, to the point that they changed her views on the subject. She said, "For years I told people that stress made them sick. But I learned that the best way to deal with it is not to reduce or avoid it, but to change how we interpret it. So my objective as a health psychologist completely changed. I don't want to help people free themselves of stress anymore. I want to help them become better at navigating it."[4] She does this by helping people change their mindset when dealing with difficult situations.

Seeing the positive aspects of stress will not render your life free of suffering, but it will allow you to reframe difficult situations as challenges rather than threats, which will have a significant impact on your actions. People who view stress as harmful will take the first sign of it as a cue to escape or run away. Their strategies for dealing with a stressful situation are to attempt to distract themselves rather than deal with it or to expend energy and effort in trying to rid themselves of the discomfort rather than seeking ways to resolve whatever is causing the stress.

People who believe stress can be useful are more likely to deal with it proactively. They try to make the most of the situation, seeing it as an opportunity for growth and looking for effective ways to overcome, remove, or alter the source of stress.

The Muscular System

Our muscles are part of a system that is naturally antifragile. When we increase the load during an exercise routine, we stress the muscles, and this causes microscopic ruptures to their fibers. Given time to recover, the muscles not only will regenerate but also will become bigger, stronger, and capable of handling heavier loads.

People who perform physical exercise generally know that pain is part of the process and maintain a positive mindset, welcoming the discomfort because they know that pain is positive. We feel the discomfort but know it is necessary for our growth and development, so instead of avoiding it, we choose to face it. Consistent exercise not only makes our muscles stronger but also enables us to become more tolerant of pain, which, in turn, expands our potential to grow.

In a study published in the scientific journal *Pain*, researchers from the University of Heidelberg, Germany, analyzed how athletes differ from physically active nonathletes with respect to their pain threshold. They found that the thresholds were similar for the two groups, but the athletes had greater pain tolerance. In other words, the onset of pain is the same for both athletes and nonathletes, but athletes recognize the benefits and, consequently, are more tolerant.

Our bodies ache when we are in high-performance mode, and as athletes, we learn to cope with this pain, which represents the enhancement of our abilities. The challenge is usually to respect the need for short breaks and recovery—which I will discuss further in chapter 6—and to recognize that pain can also act as a warning with respect to potential injury and, thus, merits special care, such as a longer period of recovery or the support of health professionals.

Once, while I was playing in a tournament in Fort Lauderdale, Florida, my shoulder locked up. I wanted to enter the water and play and did not mind the pain but was unable to raise my arms. I was immobilized. I could not rotate my arm to swim, let alone shoot at goal. My father tried to apply some *do-in*[7] techniques, but it was not enough. The doctors who were there took a look, realized it was nothing serious, asked if I could

---

[7] Do-in is a self-massage technique based on traditional Chinese medicine that uses the same points as acupuncture in promoting mental and physical health.

bear the pain, and performed a maneuver. In a few minutes, I was able to move again. I had never witnessed such an effective way of alleviating pain and loosening up the muscles ahead of a game. After the game, I took extra care, with ice and recovery.

With self-awareness and a focus on the present moment, we develop our ability to recognize when we can go ahead despite the pain and when we need to take action to slow down and seek help.

Recovery from Injury

Serious injuries can be difficult to deal with. Their impact goes beyond the physical aspects. They add a significant mental burden. There is disruption to the athlete's routine, as well as self-doubt with respect to training and the risk of exacerbating the problem, for example. Depending on the situation, the level of performance and even the future career may be at risk.

Mental preparation is needed to deal with the emotional consequences of physical injury, just as it is in handling any other adversity we may face in life. The willingness to go beyond the comfort zone, with gradual exposure to stress, expands our capabilities and our tolerance for pain. This is true for both physical and emotional pain.

Brazilian Kahena Kunze, Olympic and world champion in the 49er FX class, was considered the best sailor in the world in 2014, along with partner and helmsman Martine Grael. However, when she was preparing for the 2016 Rio Olympics, she injured her knee. When she spoke with me, she revealed that the injury upset her a great deal, as she did not want to let down her partner or everyone else involved. She said, "I'm not alone on the boat. I have a team."

However, she ended up reframing the injury in order to move forward. She told me, "Maybe the team was not completely aligned at the time, and that break enabled us to reorganize. It was a tricky situation, but it turned out for the best, as it gave us a chance to step back and think about where we were and where we wanted to get to."

The pair managed to come back even stronger, rising to the top of the Olympic podium and winning the first Brazilian women's yachting gold medal in the history of the games.

Despite the tension over the injury, Kahena believes she was always able to improve, even when she could not practice. She said, "Nowadays, the mental aspect is more important than physical preparation. I work hard on my psychological preparation. Even from the sidelines, I would place my mind in a regatta, which often works even better than training on the boat."

In July 2021, Kahena and Martine defended their title in the 49er FX class at the 2020 Tokyo games—and took gold again!

The possibility of injuries always haunts top athletes, who may develop a sense that their value to society is directly linked to their sporting performance. Therefore, they prepare so much in advance. At the same time, if the athlete understands that sport, by its nature, occasionally leads to injuries, he or she will tend to make the best use of the period of physical rehabilitation to also train in another way, such as through visualization exercises and mental preparation.

Six months before the Beijing Olympics in 2008, three-time world champion Canadian rower Adam Kreek had a herniated disk, along with excruciating back pain. "The physical pain was unbearable, but the psychological challenges compounded the pain exponentially. At first, I was relieved because I could take a couple days off training. However, relief turned to panic and hopelessness. I hit my low point about two weeks after I incurred the injury. One of my doctors told me that my injury would not allow me to compete again. This hopeless future combined with my inability to train fueled a painful depression," said Kreek.[5]

In his case, it was a major change in the way he looked at the situation that helped him to recover and participate in the competitions that earned him Olympic gold. "The goal remains. The path has just changed," Bruce Pinel, his sports psychologist, told him.

With that in mind, instead of training for six hours per day, he committed to his treatment and recovery for six hours per day. After an injury that typically takes a year and a half to heal, he was back in training in eight weeks. He and his teammates brought home the gold medal in Beijing in the M8+ (men's eight with coxswain) category.[8]

---

[8] The most classic race in rowing, a part of all the Olympics since 1900, in which the boat is steered by a cox (who sets the pace for the rowers) and eight oarsmen.

Getting injured during a competition can be the point when an athlete has to overcome the odds. When Brazilian judoka Leandro Guilheiro dreamed of going to the Olympics, he imagined he would be at the peak of his powers and in the best physical shape—and never imagined he would have to fight with a broken hand in Athens in 2004 or with a herniated disk in Beijing in 2008. "But the truth is that the ideal moment never comes, and we must do our best with the circumstances that present themselves," he told me. "Since I was very young, I have been trained to overcome pain, and during my career as an athlete, my pain threshold has grown even greater. I have fought with fever and with chickenpox and had to train many times when in pain. I believe that being injured in these situations ended up giving me an inner strength. I needed to dig deep and work on my approach mentally, and that led me to feel even more focused for each fight. Sometimes I ask myself, *If I had been in perfect shape, would I have been able to summon such strength?* In Beijing, for example, I was very limited because of the hernia. I was not able to raise my right leg. I was only able to land a single strike. This situation forced me to get the very best out of myself," said Leandro, who took the bronze medal in both of the Olympics he fought in while injured.

Mental Preparation Begins in Childhood

Downtime at home was always filled with sports activities. Thus, I acquired a taste for pushing myself at an early age. My parents were good at regulating the levels of support and encouragement they offered my brothers and me, so we could learn to deal with challenging situations.

By age thirteen, I had already learned from my father how to watch and respect the sea. With him, I spent hours learning concepts from physics in adjusting my body to the flow of the surf so as not to fight against nature but, rather, to respond to it. On one occasion, the waves were huge. There were only a few surfers, and the bathers did not dare go deeper than their waists. I decided to be bold and command nature instead of obeying it. I entered the water and—using my knowledge of the waves and all my swimming skills—managed to safely negotiate the surf. Suddenly, stronger and stronger series of waves began to form and break violently around me. I was unable to escape and exit the water. Each time I tried, an even bigger wave would take me.

My father was watching me alertly from the shore. When he realized I was struggling, he dove into the water to help. He knew I was not in danger, as I was a strong swimmer. I was just not able to execute the move I wanted. When he caught up with me, he said, "Cris, are you all right?" I replied that I was, but I wanted to catch a wave. "You want help?" he asked.

"No, I want to try this myself."

He respected my decision and went back to shore.

I must have been there trying for around three hours, over and over, until he came back into the sea and said, "Shall we do this together?"

I finally accepted his help. I came out of the sea exhausted.

The first time my father entered the water, he could have discouraged me and urged me to get out. Instead, he chose to endure the anguish of watching me try something I was not yet capable of doing. But because of this, instead of feeling deflated, I came out of the water feeling proud of my intense, challenging morning and having learned more about my limits.

When I decided at age fifteen that I wanted to do an exchange program in the United States, my parents initially resisted but ultimately decided to support me. They chose a boarding school in Maryland, and I agreed. My mother took me while my father stayed in Brazil with my brothers. My arrival was full of novelties and surprises, but as soon as my mother left, I was gripped by panic. It was all different from how I had imagined. The school laid out a strict study timetable, and by five o'clock in the afternoon, it was dark already. Above all, my new home was very different from the one I had lived in to that point. I had gone from an apartment filled with a family of five to a school dorm with a roommate who was never there, which made me feel lonely. I was afraid. I thought I would not be able to adapt. I called my father and said, "I want to come home. It's not what I imagined. I can't do this."

He replied, "Cristiana, can you take another two days?" I did not understand his question, so he added, "That's how long I need to buy a ticket to come fetch you."

My father humored me. He was not about to tell me that I had made a choice and therefore had to live with it. He also did not make a big deal of the situation. He just told me he was willing to help, while at the same time, with his question, making it clear that the escape hatch was prepared if it was a radical exit I needed. But that was not the case.

When he spoke of my holding out for two more days, I remembered what he had told me as a child: "Slice up the mountain." Whenever I wanted to take on something that seemed way beyond my capabilities, he suggested breaking the challenge down into smaller goals, so I could focus on the steps I needed to take at that moment, which would ultimately lead me to my greater goal. In achieving each lesser goal, I gained more confidence.

Still on the same phone call, I caught my breath and said, "Let's wait. I have just gotten here. If it doesn't work out, I'll let you know."

My experience in Maryland was challenging in many ways but, at the same time, extremely enriching. The strategy of slicing up the mountain, together with the safety net of having an alternative if I needed one, worked so well that I ended up deciding to extend my stay for a year.

To develop resilience and antifragility, children need caregivers who are sensitive to their needs, identify when they are able to manage a tricky situation without adult intervention, and guide them when things get really tough. If parents constantly intervene before children get a chance to tackle challenges independently, they may unwittingly impede the development of skills that are essential to navigating the challenges encountered later in life. I am grateful to my parents for how they chose to lead me through the difficult situations I went through during my development. Today, as a mother, I am fully aware that it is no easy task to find balance in providing a safe and emotionally supportive environment for children without overprotecting them or limiting their autonomy.

Permission to Be Human

Facing grief, people commonly divide into two groups with respect to their immediate reactions: (1) those who automatically don their armor and claim to be strong—they are survivors—while not truly allowing themselves to grieve the loss of the person they loved and (2) those who experience a deep sense of sadness and weep, sometimes causing concern to those around them with how intensely they experience the pain.

There is a tendency in our society to consider the people in the first group to be better prepared over the long run. But in reality, one year on, the people who allowed themselves to truly feel the pain and fully express their grief are the ones who will be stronger emotionally.

Deeply ingrained in our culture is the idea that if we are sad, frustrated, angry, afraid, or ashamed, there is something wrong with us. We categorize emotions as positive or negative and seek to reject those that make us uncomfortable, believing that will make us happier. But this is not the way our emotions work.

Brené Brown, a researcher at the University of Houston, argues that it is not possible to selectively anesthetize an emotion. You cannot say, "Here are the things I don't want to feel," and just ignore specific emotions. If you try to suppress sadness, you will also suppress your ability to feel enthusiasm. If you reject fear, you also reject love.

This emphasizes the importance of accepting our own vulnerabilities in the name of enjoying a happier and more authentic life.[6] If we want to live life well, connect to our goals, and reach our full potential, we must first give ourselves permission to be human.

"These days, I realize that it's even harder for people to give themselves permission to be human. With social media, we see images of perfection the whole time. Accepting life's struggle and hardships is thus becoming increasingly difficult. This is especially a problem for the new generations," Adam Krikorian has said. As an Olympic coach, he does not restrict the use of cell phones by athletes, but he leads an educational process, guiding and alerting them to the negative aspects of social networks and the importance of embracing all of their emotions.

When we accept painful feelings, we realize that our emotions are, by their very nature, temporary. Every emotion has a beginning and an end. There is a flow, and emotions leave the same way they came. But this only happens if you do not make a conscious effort to reject them. In that case, they are amplified.

"The only way to eventually free ourselves from debilitating pain, therefore, is to be with it as it is. The only way out is through. We need to bravely turn toward our suffering, comforting ourselves in the process, so that time can work its healing magic," wrote Kristin Neff, author of the book *Self-Compassion: The proven power of being kind to yourself.*[7] She was one of the first academics to scientifically study self-compassion, defining it as treating yourself with the same kindness you would offer a friend.

Allowing a painful emotion to flow through us, paradoxically, causes it to lose strength and enables us to regain control over our actions. Self-compassion, therefore, has nothing to do with self-pity or a conformist attitude toward situations. On the contrary, when we give ourselves permission to be human, we free ourselves from self-criticism and the unnecessary waste of energy spent in trying to avoid suffering (which we already know has the opposite effect). Thus, we generate more energy to put toward our goals and become more connected with our sense of purpose.

South African swimmer Natalie du Toit had dreamed of going to the Olympics since she was ten years old. At fourteen, she started to take part in international competitions and was proving to be a promising athlete. At seventeen, she was involved in a motorcycle accident, which led to the amputation of her left leg. That could have been the end of her Olympic dream, but her love for the sport, her perseverance, and her ability to cope with the adversity created a spectacular achievement.

Within three months, she was back in the pool—even before she had learned to walk again. She not only won thirteen gold and two silver medals in three Paralympics (at Athens in 2004, Beijing in 2008, and London in 2012), but she also was the first Paralympic athlete to qualify for the regular Olympic Games. In Beijing, she placed sixteenth in the open-water marathon and was the first athlete to be a flag bearer at the opening ceremonies for both the Olympic and Paralympic Games.

Natalie du Toit is an example of how to face adversity head-on, letting the painful emotions flow through us rather than resisting them. This is a powerful attitude that can connect us even more with our goals.

As she says, "The tragedy of life is not that we do not achieve our goals. The tragedy of life is in not having goals to achieve. The problem lies not in failing to reach the stars but in not having any stars to reach."[8]

Deep Breathing

Whenever I am having a hard time or feel tense before a performance, I find it helpful to take some deep breaths and connect with the moment. I also used to do this before important presentations when I was working at the bank and before big games. When we are anxious or nervous, our breathing becomes shallower, and oxygen flow decreases, while muscle tension increases. Taking a deep breath and exhaling slowly promotes an internal response that relaxes us. This is something that is easy to put in practice in our daily lives, yet often, we forget to do this.

Maria Eugênia Anjos of Arhka Medicina Integrativa explains that deep breathing is a powerful tool in managing painful emotions. It not only produces hormones that bring a calming effect but also helps the body disperse emotional tension. When we breathe using all our thoracic and abdominal muscles, we move regions that are usually tense when we feel fear, anxiety, anger, or sadness. These positive effects not only are felt in the short term but also can be magnified if we incorporate breathing exercises into our daily lives.

The simple act of focusing our attention on our breathing, together with the sense of amplitude it provokes, helps us to create conditions for welcoming our emotions and allowing them to pass freely through us. "It's as if we were creating an internal space specifically to feel them. And, in so doing, we can 'breathe' the fear, without being dominated by it," explains Maria Eugênia.

As we feel the flow of our breathing, we connect with the present moment, and this empowers us to see the situation more clearly. Thich Nhat Hanh, one of the world's most renowned and respected masters of Zen Buddhism, says that when we allow our minds to focus too much on past events, we are more susceptible to depression, while if we are fixed on the future, we are more prone to anxiety. Only with our minds focused on the present moment do we truly open ourselves to experiences.

Self-Control at Decisive Moments

Self-compassion and deep breathing are useful strategies for dealing with day-to-day emotions. In striving for high performance, mental preparation—before and after the event—provides us the mental vigor necessary to keep our focus on the present moment and on performing.

When there is an avalanche of pressure, such as in a deciding game, you face the true test of your mental toughness and ability to focus. In the moment of truth, all our attention and energy should be channeled into performing at our absolute best. We may experience flashes of emotion, but it is essential that we quickly regain control and connect with our self-confidence, which is something I will talk about more in the next chapter.

How to achieve this varies from person to person, but self-awareness is key. Marcelinho Huertas told me, "I try to enter the court having emptied my mind, with my full focus on the moment. During the game, I often get angry or irritated. I am a hothead. When this happens, I go to the bench, grab a towel, put it in my mouth, and let out a roar. It's my way of letting it all out. This helps me relax and regain control."

For me, the best strategy was to take a deep breath—not a slow one this time but a rhythmic one—as I sought looks of support from my team. Some players knew me and, when they saw me take a short breather, barked words of encouragement, which helped me return to high-performance mode. My father, on the other hand, used to look to his coach on the bench, and he would recover his control and focus when he heard his coach say, "Pedrinho, I need you. Let's go." This phrase always reconnected him with his sense of responsibility as captain of the team.

Reframing

When Sandy Nitta—a coach who has contributed so much to boosting the mental vigor of the Brazilian women's water polo team—asked one of the players what went through her head when she was leading a counterattack, the player replied, *"I'm going to make a mistake. I'm going to make a mistake.* That's what I am thinking." Sandy asked the question because even though this player was one of the quickest on the team, she often missed opportunities when face-to-face with the opposing goalkeeper. Given all her physical and technical preparation, these mistakes made no sense. The problem was in her mental preparation.

The way we interpret day-to-day situations affects how we feel and act. This interpretation is often done subconsciously and appears in the form of thoughts like those of the player in the example above. It is important that we are aware of them and challenge them in order to reduce their hold over us.

One way to challenge a thought is to stop seeing it as an absolute truth and to reflect on and question the idea or look for evidence that contradicts it. For example, when you think, *I can't do this*, ask yourself, *When I was able to do this, what was happening? What did I do differently? How was my body, and what was I thinking about? What skills do I still need to learn in order to execute this action successfully?*

By answering these questions, we are able to restructure our way of thinking. This reframing of our experiences is a powerful tool in the corporate world too in dealing with adversity, be it large or small.

We can look at a problem and label it either *difficult* or *challenging*. Which of these problems would you be more motivated to solve? We can interpret failure as proof of our incompetence or as an indication that we still have more to learn. While the first way of thinking might lead us to quit on our dreams, the second fuels our motivation to persevere.

A study published in the scientific journal *Clinical Practice and Epidemiology in Mental Health* reviewed several surveys about optimism and found that people who are disposed to look on the bright side of things and expect the best outcome, even in the most difficult circumstances, have a better quality of life compared to those who are less optimistic or are pessimistic.[9] Optimism can significantly influence physical and mental well-being. It is associated with improved immune response, flexibility, and problem-solving ability. It also allows us to process negative information more efficiently.

In professional sport, there is pressure from clubs, fans, and the players themselves for victory. However, our engagement is sustainable when we focus on the way we wish to achieve it—that is, on the process: through grit, discipline, strategy, and giving our all. By adopting a mindset that values the journey and not just the result, we reframe external and internal pressures and are better able to deal with defeats, which are inherent to the process, and prioritize what is most important in the present moment.

When I asked Robert Scheidt what advice he would offer the next generation, he said, "First you must have a dream, and then the dream becomes the plan. You must create a process and be faithful to it. You need to put in the effort, the work and discipline, and bring in people who are able to help you. And then you have to summon an inner strength for overcoming the obstacles that appear. It's about getting over every barrier and moving forward." Scheidt, a longtime champion, added, "When I reached the top, it was a great challenge. But staying at the top is extremely difficult. You start to get more media attention. You are touted as a national hero, and people expect you to win every time. This creates a great weight of expectation. It's not easy to deal with all this and still keep killing a lion each day. I had strong family backing and coaches who helped me a lot, but it's important to keep reinventing yourself. Be aware that what you did to win one championship won't be enough to win the next one. Mental preparation and the drive for continual improvement are factors that help keep you at the top."

When he learned that the 1963 Pan American Games would be in São Paulo, the city of his birth, my father was even keener to participate. His girlfriend and family lived there, and he would have a chance to make them all proud. Because of other commitments, such as studying for the university entrance exam, he had trained relatively little with the Brazilian national squad that year. But he was not only present for training ahead of the championship but also a standout performer. One of the coaches said, "Congratulations. You showed us you are still the best, even though you haven't trained with us much." However, there was politics involved. The coach who selected the players for the team did not get along with Emeric, who was my father's coach and mentor at Tietê, and my father did not make the cut. His frustration was enormous.

Once he had calmed down, my father realized he was mad not only about missing out on the championship but also because the situation had run contra to values that were important to him. This led him to resolve always to act in his own life with these principles in mind: justice, fair play, and meritocracy. They formed the backdrop of his successful corporate career, wherein he sought to be transparent and impartial and evaluate employees on merit.

I took what I had learned in sport about persistence and overcoming adversity into the corporate world. When I worked in the service quality and excellence area at Banco Itaú Unibanco, one of my roles was managing the customer complaints department, acting as an ombudswoman. I was often referred to as the client representative within the company. Our team was the final arbiter for resolving issues that had not been resolved through previous contact channels, such as call centers, the internet, or the branch. From recurring complaints, I began to identify improvement opportunities and learned how to enhance means of communication, which is often the main problem in a relationship. I needed to delve deeper and identify the roots of a problem to then suggest an action plan to the department responsible, with a view to delivering better customer service. This was one of my biggest lessons from corporate life. I highlighted to our team our important mission in solving the customers' problems and the art of listening to a complaint such that you can identify improvements. We started to view complaints as opportunities for the organization to learn and evolve.

The Power of Journaling

I have the habit of keeping a journal. In it, I record both the emotionally trying times in my life and all the good things for which I am grateful. I also draft up my targets and objectives and write down why they are important to me. Sometimes I like to thumb through a few pages, especially when I feel a need to reconnect with my goals.

When it was time to change direction in my professional life, I went back through some of my journals from a few years ago. As I reread and reflected on my journey and how I can leave a positive impact on the world and help others to unlock their potential, I opened to a page on which I had written about wanting to write a book with my father. The idea was to share our experiences and what we have learned from our pursuit of excellence and happiness in the worlds of sport, business, and family life, just as we are doing here. I noted that desire in my diary back in 2009. It is truly satisfying to have put into practice this long-held dream.

In addition to being a tool for self-awareness and offering an opportunity to summon and reconnect with our essence, writing in a diary is a way of making sense of and accepting painful events. We are better able to integrate and understand our experiences, which allows us to plan and reframe them.

James W. Pennebaker, a social psychologist at the University of Texas, is considered a pioneer in the study of the therapeutic benefits of writing. He suggests that writing is fundamentally an organizational system, and thus, keeping a diary helps us to organize events in our minds and make sense of them. His studies have shown that people who maintain this habit suffer fewer mood swings, sleep better, and have an improved immune response.[10] All of this suggests that writing in a journal can offer a powerful and efficient form of intervention.

Russian psychologist and Professor Sonja Lyubomirsky, who received her bachelor's degree from Harvard University and her PhD from Stanford University, conducted research in which participants were asked to mentally relive their worst experiences.[11] They were divided into three groups, with each group taking a different approach to the task: one group would write about their experiences, another would speak into a tape recorder, and the third would just silently reflect on them.

Writing or talking about the experiences was shown to bring clear positive effects, both physically and mentally, while reflecting silently produced negative effects. When we write or talk about difficult or traumatic experiences, whether in a diary, in a psychotherapy session, or in a conversation with a friend, we go into analytical mode, in which we reflect upon our experiences and are able to reframe them. When we sit silently thinking about a painful experience, we tend just to ruminate over the experience, as if mentally reliving it, and this offers no benefits.

In one study published in the journal *Psychology and Health*, researchers Chad Burton and Laura King reported the same positive effects from asking participants to write about the most wonderful experiences of their lives. The instructions were clear: "Choose a happy moment in your life and try to imagine yourself in that moment, reliving all the feelings and emotions associated with the situation. Now write about this experience, giving as much detail as possible."[12]

When journaling, sharing, or thinking about happy times, it is as if we are able to relive the well-being they brought us. It is great when we recount a special event to friends or loved ones, and they listen to us and ask for more details. We feel almost as much joy as we experienced at the time the event happened.

Stress and Social Connection

Oxytocin is known as the love hormone. It is released in women during childbirth and is associated with forming the bond between mother and baby. The hormone is also released when we hug someone or are close to someone we love. Oxytocin stimulates the social instincts in our brain, making us more willing to interact, and accentuates our propensity to be empathetic and kind.

We know that whenever we are threatened or are under stress, our brain releases a series of substances, including adrenaline, which makes our hearts beat faster and prepares us for action. But many people do not know that oxytocin is also released at these times. According to Kelly McGonigal, this biological response to stress is a prompt to seek social connection. It is as if your brain is urging you to go tell someone what you are feeling instead of keeping it to yourself.

It is important to seek help and refuge from people who care about you. I often seek out my father when I am having a hard time. This may seem counterintuitive, given that, as I mentioned earlier, my father was always one of the people who drove me hardest to push my limits and was often demanding and critical. But I turn to him because I have absolute faith in his love and support and know he will always be authentic and honest with me. The truth is that he makes me feel welcome, actively listens, reminds me of my abilities and options for dealing with the situation, and helps me think through possible solutions for things outside my control.

Seeking support from people who only wish to validate us, praise us, or tell us what we want to hear in order to cheer us up may seem like a good idea for getting through times when we are fragile or vulnerable; however, it is the beautiful enemy—the concept conjured by Ralph Waldo Emerson, introduced in chapter 1—who helps us connect with our essence, which enables us to emerge from difficult situations with greater strength and resilience.

The Arrival of the Pandemic

If ever there was a challenging year, it was 2020. The coronavirus pandemic caught everyone by surprise, causing millions of deaths across the planet and serious socioeconomic problems in several countries. Many companies and countries closed their doors, and major events had to be postponed, such as the Olympic Games in Tokyo. The year 2020 will be remembered more for the frequent, unusual, and radical changes to people's lives than for the excellent athletic performances that had been eagerly anticipated at the beginning of the year.

But even as some competitions returned, they returned to empty arenas, swimming pools, and stadiums echoing to the sound of the silence from absent fans. The few audible sounds on offer came from a ball being kicked or athletes' joy at winning a point or scoring a goal. The spectacle was incomplete. This new normal in high-performance sports confirmed the view that while a sporting spectacle may have athletes as the protagonists, the competition is only complete when accompanied by the energy of the crowd.

All of this has had a major impact on the routines of the athletes. For a top sportsperson, the Olympics represent the ultimate highlight, with maximum exposure. Many spend four years just preparing for the event. But the sudden postponement put all this preparation on hold.

In addition to the frustration of not being able to participate in the games, the athletes had to review their plans and expectations for the Olympics, which were pushed back to 2021.

Everything was abruptly postponed.

Facing constant adversity, athletes had to call upon their previous experiences to get through the moment without losing their preparation or their confidence. That was what American gymnast Simone Biles did. Winner of ten gold medals from world championships, she is the most decorated gymnast in the United States. She shone in her first Olympics in Rio in 2016, winning four gold medals and one bronze. In addition, she oozed charisma and charm, winning over the Brazilian crowd and receiving a standing ovation after her solo presentation.

She was preparing intensely for her second Olympics, when the world was downed by the pandemic. "We can only control what we do, which is the training, ... because we don't know what will happen," she said.[13]

However, not everyone has Biles's power to adapt. Many athletes were in doubt about how to maintain a top level of performance for another year, especially those who were thinking about closing out their careers in Tokyo. Then there was the renewal of sponsorships, which caused another headache for some athletes.

They had to review their routines and reframe their beliefs in order to move forward. This was illustrated by a study carried out by researchers from England and South Africa to investigate the respiratory impact of COVID-19 on some athletes while also assessing the impact on mental health. The research revealed that the continuation of training was an important component in protecting the athlete's mental health, especially in reducing the risk of anxiety and depression.[14]

With the restrictions, it was necessary to find the best way to deal with the new scenario, using flexibility and creativity. Some were able to develop training plans with their support teams, even from a distance. The current captain of the Spanish water polo team, Felipe Perrone, who has participated in four Olympic Games (for Spain at Beijing in 2008, London in 2012, and Tokyo in 2020 and for Brazil at Rio de Janeiro in 2016), challenged authorities in Barcelona by deciding to train in the sea. As it had been decreed that only sailboats, windsurfers, and surfers were authorized to enter the sea, Felipe took his surfboard along so he could carry out his swimming regimen. This defiance caught the eye of local television as an example of creativity in dealing with some of life's unexpected moments.

Ryosuke Irie, aged thirty, continued to step up his preparation for the hundred-meter and two-hundred-meter backstroke. A six-time world champion with three Olympic medals, he was seen as Japan's big star for the 2020 Olympic Games. With the delay to 2021, he and the other athletes faced a new set of challenges.

Suddenly uncertain, Irie decided to look to the future. "If the Tokyo Olympics don't happen, I believe I will go to Paris in 2024," he said during his preparation.[15] By the time of the Paris Olympics, he will have turned thirty-four, but this did not concern him. He mentioned that Olympic medalist Kosuke Kitajima only hung up his swimming goggles in 2016, when he too was thirty-four years old. In other words, if these were the circumstances that had been imposed upon him, he would just have to adapt.

Lindsay Shoop, an American rower who competed in the Beijing Olympics in 2008 and is now a coach in the sport, wrote an article in *USA Today* that reinforced how the concept of slicing the mountain has been useful for athletes in these times. One section of the article, entitled "Small habits. Big impact," gave some tips in this regard: "Stay motivated. Give yourself time to adapt. You've already made stressful life changes by self-isolating, working from home and dealing with a pandemic. Take your health one step at a time. Manage one new thing. Then add another. With a little patience and motivation, you are more than capable of creating health habits now that you'll be grateful for in the long run."[16]

She also gave some tips for accepting what you cannot control and focusing on what you can: paying attention to what you eat, being mindful of how you sleep, taking care of yourself, staying connected with the moment, having a purpose, visualizing the future, and helping people think about their priorities.

Companies and professionals from many different areas have also had to adapt. Some have bet on technology to maintain productivity and have even managed to increase profitability. Innovations that might normally have taken years have had to be accelerated, such as the creation of vaccines to combat the coronavirus. Companies that were already digitized prepared for the worst and have come out even stronger, proving themselves antifragile.

With respect to people's personal lives, even given the lockdown restrictions, many people have managed to find ways not to be alone. Some have been able to take advantage of the various digital video platforms to cultivate close relationships. They have accepted physical distancing, over which they have had no control, but have done their best to avoid social distancing, as social distancing runs against human nature.

We have a lot to learn from the adversities that arise in life, be they large or small, predictable or unexpected. Searching for meaning in each of them is key to having an existence filled with health, well-being, and happiness. Not all that happens is for the best, but it falls to each of us to choose what to do to make the most of each situation.

- Adversities can come in the form of a contretemps, a setback, or a fatality. They are part of life. Often, they offer an opportunity for personal growth.

- It is not the difficulties we face in life that matter but how we choose to respond to them. Not all that happens is for the best, but it falls to each of us to choose what to do to make the most of each situation.

- The way we perceive stress influences the way we handle it. Embracing the positive aspects promotes physiological and behavioral changes that enhance our health, productivity, learning, and growth.

- We should give ourselves permission to be human beings, accept that all of our emotions are valid, and allow ourselves to experience them.

- Slow, deep breathing brings us calm; connects us with the present; and creates space for embracing and accepting emotions.

- Reframing is a powerful tool for helping us deal with times of adversity.

- The habit of keeping a journal is an excellent practice for both enhancing the pleasure experienced during the good times and integrating and making sense of our experiences during painful and difficult times.

- Seeking help and connecting with people important to us are ways of dealing with adversity. However, we should take care not to seek out only those who will validate our actions.

- How do you deal with stressful moments in your life? Are you able to identify opportunities for learning and growth, or do you view stress as something to be avoided at all costs? How has this perspective influenced your actions?
- How do you handle moments of frustration? Have you given yourself permission to be human? What approach do you take to opening up and reflecting on such moments—a friend, a therapist, family, or perhaps a diary?

CHAPTER 5

———

BUILDING ON YOUR STRENGTHS AND GAINING **SELF-CONFIDENCE**

Everybody is a genius. But if you judge a fish by its ability to
climb a tree, it will live its whole life believing that it is stupid.
—Albert Einstein

A horse never runs so fast as when it has other
horses to catch up and outpace.
—Ovid

In the water, the Dutch seemed like giants. In the first world championship I participated in, in Australia in 1991, they were the champions. They had previously been European champions three times. The players were woven so seamlessly together that they all seemed like one. They tied their hair in a topknot, which made them seem even taller and more regal.

Over the years of facing them in the pool, I got to realize that they were not so tall after all. They were also not perfect. Like all human beings, they made mistakes.

But their secret was in their preparation before the game even started. They occupied all the spaces in the pool, creating an elaborate wall in front of the opponent, all making the same agile movements, presenting themselves in such a way that opposing players might have believed the game was already lost.

It was equivalent to the haka performed by the All Blacks, New Zealand's rugby team. They perform a traditional Maori dance to intimidate and display their passion. The ritual has become the trademark of the team and is still one of the most fearsome in world sport.

We started to do something similar with the Brazilian team. Before the games kicked off, we would get together and let loose our battle cry: "Power! Strength! As one! Let's go, Brazil! Oooh, Brazil!" Then we lined up along the edge and jumped into the pool as one and took our first powerful strokes into the middle of the pool. As we waited for the referee's whistle for the match to begin, we eyed our opponents confidently, savoring the adrenaline and the flow of energy.

As this ritual became a habit, we began to behave differently in games. There was absolute respect for the opponent, but we felt stronger and better prepared, and there were no teams who intimidated us, as had happened previously. We felt an inner strength that we could take on any team as equals.

Self-confidence can be the difference between success and failure, given the tiny margins that exist in top-level sport. Despite this, we must recognize that self-confidence is volatile, which means there are going to be highs and lows.

Act and You Will Become

"Fake it till you make it" is an expression in English that suggests if people act as if they are confident, competent, and optimistic, even though they may not be feeling it at the time, this attitude will influence how they think, behave, and feel and how others view them, which, in turn, will enhance chances of success. There is a variation on this theme that I like even more: "Act until you become it." This means trying out a behavior until you learn about new possibilities, evolve, and become what you wish to be. But how do we do this?

American social psychologist and Harvard Business School professor Amy Cuddy carried out research showing that before a job interview, just two minutes of a power pose—a confident posture with the hands on the waist or the arms outstretched, forming a *v* for *victory*—was able to impact the way candidates felt and performed, generating a positive result in interviews.

Many candidates, while waiting to begin the interview, in which they were expected to be upbeat and communicate confidently, expressed exactly the opposite in terms of their posture. They looked down, focused on a cell phone, sat with their torso hunched, or were absorbed in social media posts. These postures had a direct impact on how the candidates expressed themselves a few minutes later during the interview. In the survey led by Cuddy, the interviewers did not know which candidates had adopted the power pose before the interview, but even so, those were the ones hired.

At home, my family and I have also felt the positive impact of the power pose. I noticed before a swimming competition that my daughter Giorgia was sitting hunched over her cell phone, oblivious to the world around her. Her mental state was clear from afar. As I approached, I could see she was anxious and unsure of herself. I led her into a corner and suggested she do a power pose for just three minutes. "Let's pretend we're here talking. Turn to me, and put your hands on your hips with your body up straight. Close your eyes, and focus on taking some deep breaths," I said. Afterward, we shared a joke, and she left for her challenge. The change was impressive. The relaxed yet focused way she walked to the side of the pool, with her arms hanging loosely, was reflected in her performance. In just three minutes, she had transformed.

It is not just posture that influences our emotions and behavior. Facial expressions can have the same effect. A steady look around with a smile on our face ahead of a match also increases feelings of self-confidence and well-being. It is important to think about our body language from head to toe.

In one of the most popular talks in the history of TED Talks, Amy shared a personal story that illustrates the power of how we comport ourselves in life.[1] When she was nineteen, she was involved in a serious car accident. Wanting to return to college, she was discouraged by those who told her she would not be able to keep up with the program.

She continued to study and took four years longer than her classmates to graduate. When she was accepted to study for a PhD at prestigious

Princeton University, she had to give a presentation to twenty people. She felt insecure, as if she were an imposter. She told her adviser, psychologist Susan Fiske, she would give up her place. Fiske said, "You are not quitting. ... You are going to stay and this is what you're gonna do. ... You're gonna do every talk you ever get asked to do. You're just going to do it and do it and do it—even if you are terrified and just paralyzed ... —until you have this moment where you say, 'Oh my God, I'm doing it! Like, I have become this. I am actually doing this.'" So that was what she did, and when she least expected it, she joined the faculty at Harvard University.

William James, who was one of the leading thinkers of the late nineteenth century and is considered the father of American psychology, said, "If you want a quality, act as if you already had it." The idea is that if you attempt to act in a certain way and stick with it, you will tend to become what you are trying to be. At first glance, this idea of acting until you become might seem to separate us from our essence, but it actually is a process of experimenting with new possibilities. We simulate a posture, as it is through action that we connect with our potential and learn. Our actions' directing our feelings demonstrate once again the integration of mind and body.

Self-Confidence Comes from Action

When people do what they enjoy, conveying a posture of power and demonstrating mastery over what they do, we see them as confident and secure in their abilities and convictions. That is, we judge other people based on their actions and behaviors.

Social psychologist Daryl Bem, professor emeritus at Cornell University, proposed the theory of self-perception, which suggests that we also judge ourselves in terms of our own behaviors. That is, if I act decisively and confidently, I start to think of myself as someone who is decisive and confident.

Building self-esteem and self-confidence and acting in line with our goals and passions is about more than merely considering the way we feel, think, or speak about ourselves. We should visualize the person we want to be—the best version of ourselves in the present moment—and start acting as if we already are that person. By adopting this approach, not only will we come to see ourselves as secure and confident, but our behaviors will become habits, at which point we will no longer need to think about them. Our conduct will become natural to us.

According to Canadian psychotherapist Nathaniel Branden, one of the world's leading experts on self-esteem, whose books have been translated into eighteen languages and have more than four million copies in print, there is a continuous feedback loop between our actions in the world and our self-esteem. The level of our self-esteem influences how we act and vice versa.

An expression often used in business is "going for the low-hanging fruit," which suggests that when standing under a tree laden with fruit, it is better to pick the fruit within our reach first. When aiming for an ambitious goal, if we begin with results that are easier to achieve, we will gain increasing confidence before moving on to bigger challenges. We thus enter a positive spiral.

With training, practice, and a focus on taking action, we develop mastery. We enhance our skills, deepen our knowledge, and learn more about ourselves. As a consequence, we increase our self-confidence and self-esteem.

Analyze What Went Well

To further build on this relationship between our actions and our self-confidence, it is important to spend some time analyzing what we actually did to achieve the positive results. American water polo coach Sandy Nitta always used to recommend that after every game—whether in practice or in competition—players reflect on what they had done. For every goal they scored and every good move, they had to consider the external and internal conditions that had helped the result to happen. She challenged us to analyze the following: "What was going through your heads? How were you feeling? What did you do that worked?"

It is common for people to engage in this type of self-reflection when faced with an error or when things have not gone as planned. I consider it important to analyze and learn from failures, but it is also fundamental that we analyze our successes. "We are used to holding ourselves to account for what went wrong but not for what went right. We need to give ourselves credit for what we've done well and to explore the key elements of the success. This is what helps build our self-confidence," Sandy told us.

This approach can also be helpful when educating our children. We should support them in learning from errors as well as celebrate their efforts when they succeed. How we go about this is crucial, since it is in childhood that we start to form our self-perceptions and our beliefs about our own abilities.

Carol Dweck, professor at Stanford University and author of *Mindset: The New Psychology of Success*, highlights the importance of praising children wisely. As previously discussed, rather than associating children's achievements with a characteristic or a result, such as praising them for being smart after they get a good grade on a test, we should congratulate them on the process and how hard they worked and focused and on the strategy they used. If, instead of simply celebrating their achievements, we ask questions that help them reflect on the process, there is a greater boost to confidence, as it allows them to learn more about what they did to achieve the result and develop their own bank of knowledge to call upon when next faced with new challenges.

After celebrating with one of my daughters her performance at the state championship, in which she had recorded personal bests in the four events she competed in, we went on to analyze what had led her to that level of consistent performance. I asked, "What have you done along the way to get to this point?" One important insight she gained was in how she was spending the period between races: listening to music, staying quietly focused, and avoiding the anxiety that comes naturally at such moments. I noticed that type of reflection made my daughter more aware of what worked for her and gave her more confidence and autonomy in facing the next tests, whether in sport, at school, or in life.

This also holds true for corporate life. I often took part in teams that were formed to identify the root cause of what had gone wrong and reduce the operational risk of new failures. This was important, of course; however, reviewing a project that launched successfully, for example, can highlight new ways of achieving extraordinary results. When I worked as a quality manager, I was delighted with the forum we held with clients.

We learned a lot from giving customers a chance to describe how they had learned about the launch of a new product; what had attracted them in the communication materials; which means of contact with the bank they preferred and why; whether the initial sign-up and user experience had been welcoming and friendly; and what made them continue to use the product. Each of these conversations allowed us to create formulas for success that could be rolled out to other projects at the company. It was important to identify the key success factors in generating a positive result, from the process that conceived of the idea to testing the concept with customers, so that new insights could be incorporated into the company's bank of knowledge, which led to performance excellence and customer satisfaction.

Focus on the Strengths

Many people believe that in order to achieve excellence, we should focus on identifying our weaknesses and invest a good deal of time in either eliminating them or turning them into strengths. But this is actually not the best approach. In seeking high performance, our focus should be on our strengths. They are what lead us to stand out, excel, and break records. By practicing what we are already good at, we become even better and gain more confidence in ourselves. But what about our potential limiting factors? Should we just ignore them?

Austrian writer, professor, and consultant Peter Drucker has demonstrated that we should expend as little effort as possible in improving areas of low competence. After all, it takes a lot more effort and energy to go from incompetent to mediocre than it does to go from excellent to exceptional. But there is more to it than that.

As both an athlete and an executive, I sometimes came across people who focused solely on what was not working well—that is, on the empty half of the glass. It is difficult to cultivate self-esteem, emotional balance, and intellectual well-being without also focusing—emphasis on the word *also*—on the positives, the things we are good at, and the aspects of life that are going well.

Yes, we should identify and recognize our weaknesses, which I prefer to call *potential limiters* to avoid the fatalistic tone that the term *weakness* can convey. But the aim is to leverage our strengths. If a soccer player's main strength is shooting, but he lacks pace, he should work on becoming quicker in order to increase his opportunities in front of goal to do what he does best: shooting.

When Sandy coached our team, she identified that our main strength was our creative offense. "You Brazilians love to attack and be creative in front of goal," she joked, encouraging us to develop our skills in that area. However, we had limitations in defense, and our performance tended to drop off when the game got more demanding physically. She had us boxing and doing martial arts, which improved our confidence in our ability to defend ourselves and also improved our breathing to engage the right muscles. We worked intensively on defensive tactics and body positioning and observed what other teams were doing who were strong defensively. All of this helped to consolidate our performance in the area where we excelled: our powerful offense.

Robert Scheidt, who is participating in his seventh Olympiad, recognizes that the physical side can be a limiting factor in facing competitors younger than he is. To combat this, he invests time in physical preparation and recovery. However, his main focus remains on perfecting and exploiting his strengths, which are his tactical skills, his experience with different types of winds, and his mental preparation.

"Sailing is a sport that mixes physical demands with the strategic and tactical aspects of a regatta. My experience in having already faced many crucial decisions at key moments of competitions, with pressure from all sides, can help me. I feel more prepared for these moments than those who might be competing in their first Olympics. My strength is in my experience and knowing what routine works for me," he told me. In addition, he has a long and successful track record, which only serves to boost his confidence further. "The fact that I have achieved the previous results gives me greater confidence. After winning the first time, you already know that road. Of course, repeating the feat isn't easy, but you've been through it before."

I talked to Martine Grael and Kahena Kunze, Olympic champions in Rio in 2016 and Tokyo in 2020 and world yachting champions in the 49er FX class. They told me, ahead of the 2020 games, that they had also been working on their strengths in preparation for the upcoming Olympics.

"In sailing, there are specialists, those who are very good in strong winds and those who do well when the wind is light, for example. But our main strength is our ability to adapt to changing conditions quickly," Martine told me. Thus, instead of trying to specialize in one type of wind or another, they have worked on enhancing their adaptability.

Before I entered the pool for key games, my father used to remind me of all the things I did well. My confidence got an immediate boost. It influenced my posture in walking up to the pool, my thought patterns, my level of concentration, and how I dealt with those pregame moments.

Immediately after a game, I would receive some brief feedback. Then, at home, more at ease, we focused on the areas I had performed well and those I needed to improve. At first, we focused more on the technical aspects, such as body positioning, how to get more swerve on a shot, or a specific form of defense. As time passed, the focus shifted to how I could make more of the opportunities arising in a game, using the game clock to enhance the timing of my drills, such as anticipating a ball and starting a counterattack; eluding a specific type of marking; and reading the goalkeeper better. These reflections on the game, coupled with my coach's comments, inspired me in my next training sessions to seek to perfect what I had done well and reduce the risk arising from the potential limiters.

Performance and Passion

We were on our way to the 1999 Winnipeg Pan American Championship, when my father handed me a letter that read,

> Today, you represent 170 million Brazilians. Winning the medal will build a deeper awareness and more confident sense of citizenship, which is key to the future of our nation. Bear with you the spirit of patriotism, courage and bravery. Do what you have trained so hard to do—players, coaches and managers—and it will be enough. With the medal, you will be on the side of history and glory, but even without it, this is already a great (if not the greatest) performance in the history of Brazilian water

polo abroad. Show the devastating attack that you have; and your true wall of a defense; and the togetherness and spirit of this team, of which there has never been the like. Rest assured that when you hold the ball, your opponent will tremble, as they know the goal threat that you carry from any and every position. Do what only you know how to do, with the full knowledge and desire, passion, skill and talent that God has given you. And the medal will come, naturally, through persistence and dedication, without a doubt, but with a sacred blessing that will touch your grandchildren and great-grandchildren, and go down in our folklore.

While some of our strengths are performance-related, we also have strengths arising from our passion. The first group relates to our skills and abilities—what we do well or what gives us the greatest potential to become an expert. Passion-related strengths are activities that light a fire within us, that we love to do, and that give us great pleasure.

To identify your performance-related strengths, ask yourself the following: *Which tasks do I learn easily? What do I do well? What kind of activities have I been most successful at in the past?* To identify your passion-related strengths, ask yourself the following: *What do I love to do? What activities fill me with energy? What do I achieve that makes me feel like my true self?'*

Think of someone you consider extraordinary, such as a champion or a successful executive, for example. You may be thinking of someone who is highly competent and passionate about what he or she does, for it is the union of these two traits that leads us into a virtuous circle toward excellence.

When we apply our performance-related and passion-related strengths in unison, we enter our zone of peak performance, and our confidence level increases. The more we experience situations that lead us to peak performance, the more we will feel fulfilled while doing what gives us pleasure and success, thus creating a virtuous circle.

Meditation in Action

Hungarian American Mihaly Csikszentmihalyi is one of the world's leading researchers in positive psychology. He coined the term *flow* to describe a highly focused state of mind.

We experience flow when we are totally immersed and absorbed in an experience, such as when we are engrossed in a book, oblivious to the hours passing. We can also experience this when interacting with a friend or when working. It is as if we are at one with the moment, ourselves, and the experience—a single entity.

Sportsmen and sportswomen often experience this flow when they are fully engaged in a match. When I was in the middle of a game or a practice, if someone beyond the pool tried to attract my attention, he or she had to call out more than once, as I hardly heard anything that was alien to the game experience.

Flow represents meditation in action, which takes place when we reach our peak performance. In it, we feel self-confident and are totally focused on the activity we are doing. By performing at our best, we learn, grow, improve, and advance toward our next goal.

In order to get in the zone, there needs to be a balance between the level of our ability and the level of challenge we are facing. If the difficulty of a task exceeds our ability to deliver, we feel anxious. If our abilities exceed the level of the task, we become bored and dissatisfied.

The key to generating more moments of flow is to ensure this balance. When we're facing ambitious goals, it is important to slice up the mountain and match the level of the challenge to that of our ability. On the other hand, as we develop our abilities from training and practice, we need to set ever-greater challenges.

For this reason, it is important to respect the stage of an athlete's development, as discussed in chapter 1. When our children first go to school, we hope they will feel welcome, enjoy the experience, and feel encouraged to learn, and the same applies to sport. By emphasizing the fun side, we allow the child to enjoy, and to want to continue playing, sport. As skills develop and sporting preferences become clearer, the level of demand needed for activities to challenge yet remain fun changes.

Self-Esteem

Edwin Moses won an academic scholarship to study physics and engineering at Morehouse College, Atlanta, an institution that produced African American leaders, such as Martin Luther King Jr. There were no athletics training facilities, but Moses trained anyway. "I spent 1974, 1975, and 1976 literally jumping over fences," he said. He was totally unknown when he qualified for the Olympics in Montreal in 1976. To accomplish this feat, he needed to overcome a series of political and financial obstacles, which led him to speak directly to the college's dean, Hugh Gloster. Moses requested $3,000 so he and his coach could compete in the tryouts for the Olympics. The president laid down a challenge, asking, "Do you really think you can win a gold medal?"

Moses replied, "If I get that money, I will go to the track meets, win them one by one, and break the US record as I go. And when I get to the Olympics, I'll break the world record."

With the check in hand, Moses felt like a gladiator. As he put it, "I knew I was ready. I knew I would win and break all records. And that's what I did."[2] And he achieved much more. Edwin Moses became the biggest name in the history of the four-hundred-meter hurdles. Not only is he a two-time Olympic champion and four-time world record holder, but in the decade his career lasted, he accumulated 122 wins, 107 of which were consecutive.

Self-esteem and self-confidence are not the only factors that led him to so many titles, but they certainly played a part. Having high self-esteem is a crucial factor in drawing up targets for our lives and then striving to achieve them. According to Nathaniel Branden, self-esteem creates a set of implicit expectations regarding what is possible and appropriate for us, and these expectations end up becoming self-fulfilling prophecies.

A self-fulfilling prophecy occurs when someone makes a prediction regarding what will happen and then acts as if the prediction is already reality, creating a process to achieve it and, in effect, making it happen.

Self-esteem is comprised of both internal factors—our own beliefs, thoughts, practices, and behaviors—and external factors—messages, criticism, and feedback we receive from others. It is, therefore, important to reflect on the way parents, teachers, coaches, or managers praise or criticize children, athletes, or company employees. Depending on the manner and degree of criticism, the risk of imposing labels on the other person is high and should be avoided, so those labels do not become part of that person's reality and limit performance improvement.

The risk is that those receiving such labels will give up in the face of obstacles and become guided more by a desire to avoid suffering than by satisfaction or enjoyment. Thus, they end up not achieving their goals, reinforcing their self-perception. People with high self-esteem, on the other hand, make optimistic predictions about their own futures and tend to persist when faced with difficulties, giving their all to attain their goals, which increases the chance of success.

In the book *The Six Pillars of Self-Esteem*, Branden argues that self-esteem works as an immune system for the conscious mind, providing us with endurance, strength, and the capacity for regeneration. He writes, "Just as our body's immune system does not guarantee that we will never become ill, but makes us less vulnerable to illnesses and better equipped to overcome them, so a healthy self-esteem does not guarantee we will not suffer from anxiety or depression when faced with life's difficulties, but does make us less susceptible and better equipped to recover and transcend these situations."

As a psychotherapist, he has developed a technique that helps people to enhance their self-awareness and produce significant changes in their lives, thus increasing their self-esteem.[3] It is a technique involving sentence completion,[9] in which the subject is presented with incomplete sentences and invited to suggest as many endings as possible.

The idea is to do this quickly, without thinking critically.

Reflection only comes after we finish the task. Some examples of incomplete sentences are the following:

- If I bring 5 percent more attention to my life …
- The things that make me happy are …
- If I were more attentive to satisfying my desires …
- If I brought 5 percent more integrity to my life …
- If I say yes when I want to say yes and no when I want to say no …

---

[9] A complete guide to the technique can be found at http:// www. nathanielbranden. com/sentence-completion-i.

The idea is to create at least six endings for each of these sentences. After creating the answers for that week, we should review them, see what we have learned from them, and choose one or two actions to put into practice. We can repeat this exercise as many times as we wish, and the more we do so, the greater our self-awareness, the more we will experiment with new possibilities, and the more we will act on what is key to enhancing our self-esteem.

Permission to Be Happy

It is common in Western culture for people to feel some sense of hesitation when it comes to happiness. Presented with emotions of joy and contentment, an inner voice tells us, "I don't deserve this," "It won't last," "This is too good to be true," or "Something bad could happen at any time." It is as if we feel guilty about being in a good place.

As paradoxical as it may seem, we need to give ourselves permission to be happy, enjoy the things that give us pleasure, and savor the fruits of our endeavors. The celebration of victories and successes helps build our self-confidence and promotes a sense of well-being.

We should cultivate pleasurable emotions not only as an end in itself but also as a means to strengthen and evolve psychologically. Barbara Fredrickson, a professor at the University of North Carolina, published an article in the scientific journal the *American Psychologist* wherein she presents her theory about the importance of letting pleasant emotions flow through us (just as we should allow painful ones).[4]

Positive emotions, such as love, joy, and pride, have an evolutionary function. When we experience them, momentarily, it is as if we broaden our view of situations, with new insights and perspectives. Over time, these experiences lead us to develop our own way of dealing with adversity. Pleasant emotions make us healthier and more creative, resilient, and socially integrated. They can boost our motivation and energy levels.

When we feel good about ourselves and how things are going in our lives, we have more energy and engage more in what we set out to do.

Best of all, happiness is contagious! When we improve our own well-being, we contribute to the well-being of those around us. Laughs and smiles are the most obvious indicators of positive emotions and are highly contagious. If we wish our family, friends, teammates, and coworkers to lead successful and happy lives, we should start with ourselves.

Stretching Limits

Yusra Mardini started swimming when she was three years old, in her home city of Damascus, Syria. At nine, she already dreamed of going to the Olympics. When she was twelve, civil war broke out. They were tense times, although she continued with her studies and training. Heavy ordinance bombing attacks were frequent, and she lost many friends during that period.

In August 2015, Yusra and her sister Sarah decided to flee to Germany, in a saga that lasted twenty-five days. At one point on the trip, they and eighteen other refugees boarded a boat designed to hold up to six. The journey from Turkey to Greece was expected to take forty-five minutes, but after just fifteen, the boat's engine stopped, and the boat began to fill with water in the middle of the Aegean Sea. Mardini, her sister, and two male refugees jumped into the water and pushed the boat for three and a half hours until they reached shore.

"It was at this point I realized that I was so strong inside. I felt brave enough to do anything with my life," said Mardini. Soon after her arrival in Germany, she returned to the pool. "When I'm in the pool, I just focus on swimming and doing my best, and that helps me deal with the tough times in life."[5]

The 2016 Rio Olympics were the first to feature a team of refugee athletes, who competed under the Olympic banner. Yusra Mardini was one of the athletes who qualified. "We were one team, united in representing diversity and the Olympic spirit. We had all had to fight to get there," she said. For Mardini, being part of that historic moment was more important than realizing her dream of competing in the Olympics. "I realized that I represented many people. I was a role model for refugees, and even today I receive letters from children inspired by my story." She qualified again as part of the refugee team for Tokyo in 2020 and became a goodwill ambassador for the UN Refugee Agency (UNHCR).

How we react to adversity can enable us to grow and evolve—as discussed in chapter 4—and one of the effects of this growth arising from challenging times is a boost to our self-confidence. When faced with adversity, we create our own method for dealing with situations, which we call upon again in the future. When we understand our ability to deal with painful situations, we recognize that there is a strength within us, as we know we are capable of surviving or overcoming the difficulty.

This idea is also behind training regimens that take athletes to extremes, such as those of Croatian coach Ratko Rudić. When we push beyond our limits, we reap the rewards of our efforts and gain a new perspective on our abilities.

Brazilian water polo player Felipe Perrone, a naturalized Spaniard, played in the 2008 and 2012 Olympics for Spain and in the 2016 games for Brazil. He was the captain of the team coached by Rudić. He stressed that the coach not only pushed them to the limit but also prepared them mentally at the same time. He said, "He was preparing us for the final, creating a scenario more akin to the feelings we might have in an extreme situation. There were players who fell by the wayside, who said, 'I can't take this. I can't handle it,' and left. Those who remained were left feeling they could handle anything that life threw at them."

Felipe also stressed that these insights he gained about himself hold true even today and are not restricted to water polo: "I truly believe that I'm ready to face anything, regardless of the context." This reinforces the view I have always held about playing sport and its power to build our self-confidence during different stages of our lives.

This happens not purely through stretching our own limits but also through observing and competing against the best in our sport.

Competitiveness

"I don't believe in tournaments in which everyone who takes part gets a prize," Frank Steel, head of Gulliver Schools, told me. He believes that competition has merit and should be encouraged, as it gives people a chance to test their abilities. In our conversation, he explained that competition gives us a point of reference regarding how we can improve and, thus, encourages us to work harder, overcome perceived barriers, and strive to get better. This often stretches the limits of what we think we are capable of and boosts our self-confidence.

My father always used to say, "Aim to be second best, because when you are the best at something, you stagnate. You stop evolving." If there is someone better than you, it is as if there is a tangible goal against which you can set your targets. He also said, "If you get closer to your idols, you will see what it takes to get there, given the right level of dedication and extra work."

In 1959, the great forward Aladar Szabo, a Hungarian naturalized Brazilian water polo player, was invited to represent Brazil. His arrival attracted the media and the public to the national team's games. He was the idol we had been waiting for. My father was just starting out in the sport when he arrived to train with the Brazilian national team ahead of the Rome Olympics and met Szabo in person in July 1960.

Szabo was a fearless attacker and possessed one of the best shots in the world, as well as having exceptional ability in the water. However, he was a human being, willing to go the extra mile to achieve excellence through effort, practice, and persistence. "All you have to do is touch a legend whose achievements have bestowed immortality to realize that he is also human in having virtues and flaws," said my father.

Since first beginning in the sport, he had learned to admire and copy the great Hungarian players in Béla Rajki's book, and then he had the opportunity to play with his idols, three-time Olympic champions Dezső Gyarmati and György Kárpáti, at the Universiade of 1963, held in Porto Alegre, Brazil. "I realized that while I may have felt unsure of myself, so did they, and that gave me more confidence to play," he said.

Sporting legends are not unreachable gods. In reality, they are people who spend hours practicing their skills and techniques in the pool or on the court, track, or field while also working on the mental side. By aiming to follow their examples, we will always be pursuing excellence rather than being satisfied with good.

This fact, which is evident in sport, also holds true in school, in the family, or at work. You can raise your performance to be closer to the performances of those you most admire, and competing with or against them can help in this development.

High-performance athletes develop the habit of being competitive the whole time. Preparing for his seventh Olympiad, at the age of forty-seven, yachtsman Robert Scheidt told me he did not want to go to Japan just to be the oldest Brazilian athlete ever to compete at an Olympics. More than anything, he wanted to be competitive. "The Olympics is a place to perform, not a place to participate. If I thought I had no chance of winning, I wouldn't even try," he said.

In one of the funniest scenes in the Netflix documentary *The Last Dance*, NBA star Michael Jordan battles his bodyguard, John Michael Wozniak, in a game of pitching pennies. Jordan not only loses this contest but also has to contend with the bouncer performing his classic shrug celebration. This makes Jordan mad, as if he has just lost a championship game.

Competing implies learning in both victory and defeat, recognizing strengths and potential limiters, and constantly focusing on our own development. This entails making choices, anticipating and correcting errors, and becoming more careful and attentive. Regardless of the result, each experience moves you closer to improving your performance. Whoever wins wants the new challenge of staying a winner. Whoever loses wants another chance.

In my own experience, what attracted me to the sport was its competitiveness. I always liked the idea of continually improving and testing myself against other teams. As my sports career progressed, I discovered that there were always people more talented than I was and that if I focused purely on comparing myself to them, I would be disappointed. Therefore, although I copied those I admired, my targets, while always challenging, were based on what I might be able to achieve, rather than focusing on other people.

Something I took with me from sport into the executive world is that running alongside the competitive tussle for victory is the need for respect, integrity, and responsibility.

A team or company that seeks high performance and sustainable results rightly needs to have a competitive spirit, but equally, it should also stay true to its values and principles. Competitiveness, so important in the pursuit of success, calls for technical and moral integrity.

To follow the path to excellence and happiness, it is important to develop self-confidence and focus on both what we enjoy and what we are good at, working to project the image of what we aspire to become and seeking the competitiveness to recognize and exceed our own limitations.

Main Points Covered in This Chapter

- Self-esteem and self-confidence are key to achieving and sustaining high performance. To cultivate them, we should focus not only on the way we feel or think about ourselves but also on the way we act. Behaving confidently and self-assuredly makes us more confident and secure.

- Start with what you do well and what is most within your reach, and then focus on incremental improvements. Adapt the size of the challenge to your skill level, and keep pushing yourself.

- Get to know your abilities intimately. Invest more time and energy in building on your strengths. Be aware of the potential limiters, and work on them in order that you might further enhance your strengths.

- We achieve peak performance when we combine what we do well with what drives us: our passion.

- Learn not only from your mistakes but also from your successes. Allow yourself to be happy. Celebrate your achievements, identify the process that led to the result, and appreciate what you have achieved, in order to create a state of constant evolution.

- Competition offers opportunities to learn about our own abilities and motivates us to continually evolve.

- Do your actions and behaviors demonstrate confidence and self-assurance?
- What are your strengths, and what have you been doing to enhance them?
- What do you find easy to do well?
- What activity brings you the most joy?
- When did you perform at your best? Whom were you with? How did you feel? What were you doing?

CHAPTER 6

REENERGIZING ROUTINES FOR
HIGH-PERFORMANCE

We live in a world that celebrates work and activity,
ignores renewal and recovery, and fails to recognize that
both are necessary for sustained high-performance.
—Jim Loehr and Tony Schwartz

My thoughts before a big race are usually pretty simple. I tell
myself: Get out of the blocks, run your race, stay relaxed. If you
run your race, you'll win … channel your energy. Focus.
—Carl Lewis

Vanish, o night! Fade you, stars! Fade you, stars!
At dawn, I will win! I will win! I will win!
—Puccini, "Nessun Dorma"

"Nessun Dorma" is the final act of Puccini's opera *Turandot*, which gained even more fame through the voice of tenor Luciano Pavarotti. When I played for Sicily in Italy, we used to play this song ahead of big games. We used to sit in silence on the bus en route to the pool, savoring every word. The energy the song carried made our hearts beat faster as we slowly entered a state of greater focus and concentration. The lyrics *"Vincerò!*

Vincerò!" (I will win! I will win!) in the final verse brought the ritual to a crescendo that lifted our spirits and got us up for the challenge.

In my childhood and adolescence, in place of Puccini's night and stars, my parents invoked the sun, telling me, "Feel it shine. You shouldn't look straight at it, but feel its energy run through your fingertips." They taught me to take nourishment from the forces of nature—to sense the earth, walk on the grass, and feel the energy emanating from the soil. Before competitions, my father advised me, "Do some stretching while leaning back against that tree. Feel its energy passing through you, boosting your inner strength." Finally, my parents and I would touch at the fingertips, which gave me an emotional comfort that prepared me for the test ahead. The act was simple yet so powerful that it made me feel strong and capable.

Over time, I created my own routines. I always liked to listen to music in the days and hours leading up to tournaments. Often, on trips with the national team, we would journey to the game, and the energy would start to flow as we sang, as one, the Brazilian popular music that kept us in touch with our roots. As I progressed in the sport, my routines improved too. Routines and rituals do not have to be rigid but can be adapted to the needs of the moment. In long tournaments, where I needed focus and energy for each game, I learned to use meditation, breathing, and visualization to improve concentration. As the human mind is the most powerful simulator there is, visualization enabled me to prepare myself mentally and to summon the intensity and moves I was planning in the game.

With the Brazilian national team, official protocols often dictated our activities just before a match. After warming up in the water, we would put on our robes and form a line in front of the spectators. As each of our names was announced, we would acknowledge the crowd, to be greeted by a familiar rhythmic clapping.

Once the national anthem began to play, I tried to focus and tap into the positive vibes of the whole country we were representing. This was a key moment for me. I let the emotion enter my soul, as I knew it would give me inner strength and spirit during the game. As captain, I could not help but notice how some players got emotional in other ways as prematch nerves intensified. I asked myself how we could transform the importance of this moment into a positive, contagious energy among us and generate the focus and balance needed for when the game began.

We also developed in terms of planning our routines after each match. In victory or defeat, the desire was always to exit the pool right away, either to celebrate or to wind down with our team. However, small improvements we added to our routines started to make a significant difference. Rituals have the power to create symbolic subliminal messages that enhance our performance. In Sicily, when the Sunday matches were finished, knowing we would not be back in the pool until the following week, my teammates and I had a ritual I used to love of going to a restaurant by the sea to enjoy a delicious seafood salad and pasta. It is a ritual I still try to uphold with my family today, even though we are far from the Mediterranean. These moments of relaxing, laughing, and discussing all manner of topics with friends generate positive energy, which is often enough to trigger an upward spiral to our day and to a season.

A period of recovery after a game, or after an important task or challenge at work or in our family lives, is essential for us to recharge our batteries.

Taking Care of Our Energy Reserves

In the first part of the book, I talked about the foundations of high-performance: having a support network, investing in consistent practice, taking care of the details, and adopting a healthy lifestyle. In this second part, I have talked about how we can prepare mentally, learn and grow from adversity, and develop self-confidence. All of this is important in the quest for excellence, but there is a key ingredient that needs to be added to the above if we are to realize our full potential: the energy reserves.

Energy is our fuel. As much as we need to devote ourselves to developing our abilities, it is difficult to sustain high performance without also ensuring the necessary energy levels. Imagine winning a brand-new Ferrari with a full tank but one small factory defect: once the tank is empty, you will not be able to refuel. Either you will experience its full potential and afterward have an unused supercar sitting in the garage, or you will try to conserve fuel so you may use the Ferrari for longer, but you will never really make the most of its potential.

As with the Ferrari, our performance and health depend on careful energy management. This means establishing ways to tap into it before and during an important activity and ways to replenish our energy tanks after use. Another interesting analogy is the importance of the pit stop in a Formula One race. If the driver does not stop at the right time, a tire may give out, or the car may run out of gas. In either case, the race is lost.

So how do we replenish our energy reserves? By creating reenergizing recovery routines. These are positive, habit-forming routines we perform repeatedly until they become automatic to help ourselves manage our internal reservoir in the best way possible. They help us to make a conscious effort to use the least amount of energy possible, so we can maximize the energy available when it is really needed. This leaves us with greater freedom to expend our energy creatively and strategically.

One of the greatest players in NBA history, Kobe Bryant, talked about his habits in his book *Mamba Mentality*. When he and center Shaquille O'Neal led the Los Angeles Lakers to three championships between 2000 and 2002, he used to have his own routine he followed religiously before heading onto the court.

Prior to each game, he used to undergo contrast therapy to help loosen his joints or anaesthetize certain parts of his body. It started with four minutes of very cold water, followed by three minutes of hot water, two minutes of cold, two minutes of hot, and, finally, cold. It was always the same.

Then he would do some stretching and, as game time approached, would increase the elasticity of his stretches. Then he and Shaquille O'Neal would each tape their fingers, which gave them the opportunity to banter. As the two stars were the players the younger ones looked up to, their cheerful exchanges boosted the team. As the clock got closer to game time, they both fell quiet and focused, thus signaling the rest of the team to do the same. As Bryant matured to become the NBA scoring champion three years in a row, his routines evolved, but one aspect never changed: the importance he placed on listening to his body and adapting his preparations accordingly.

Aníbal Sánchez has spent sixteen years in Major League Baseball, the highest level of the sport in the United States. He told me he follows a well-structured routine on game days in order to arrive prepared to give his best. He said, "When I wake up in the morning, I try to stay relaxed, with a clear head. I don't think too much about the game, because if you start preparing too early, come game time, you're already tired mentally. Usually, my wife makes pancakes so I can put some carbs into my body. Between 10:00 a.m. and 12:00 p.m., I keep to myself. I listen to a song, reflect on things, and visualize what I'm going to do in the game. Around 2:30 p.m., I leave the house and go to the stadium. There I stay focused, incommunicado, for two to three hours. An hour and a half before the game, I try to relax again, make small talk, and chat with my wife. Then I'm good to go."

Types of Energy and Performance Zones

As Abraham Maslow, the father of humanistic psychology, suggested, if we wish to learn more about the extraordinary, about the limits of human potential, we should study those who have achieved excellence. Thus did Jim Loehr, world-renowned psychologist and founder of the Human Performance Institute, and Tony Schwartz, journalist and president of the Energy Project. They began by studying elite athletes and went on to observe other individuals who are successful in high-pressure situations, such as Special Forces soldiers, FBI agents specializing in hostage rescue, emergency-room surgeons, and senior executives of large corporations. After more than thirty years of research, they have concluded that what sets the best apart from the rest, including the very good, is that they are masters at energy management.

We have four energy sources in our body: physical, emotional, mental, and spiritual. Physical energy, at its base level, boils down to oxygen, glucose, nutrition, rest, and physical recovery. Emotional energy is fed by positive experiences, such as joy, pleasure, confidence, and pride, and is associated with having the emotional flexibility to turn adversity into challenges. Mental energy is the ability to focus our attention on where it will serve us best. Finally, spiritual energy, which does not necessarily have a religious component, is linked to doing something meaningful and aligned to our goals and values. I will explore this theme further in chapter 11.

The four energy sources connect at tenuous intersections. High performance is the result of all four operating in harmony. In other words, to achieve our best performance, we must be physically energized, emotionally connected, mentally focused, and spiritually aligned to our purposes and values.

We can also think of our energy in terms of quantity and quality.

When we can tap into a large quantity of high-quality energy, we are in the zone. We both feel and perform in a way that is powerful, strong, confident, proud, happy, and focused. We need to be in this zone if we want to give our best. This holds true whether in a game situation, a key tournament, or an important company presentation.

When we feel a large quantity of energy but the energy quality is that associated with tension or fear, we are in the survival zone. Due to the volume of energy, our performance is explosive, but operating in this zone should be reserved for survival situations, such as when catching one of the biggest waves in the world. Any mistake could be decisive. Tapping into our energy and running on emotions of tension is physiologically helpful in these situations, but in the long run, it is unsustainable and harmful. When we are in this zone, we are in fight-or-flight mode. We are fully alert to every signal coming from the environment in order to make the best decision in a short space of time.

However, many people go into fight-or-flight mode in day-to-day settings, where it is not necessary, as the situation is not threatening and does not demand this state of mind. Former American tennis star John McEnroe is an example of an athlete who achieved exceptional results but spent a lot of time in the survival zone. He was in the habit of confronting the crowd, throwing and breaking his rackets, and complaining to the referee. He became known for his trademark phrase "You cannot be serious," which he aimed at umpires. He became one of Wimbledon's youngest men's singles champions at just twenty years old, but his career was cut short. He won his last Grand Slam title at the age of twenty-five and retired from the professional circuit at thirty-one, while other players, such as Andre Agassi and Roger Federer, remained at an elite level beyond the age of thirty-five.

Staying too long in the survival zone can lead to the burnout zone. This occurs when we operate with low or negative energy levels. All athletes wish to avoid this zone, as the physical or mental exhaustion is such that it usually takes a long time to recover. Operating in this zone, we produce our worst levels of performance and can feel depressed, drained, and unhappy. In sport, we notice the impact of burnout when activities we used to do with ease become impossible. The athlete enters a vicious circle. The body does not respond as it did, and our mind no longer seems to have the strength to raise the levels of performance. In the corporate world, people who spend a lot of time in areas where they face continually aggressive targets under a lot of pressure to deliver tend to fall into this zone and may need a significant period of sick leave to fully recover.

There is also a fourth stage known as the recovery zone, which includes periods of rest and energy renewal. This zone is often neglected, undervalued, and underutilized in many settings but is especially so in the corporate environment. High-performance athletes, on the other hand, recognize how essential it is to schedule and respect this recovery period. Just as finding the correct balance between the high-performance zone and the recovery zone is essential to sustaining excellence, people in the survival and burnout zones need a significant period of recovery in order to exit the critical condition in which they find themselves.

Athletes are generally aware of the importance of dividing their preparation into periods of intense training and rest. A good example of someone successfully balancing the high-performance and recovery zones is Leandro Guilheiro. For many years, he was among the best judokas in the world rankings, earning two bronze medals, at Athens in 2004 and Beijing in 2008. Between 2008 and 2012, he completed the most intense cycle of competitions that any Brazilian has completed in the history of judo. He told me that to sustain his performance, he introduced into his routine something he'd learned from reading the biography of Roger Federer. Leandro pointed to the key takeaway: "I liked the way that he organized his season. He took a week's vacation at the end of each significant cycle. I saw that I could do something similar. I organized the calendar, and for each block of competition, I took a week off. And it ended up working out really well."

The recovery period after playing sport is fundamental, and it has benefited from continual advances in scientific research and technology. Marcelinho Huertas told me that in addition to an ice bath, he usually takes on proteins and natural juices right after games. "What you consume in the first hour after a game is essential for energy recovery," he said. "I try to eat something high quality. A lot of people think, *The game is over. I'm gonna eat a hamburger and fries,* but this is the worst thing you could do to your body just at that point when it's trying to replenish the energy it has spent."

When I talk about the balance between high performance and recovery, I am not suggesting you spend half your time doing one and the other half doing the other but, rather, find your own balance between the two.

Consultant, author, and researcher Jim Collins, a graduate of Stanford University, specializes in topics such as business management and sustainability. In partnership with Jerry Porras, professor emeritus of behavior and organizational change, he wrote the best-selling book *Built to Last: Successful Habits of Visionary Companies.*

This work introduces the concepts of the tyranny of the *or* and the genius of the *and*.[1] The tyranny of the *or* relates to a common view that we cannot accept paradoxes and that it is not possible to experience two apparently contradictory forces or ideas at the same time. The genius of the *and* stems from the possibility of the coexistence of extremes and the benefits of diversity.

For the authors, visionary companies are those that free themselves from the *or* and invest in the *and*. This way, they do not have to choose between focusing on purpose or profit, stability or innovation, continuity or change, or short-term or long-term gains. On the contrary, they find a way to keep both on their radar at the same time.

Whether in a corporate setting or any other context, the genius of the *and*, when applied to energy management, is in reconciling periods when we are full on with periods of rest, silence, and recovery.

Expanding Our Energy Capacity

Often, we wish the day had more than twenty-four hours so we could do everything we would like to achieve, do we not? Time management is something that athletes learn to do well, as we divide up the schedule between the many day-to-day commitments and the need to devote hours on end to training and practice. But managing our time effectively does not guarantee that we will have enough energy to do everything we aim to achieve.

Energy is the reserve currency of high performance. For example, as you read this book, are you fully engaged? What about your mind and body? Are you using your energy to focus on the present moment and take in the text? There can be a gap between dedicating time to a task and being fully focused on it. To close this gap, it is necessary to train, generate self-awareness, and manage our energy levels appropriately.

Energy management does not follow the same logic as schedule management, as time is a precise and limited quantity, whereas our energy can be expanded. But how can we do this? By combining periods of intense performance with periods of energy replenishment. As we saw previously, periods of stress, followed by appropriate recovery, have the potential to expand our energy capacity once we have learned how to deal with challenging situations.

Performing continually below our energy capacity, or just at our limit, without seeking to expand it drains our energy reserves over time, as does a lack of recovery.

As we saw in chapter 4, the real enemy of high performance is not stress, which in fact stimulates growth, but, rather, an absence of disciplined periodic recovery. Chronic stress without recovery consumes energy reserves, leads to burnout, and ultimately impairs performance.

Intermittent Recovery

"My coach told me, 'You can't travel without your bike, because it's key to your inner peace,'" Martine Grael, a sailor and gold medalist at the 2016 Rio and 2020 Tokyo Olympics, told me while talking about the importance of nature and bike rides to feeling balanced and energized. "I need to feel close to nature, the land, and the sea. I really enjoy cycling. When I am pedaling, I feel the wind on my face. Sometimes I think about life. Sometimes I don't think about anything; I just pedal. If I feel like cycling to the cliffs, I will. If I just want to go as far as the corner, then that works too. When I'm stressed, I get on my bike. It's my therapy."

Recovery is a means of detoxifying and replenishing our energy reserves so we go back to our activities with a sense of renewal. Recovery routines exist at several levels. In life and at work, we know the importance of respecting vacation periods. This is something that applies to everyone, whether he or she is an athlete, self-employed, or a corporate executive. It is common for executives not to switch off their smartphones or laptops while on vacation, as they feel indispensable. This compromises the recovery process and has the potential to impact their performance over the long term. With modern technology enabling us to access our work anywhere, most of us have unlearned what it means to truly rest, unwind, and switch off from all work-related thoughts.

The ideal is to have different rhythms in your life such that when you are engaged, you are highly productive and focused on the task in hand, but when you are in recovery mode, you allow yourself to soak up the moment with family, friends, and nature, exploring new places during the vacation and truly finding renewal.

This is a physiological phenomenon. Our bodies pulse, our hearts ramp up and down, and our muscles contract and relax. Passing between moments of intense activity and moments of rest is part of human nature.

This takes us back to the teachings of Francis Bacon, the seventeenth-century English philosopher, who believed that reality can be better understood when we study nature. He said, "Nature, to be commanded, must be obeyed." The deeper we explore and comprehend our human nature, the better we will coordinate the rhythms and routines in our lives to optimize our energy.

At a base level, we can arrange to take a day off from work after a demanding period or manage our sleep routine so that we gain a sufficient number of hours to feel refreshed. At a micro level, we can take breaks during the day to meditate or carry out some deep-breathing exercises, go out to lunch with a friend, go to the gym, or walk the dog. These are small routines we can incorporate into our daily lives that leave us feeling refreshed and reinvigorated.

We should learn to build checkpoints into our day, inviolable times when we take a respite from processing information or, in the case of athletes, physical training and switch our focus from performance to recovery.

I took advantage of meditation during my last years in sport and used it increasingly after having my second child, when trying to reconcile the demands of motherhood, work, and family. The Tibetan word *gom*, or *meditation* in English, represents the idea of entering a positive state of mind. The mind is depicted as a monkey that does not stand still for a single moment. Its positive state can be unlocked by a sensation or emotion felt when we focus on our breathing or on music. Meditation is not relaxation but, rather, the practice of developing a highly focused state of mind that allows us to calm the rhythm of our thoughts and access the deep knowledge and insights within us.

Just as we are in the habit of brushing our teeth every morning for the benefit of our health, in addition to feeling good, meditation represents mental hygiene, which cleans and fortifies the brain's synaptic connections. Meditation helps me tap into a deeper power, whether before an important event or in taking a break during the day, even if it lasts only three minutes. It creates islands of sanity by giving our mind a chance to rest and focus on a single thing. The stillness of the moment helps to alter the rhythm of the mind and restore calm amid the natural turmoil of the day.

Author, philosopher, and Buddhist monk Allan Wallace studies the relationship between Buddhism and the science and philosophy of the West. He has played an important role in the dialogue between the Dalai Lama and prominent scientists and has written and translated several books on the subject. Wallace stresses that the objective with Buddhist meditation is not to suspend thought but, rather, to shut out thoughts that arise automatically, which both are tiring and inhibit our ability to connect with the present moment.

Meditation is not something that occurs naturally. It requires practice. We should keep reminding ourselves to do it until it becomes a habit, part of our routine. With meditation, we learn how to center and expand our energy. It is beneficial to both the metabolism and the immune system.

I should stress here the importance of breathing as a means of reenergizing. Taking a time-out to focus on our breathing is a simple thing that takes but a few minutes, but it brings enormous benefits. Breathing is a powerful tool for self-regulation—a means of both summoning energy and relaxing deeply.

Dutch athlete Wim Hof, known as the Iceman, is the holder of several Guinness World Records for exposure to freezing temperatures (hence the nickname). He has created a training method that allows him to control his breathing, heartbeat, and blood circulation such that he can withstand the very low temperatures to which he submits himself.

His method combines cold therapy, breathing exercises, and commitment. Cold therapy involves the frequent exposure of the body to low temperatures, such as in an ice bath. His breathing technique involves inhaling deeply and allowing exhalation to occur freely. The combination of the two requires patience and dedication, which reinforces the third pillar of the method: commitment. Among the benefits generated by these routines are a faster recovery following physical exercise and gains in energy.

Other benefits from this method have been proven scientifically by studies carried out at Radboud University in Nijmegen in the Netherlands and reported by the community of people who ran the training sessions. These findings include improvements to the immune system and anti-inflammatory response, sleep, high performance, and the ability to focus with awareness of the connection between mind and body.[2]

Recovery for the Four Types of Energy

Recovery is not the same thing as lying still, prostrate, not doing anything. It can often mean engaging in activities that we enjoy or that are different from what we usually do, in which we transcend and voyage in our minds. Martine Grael told me, "For me, rest means relaxing my mind. My grandmother jokes that I rest by carrying rocks, because in my free time, I like to go hiking and cycling. The more engaged I am in another activity—my focus of attention completely changed—the more profound my rest."

Intermittent recovery is not just about replenishing physical energy levels. Any activity that is enjoyable, rewarding, and positive serves as a source of mental and emotional renewal. Among the popular expressions considered wise because they convey experiences and knowledge that can help people, I subscribe to the saying "Laughter is the best medicine."

In fact, including humor as a source of renewal can be a great strategy. When deployed at the right time—for example, with friends or family—it can help us relax, relieving pressure and anxiety and offering a chance for intermittent recovery.

Coaches can also add fun games and exercises to certain aspects of physical and mental preparation. When I was a swimmer, there were countless coaches who would propose a game of water polo as a way to relax. On my water polo teams, we would hold relay medleys of breaststroke, backstroke, or swimming backward. Such a break in the routine can usually be fun, even during an intense training session.

Adam Krikorian, coach of the US women's water polo team, distinguishes between fun and enjoyment. He said, "It's impossible to have fun all the time, but we can be enjoying ourselves even during moments when we are being challenged. It's enjoyable when we're focused! The feeling of being so passionately involved in something is incredibly enjoyable." It is fundamental that we understand that enjoyment goes beyond laughs and smiles, because if we only think of it this way, we train our minds to understand that we are not enjoying ourselves when we are focused, for example. "When we played the final, which earned us gold at the 2016 Rio Olympics, we weren't smiling, but do you think we weren't enjoying ourselves? The team were focused and in sync, and we felt the energy around us. That's fun too," Adam added.

Other sources of enjoyment include spending time with loved ones, reading a good book, or watching a good movie. Swimming in the sea; traveling with my family; and listening to "La Cumparsita"[10] on the piano, which triggers a special memory of my grandmother playing this song, are activities that are reinvigorating to me. Engaging in activities

---

[10] Created by Uruguayan musician Gerardo Matos, this tango is considered the most popular tango in the world.

that involve creativity is one way to refresh mental energy. When it comes to spiritual energy, the expending and replacement of energy are fundamentally important and interconnected. Performing activities related to our sense of purpose and values can be demanding but, at the same time, relaxing.

This not only applies to athletes but also is essential for executives, entrepreneurs, the self-employed, teachers, students, and anyone else. A life of excellence and happiness is characterized by the ability to fully engage in the challenge but also unplug occasionally and seek renewal.

In addition to the importance of refueling, tapping into and managing our energy reserves is fundamental to achieving our goals and sustaining the high-performance state over a longer period of time.

Exploring New Routines

"I am strong and powerful. I believe in everything I do. I don't doubt my potential. The greatest power is in the mind." Repeat this sentence fixedly in front of the mirror a few times, and watch what happens. This is what judo coach João Gonçalves suggested his judokas do daily during competitions.

Before dedicating himself full-time to judo, João Gonçalves participated in five Olympics as an athlete—two as a swimmer and three as a water polo player. In the last two, he and my father were on the Brazilian team. "He was in extraordinary physical shape and tormented defenses, even the toughest ones," my father told me. When the rest of the team tired, they just threw the ball to João, who was still full of energy. Even in 1968, when he was thirty-five years old, his conditioning was impressive.

Later in his career, he began to focus solely on judo and became one of the most important coaches in the history of the sport in Brazil, putting the country among the elite in the purest of the martial arts.

João Gonçalves revolutionized the mentality of the sport, becoming responsible for producing and influencing an entire generation of Olympic medalists, such as Aurélio Miguel (gold and bronze medalist), Thiago Camilo (gold medalist), Douglas Vieira (the first Brazilian to reach an

Olympic final in the sport, in 1984, earning silver), and Leandro Guilheiro (two-time bronze medalist).

Gonçalves identified that the Brazilians had good technique but lacked the necessary physical and mental preparation, so he developed more intensive training programs to close this gap. In addition, he used to read a lot about the powers of autosuggestion, chromotherapy, and hypnosis, deploying these methods in preparing the judokas. "Everyone arrives at the Olympics in good shape technically and physically, but the resolve to become champion, which is in the head, is what leads an athlete to the gold medal," said the coach.

The judokas not only used to repeat positive mantras before entering the tatamis but also heard them repeatedly from their coach, both during preparation and during the fight itself. Douglas Vieira said, in a documentary on João's life, that his gravelly voice filled their heads.[3]

Repeating empowering statements creates a positive environment for your thoughts and is a great way to access your energy reserves. Phrases such as "Today I am the best version of myself" and "Every game, I start strong and finish even stronger" can change the way we feel and be reflected in our attitudes.

Empowering statements can be great energizing routines, but they do not necessarily work for everyone in the same way. The main thing is for each of us to find statements that speak to us, exploring the possibilities and seeing what works in practice. Leandro Guilheiro, for example, told me that what worked for him was going through the technical aspects of the fight in his head, which reassured him of his mastery. He said, "What ran through my head were the tactical issues and what I would or wouldn't do once out on the tatamis."

He also used other strategies: "When I used to warm up, it wasn't just about warming up the body. I knew the importance of preparing the mind, so I wasn't just daydreaming. The key for me was to breathe. When you focus on your breathing, you are focusing on something that is part of your essence. I also visualized the task ahead—very basic things, like what I would do when I entered the fight."

To clear his mind ahead of a competition, he trained his thoughts on the here and now. He looked about him and tried to describe each detail of the environment to himself, such as the colors of the carpet, wall, and ceiling. "I kept repeating, *Red. Blue*," he said. "It was a way of reining in my attention so as to be in the moment."

For me personally, visualization, which I learned from my parents at an early age, was always a powerful energizing routine. My routine before an important event was to visualize my arrival at the pool and each step I was going to take leading up to the start of the match. In my mind, I saw and absorbed every detail of the environment—the opposing team warming up, the temperature of the water, and so on. I warmed up the same way as always: I visualized the initial swim-off that starts the game and mentally rehearsed some moves I had practiced that would be key come game time. This exercise allowed me to establish the energy settings, or wavelength, I required for competition, preparing my mind and body to tap into this energy.

Born in 1940, American Jack Nicklaus is regarded as one of the best golfers of all time, having won a record eighteen major championships collected over a quarter of a century—a total that is three higher than that of Tiger Woods, who holds the second most major wins. Nicklaus describes the technique he used to visualize the scene before the start of a round as follows: "I never hit a shot, not even in practice, without having a very sharp, in-focus picture of it in my head. It's like a color movie. First I 'see' where I want it to finish, nice and white and sitting up high on the bright green grass. Then the scene quickly changes and I 'see' the ball going there: its path, trajectory, and shape, even its behavior on landing. Then there is this sort of fadeout, and the next scene shows me making the kind of swing that will turn the previous images to reality."[4]

The creation of energizing routines ahead of high performance is not something unique to athletes. How we prepare for a speech, a job interview, or an important conversation, for example, is crucial to our performance. You can visualize these scenarios and rehearse the way you intend to behave and the opening lines of your speech, including an initial icebreaker, such as an amusing anecdote to relax the atmosphere or an enticing question to pique the audience's curiosity in the case of a lecture.

There are many routines that can help us access our energy and focus in these situations. My father was always punctual for his appointments or important presentations. Furthermore, he would arrive early to familiarize himself with the environment and watch the people arriving; thus, he felt in greater control of the situation.

The Team Also Needs to Be Energized

Felipe Perrone, captain of the Brazilian water polo team at the 2016 Rio Olympics, told me about a ritual the team developed before competing. It is worth remembering that the coach of the national team was Croatian Ratko Rudić, who stands out for his striking presence—reassuring, inspiring body language to add to the confidence he already transmits just through his track record. "He had already won four Olympic gold medals, so if he said, 'Let's go,' we followed him," joked Felipe. "Before entering the water, we would listen first to Rudić's firm, energizing messages and then to those of the fitness coach, Williams Morales, who gave a more emotional speech with a different energy. Then we would form a circle, and I would get to have the last word. I took my cue for my speech from what we had just heard, the previous messages from the coach and fitness coach, and from assessing what we needed to hear at the moment— whether to pump it up or calm things down. Then together we would jump in the pool."

For the team as a whole to perform to its best, it is important that everyone is on the same energy wavelength. Whether in sport or in a corporate context, individual routines are not sufficient.

We should remember that our energy is contagious. It is especially important for people in leadership roles to look after their energy levels, as this directly affects others under their command.

While coaching the Brazilian team, Rudić demanded that players surpass their limits in training. The players came out of the pool exhausted, and some made little effort to hide the fact, complaining and placing ice packs on their shoulders.

In preseason training, when Rudić saw this kind of behavior, he wasted no time in getting involved. "Are you in trouble?" he would ask the player, promptly dropping him from the next game. Soon the players got the message that they could use ice packs, or whatever they needed to recover, once they were somewhere discreet but not in front of others. Rudić expected his players to behave like true warriors, proud and defiant.

Being the great leader that he is, he knew the importance of managing the energy of the team as a whole. Observing teammates with low energy can influence the wider environment, which is not good. I should stress here that while it is important to give ourselves permission to be human, accepting our physical and emotional pain, there is a time and a place to do this, especially when building a team aiming high at the Olympics. Knowing the right moments to work on a weakness and suck up the pain is key to boosting the energy of the group.

When my father was captain of the Brazilian water polo team, he noticed that right after a game, players were not very receptive to the coach's feedback—neither praise nor criticism and much less to technical details. So he suggested to the coach a new rule: game comments and feedback only after twenty-four hours.

Mental Anchor

Before going to the 1999 Pan American Games in Winnipeg, we attended a workshop with Roberto Shinyashiki, a renowned Brazilian speaker, psychiatrist, and author of more than thirty-one books on high performance and happiness.

Throughout the workshop, we performed a series of activities designed to raise self-awareness of our thoughts and emotions and the power they had over our behavior. We practiced using a mental anchor that connects us with high performance. In our case, the word was *now*.

The training progressed such that by the end of that day, he offered us the chance to walk barefoot over glowing embers. There was a corridor of around ten meters covered with red-hot coals. I mentally repeated, *Now!* and then, as captain, set the example by being the first to cross. I felt so confident that I barely felt the heat under my feet. Once I had crossed, I could hardly believe what had happened, and I asked to go again. It was a powerful demonstration of the power of our minds over our bodies.

Anchors are power words that can be chanted by the player, coach, or team captain to condition our minds to release our energy and maintain our focus. Anchors help us exit a mental state filled with emotions that add no value, such as nervousness and anxiety, and enter one with positive emotions, such as courage and confidence, which add focus and raise performance. In the same way that an anchor stops a boat from getting swept away by the current, the mental anchor is a way of centering ourselves and protects us from getting swept away by the tide of negative thoughts.

Martine Grael told me that when something goes wrong in the middle of a race, she repeats to herself in her mind, *What's the next step? What's the next step?* This conscious reset helps to bring her focus back to the present moment, disrupting the tendency to start analyzing what just happened.

Felipe Perrone uses an anchor not just for himself but also for raising the confidence of the whole team. He said, "Often, when things have gone against us and we realize we are losing, there is silence. This is when I get vocal with the team. I speak loudly or even scream, if needed, to shatter the silence. I also make a show of stepping up my own game so as to set an example for my teammates."

Felipe told me how he used this technique in Brazil's first game at the Rio Olympics, against Australia: "The stands were packed. There were about four thousand people there. Most of the players had never played in front of such a crowd. As well as we had prepared, I saw that the pressure was starting to tell, and some players were getting tense. The noise was deafening. I couldn't hear anything, but I screamed like never before and summoned that game-time intensity." It worked. Brazil won 8–7.

Brazil also won the next game against Japan and went on to face Serbia, the reigning world champions. "With this game, having won the previous matchups, we were more relaxed and confident and totally got into the flow—which represents meditation in action. Both defense and attack were in harmony," the Brazilian captain told me. They secured a thrilling victory over the Serbian dream team (who wound up with the gold medal). "Beating the favorites in that first phase was what made it all worthwhile," said Felipe, visibly moved.

As captain of the Brazilian team, I used to try to make a great play— by making a sprint or setting up a shot with a perfect pass, stealing a ball, or taking a shot on goal—as a way of visibly showing the team that we were able to recover our energy and focus when it was starting to drop off. By celebrating unrestrainedly, we were able to reconnect with the high-performance state. Later, this experience was of benefit to me when dealing with unexpected situations at work and even with my family.

In individual terms, taking a deep breath, bringing my mind back to the present moment, and focusing it on the next step has always been my main routine when I need instant access to my energy reserves, whether in the middle of a game or during an important presentation.

The Priming Effect

Researcher and social psychologist John Bargh, currently working at Yale University, asked students to construct phrases from a few previously selected words. One group was exposed to words typically associated with the elderly (*Florida, forgetful, bald, gray,* and *wrinkled*), and the other group was exposed to more neutral words. After completing the task, the students were directed to a room at the end of the corridor. They did not know that this short walk was the focus of the experiment. The researchers measured the time that the students took to complete the distance and noticed that those who had been working with words associated with the elderly walked much more slowly than the control group.[5] In other words, the mere exposure to certain concepts can activate subliminal associations in our brain that can influence the way we behave without our even being aware of it. This has been termed the *priming effect*.

In 1979, psychologist and Harvard University professor Ellen Langer, whose best-known work is *Counterclockwise*, took a group of men between the ages of seventy and eighty on retreat to a location that had been adapted to appear as it had twenty years earlier. The furniture, decor, music, television programs, and movies were all from the 1950s, and the participants, although aware of the current date, were encouraged to behave as though they were younger. The results were surprising. Participants showed improvements in the flexibility of their joints, in their arthritic conditions, in their posture, and in their manual dexterity. They also performed better in tests of memory and intelligence and, by the end of the research, had rejuvenated in many ways.[6]

These two groundbreaking experiments demonstrate the power and influence that our environment can have over our bodies, our cognitive and intellectual abilities, and our behavior—including our energy.

In other words, our energy reserves are also influenced by the environment around us. Without our noticing, words and phrases—or photos on our walls, cell phones, or desks—can drain or amplify our vitality.

In summary, our energy is a precious resource that should be managed and nurtured appropriately so we can experience true engagement in its purest form. Unlike time, which is finite, energy can be expanded—by alternating between periods of pushing beyond our limits and periods of recovery. By creating energizing and recovery routines, we optimize our ability to access and replenish our reserves. No less important is taking care of the environment in which we operate, something that contributes to the strategic management of our energy levels.

Main Points Covered in This Chapter

- Energy is our fuel. Without it, no matter how much we devote ourselves to developing our skills, we cannot sustain high performance.
- What sets apart those who achieve excellence is how they manage their energy levels.
- There are four types of energy—physical, emotional, mental, and spiritual—which are interconnected and need nurturing for us to optimize our performance.
- We can operate in four performance zones: high performance, survival, burnout, and recovery. It is important to alternate between the high-performance and recovery zones.
- Our energy can be expanded. To achieve this, we must combine moments of surpassing our limits with moments of renewal.
- Recovery routines should involve the four types of energy and operate at three levels: macro (e.g., taking an annual vacation), meso (e.g., respecting sleeping hours), and micro (e.g., taking short breaks throughout the day to engage in exercises such as breathing and meditation).
- Preperformance, individual, and team energizing routines are important in helping us summon our high-performance mode when needed.
- Creating routines and rituals that enable us to access our energy reserves while competing is essential to recapturing high performance when facing setbacks.
- Energy is highly contagious and is influenced by both the people involved and the surrounding environment.

- What have you been doing to enhance your physical, emotional, mental, and spiritual energy levels?
- What are your routines and rituals before an important event that help you tap into your energy reserves?
- What works best for you in recovering and replenishing your energy reserves after major events? How much attention have you paid to this?

CONCLUSIONS FROM DIMENSION 2:
INNER ENERGY

———

In this second part of the book, I have presented the aspects related to our core, the center of our vitality, which provides a second layer in reinforcing, developing, and supporting our actions.

To achieve excellence and happiness, we need to connect with our inner energy in order to overcome difficult or challenging situations, from which we can extract a learning process, building our repertoire of knowledge and actions that make us more engaged with our dreams and boost our self-confidence.

With the WeTeam method, my work is focused primarily on building mental vigor, finding growth out of adversity, developing self-confidence, and managing internal energy reserves.

DIMENSION 3

—

COURAGE AND COLLABORATION

CHAPTER 7

ACT AND REFLECT: LIMITATIONS FROM THE FEAR OF FAILURE

The mind, once stretched by a new idea, never
returns to its original dimensions.
—Ralph Waldo Emerson

The greatest mistake you can make in life is to be
continually fearing you will make one.
—Elber Hubbart

In 1986, women's water polo began to be played in Brazil. The pioneers of the sport were found in three clubs, two in São Paulo and one in Rio de Janeiro. Three years later, a tournament was to be held in Alhambra, California, uniting teams from the United States, Canada, and Mexico. My mother, on seeing my interest and that of the other players dedicated to establishing this new sport in Brazil, decided to get in touch with the Brazilian Confederation of Water Sports (CBDA) to see if we could take a team to represent our own country. The answer, in keeping with strict protocol, was that women's water polo was not an official sport in Brazil.

We persisted with the idea and started to gather a group of committed players and parents, ready to embark on our first international trip with the sport. We organized different events to raise the necessary funds, from holding a prize draw for a bicycle to ticket-only parties. We received a donation of T-shirts and made full use of everyone's contribution. In short order, we had raised the money we needed. At that point, my mother called the CBDA again, telling them that she had both the funds for the trip and a group of players ready to roll—and that we would like to play under the name of the Brazilian women's national team. This time, the answer came back in the affirmative!

This was a landmark occasion for us all. I was fifteen years old. To wear the colors of our country in an international tournament was every player's pride and dream. Once there, we were even more excited to see so many players from different nationalities playing the sport at such a high level. It was impressive to watch the goalkeepers leap so lithely to block shots, the speed of the counterattacks that left nothing but foam, and the overall pace of the game. Each team had its own style of play, enchanting us with slick, well-rehearsed moves.

When we arrived home, our campaign encouraged other clubs to take up women's water polo, and the number of players started to grow. In order to continue training and flying the flag for the Brazilian team unfunded, the local players hosted those from out of state, and my mother helped out by trying to organize bus tickets through well-known businessmen.

In 1991, women's polo participated in the World Swimming Championship for the first time, in Perth, Australia. The heads of the other teams started to take an interest in us, as they wanted more nations playing the sport, especially from South America. They sought the manager of the sport for Brazil, but the position was yet to be made official. At that point, the CBDA invited my mother to become the director of women's polo. During the world championship, Dona Olga, as she became known, proudly represented her country. At the official meetings, she retold our story of the challenges in setting up the sport in our country. Backed by data, she demonstrated, promoted, and defended the growth potential of women's water polo in Brazil. Several interviews followed. Even though we were novices playing against teams who had years of experience, we were singled out in the local press for our enthusiasm, natural talent, and initiative in developing the sport.

My mother made her acceptance of the director's position conditional on having a free hand in managing all aspects—administrative, financial, and planning—with a view to developing the sport both in Brazil and internationally. So it came to pass.

Back in Brazil, we started to hold an increasing number of regional championships, and the number of teams increased throughout the country. Our director called clubs in different states, presenting the sport and the opportunity it presented to develop young athletes. She also supported them by providing caps, balls, goals, and whatever they needed to form a local team. Women's water polo expanded throughout Brazil. Soon the sport was no longer restricted to the Rio–São Paulo axis. We had a national championship.

The next step was to develop internationally, promoting not only tournaments with different nations, such as Hungary, Italy, and the United States, in order to develop the level of our players but also clinics with experienced coaches from other countries to enhance the knowledge of everyone involved in the sport. As the years passed, in addition to the coaches, for the first time, we had the support of a physical trainer and nutritionists. As results improved, we captured more coverage in the news and television media, which helped us to promote the sport and reach out to potential sponsors.

There followed several years of teamwork, persistence, and creativity in overcoming the challenges of establishing the team, until we had a group of players who were united, confident, coordinated, and operating at a competitive level internationally. A team was born that, for several years, troubled its opponents and earned its colors.

The long-awaited day arrived, and the women's game was finally accepted as an Olympic event. As a consequence, we had our first official participation in the Pan American Games in Winnipeg in 1999, which was also a qualifying event for the Olympic Games. It was the same venue and championship my father had played in thirty-two years earlier, winning the silver medal. We faced structure and planning we had never witnessed before. Days before the competition, we participated in a tournament in Montreal as the final step in our preparations. The organization was impeccable, from our uniforms to the logistics, the attention to the quality of food, the psychological work, and the fact that we could count on the experience of American coach Sandy Nitta and the vitality of Brazilian coach Rodney Bell. We captured the bronze medal.

Olga always stressed that she accepted this challenge because she believed in the growth of the sport in her country; in gender equality in water polo; and, above all, in providing opportunities for young athletes to develop new horizons and choices for their futures. "My goal was for those athletes to develop a purpose in their lives and to understand the importance of teamwork and the effectiveness of a well-structured program so that they could evolve as individuals and as citizens. I have always believed that the advancement of women's water polo would also advance the social inclusion of young athletes. Through sport, they would have the chance to see the world, experience new cultures, and build bonds of friendship that would last a lifetime," she said.

Today she is proud to see the results of her work. Every time she meets current or former national players, they embrace her and point to her contribution to the national game, and her eyes fill with emotion. This is a clear example of how, if we believe, we have the power to make our dreams come true.

When I interviewed my mother for this book so she could share her take on how this sport has evolved, she replied, "Cris, you know I'm not a big talker." That is true. She has always been a doer. It was through her many actions that she became one of the main leaders of this process. So I told her, "You are in the right chapter."

With her modus operandi all about action, persistence, and uniting the contributions of a range of people and entities, she managed not only to transform the sport of water polo in Brazil but also to transform women's place in the world with respect to the sport.

Curiosity and Willingness to Experiment

Among the key characteristics needed to achieve high performance are curiosity and a willingness to experiment. Curiosity is associated with the desire to learn more and manifests itself through a cognitive process, while openness to experimentation is associated with the desire to do more and manifests itself through a physical process.

On the one hand, if there is only curiosity without the courage to act and leave our comfort zone, there is no development of the idea, as we do not put the concept to the test. This can happen in the academic environment, for example, where many ideas and theories are developed but do not always get off the ground.

On the other hand, the courage to act without the element of reflection restricts learning. This often happens in the corporate environment, where there is a major focus on results and efficiency, with deadlines and ambitious targets, but a consequence is that many actions are implemented without due reflection.

When these two attitudes—reflection and openness to experimentation—are combined and operate in a complementary manner, we create a powerful cycle of growth, wisdom, and maturity, whether in sport, at work, or in our wider lives.

While I was working in customer relations at Itaú Unibanco, we launched a bold and well-structured program called Executive in Action. We invited the bank's most senior leaders to experience day-to-day customer relations. I remember the tension in my team when we had the CEO and various directors listening live to customer experiences and watching as the customer relations analyst sought the most appropriate solution.

When it was not possible to solve a problem during the call, the case was duly logged, and the employee had up to five days to find a solution and get back to the client. The learning experience was profound on all sides. The executive group came to understand the customers' problems in depth and the importance of clear and transparent communication when selling the product. These lessons led to new solutions that considerably improved customer perception and satisfaction.

Peter Drucker, considered the father of modern management, who studied many business leaders around the world, comments in his book *The Practice of Management* that the most common source of error in corporate decisions is the emphasis on finding the right answers rather than the right questions. The question is like a flashlight that illuminates one corner while leaving everything else dark. According to Drucker, his greatest contribution as a consultant is to be "ignorant" and ask questions.

Curiosity not only is a useful driver of our actions but also prompts reflection on the lessons to be learned from the results obtained.

Probing questions make us consider all the factors that led to a certain result, which allows us to look at mistakes and failures not as a frustration but as an opportunity to move forward.

In our pursuit to fulfill our potential and be happy, we need to constantly engage in this cycle of reflection and action. When I came home one day and mentioned to my mother that a sports club in São Paulo was going to set up a women's water polo team, her first reaction was one of surprise, as she had followed my father's entire career in water polo and had never heard of women playing the sport. But from that point on, her curiosity got the better of her; she began to do some research; and that led her to roll up her sleeves and get involved, as the women's game had already been played in the United States, Canada, and Europe for many years.

She would share her reflections during our family time. She would analyze the results from championships, the training of the national team, and the repercussions for the sport in Brazil and the wider world in order to trace out the next steps for the sport on its journey to evolve.

Elite athletes, like top executives, teachers, and successful people from different walks of life, possess a deep curiosity and desire to improve their skills, broaden their knowledge, and reinvent themselves through research and experience. For an athlete, this process comes naturally, as this willingness to experiment, act, and reflect on what has been learned is already embedded in competitive sport.

The Beginner's Mind

After calling it a day on his successful career as a water polo player, Croatian Ratko Rudić began to study the dynamics and methodology employed in different sports and the secrets to building a winning team. "For me, being a coach was as fascinating as being a player. I had to keep learning, even after I had achieved a goal. I spoke with many coaches and colleagues, not only about polo but about all sports," Rudić told me.

In Zen Buddhism, the term *beginner's mind* refers to an openness and eagerness to learn and, at the same time, abandon our paradigms when studying a given subject. Shunryu Suzuki, one of the most influential Zen masters of this century, said that in the beginner's mind, there are many possibilities, while in the expert mind, there are only a few. By maintaining a childlike curiosity and enthusiasm, even when dealing with something we already have some knowledge of, we expand our ability to learn and truly fulfill our potential.

According to a group of researchers led by Todd Kashdan, professor of psychology and director of the Well-Being Laboratory at George Mason University, curiosity is not a simple attitude but depends on five dimensions.[1]

The first is *joyous exploration*, which relates to a sense of fascination regarding activities, places, and things and feelings of pleasure when we learn something new about the world. The second is associated with a sense of discomfort we feel when we realize we are lacking information we desire and is termed *deprivation sensitivity*. That certain disquiet makes us want to know more about a subject and recedes only when we deepen our knowledge and understand the concept.

The third is *stress tolerance*, a characteristic needed for dealing with any discomfort that arises when we're faced with uncertainty and new information, especially if this new information challenges our beliefs. The fourth is *thrill seeking*, which refers to a willingness to experience new sensations, amplifying any anxiety experienced rather than trying to avoid or minimize it.

Finally, the authors describe a dimension related to *social curiosity*, which is one of the most efficient and effective ways to learn: by observing and communicating with other people.

Leonardo da Vinci was a genius who excelled as a scientist, mathematician, engineer, inventor, anatomist, painter, sculptor, architect, botanist, poet, and musician. Throughout his life, he struggled to understand and unravel the mysteries of each world. According to renowned American biographer Walter Isaacson, one of the ways he entertained his curiosity was through collaborating with others.[2] Da Vinci believed that creativity was like a team sport, arising from the exchange of ideas with others.

The joy of exploring and learning has been ever present in my life. This desire to have new experiences and understand a new culture motivated me to do an exchange program in the United States at the age of fifteen. Years later, when I was invited to play professional water polo in Italy, in addition to the thought of developing my skills as an athlete, my eyes sparkled at the chance to learn about a new culture, this time on the old continent.

I focused on savoring each moment and making the most of the experience. I immersed myself in the regional culture through my interactions with local families. I learned the language and kept an open mind with respect to the local culinary, artistic, and musical experiences and the regional traditions. I visited cities that told incredible stories of conquest and rebuilding and changed the way I viewed the world. I learned a lot from the traditions and rituals of each region, which made me not only more tolerant but also more appreciative of diversity. There were difficult times, especially in being away from my family and missing important occasions, such as weddings, birthdays, and the loss of a loved one, but I never thought of giving up, because I knew I would reap the rewards from those experiences for the rest of my life.

As an athlete, I experienced all the dimensions of curiosity, including deprivation sensitivity. When I missed a penalty while playing for the Brazilian team in the South American championship, I did not rest until I had improved my technique. After hours in the pool, training, I was always looking for someone to go in goal so I could take some penalties. My teammates joked that they could not take it anymore. This obsession of mine stemmed from a genuine desire to learn and improve my every move, including my preparatory routines. I was not satisfied until I could see the progress for myself and gain more confidence in making this play.

This inspired me to move beyond practice and repetition. I decided to expand my repertoire of plays by drawing inspiration from other sports and observing what other players did at decisive moments in a game. How did the best penalty-takers in soccer behave? How did basketball players behave before a free throw? A great inspiration for me was Hortência Marcari, captain of the women's Brazilian basketball team and the greatest scoring champion in its history. She won a world championship, a silver medal in Atlanta in 1996, and a Pan American championship in Havana in 1994 (after an epic final against the host country). Before a free throw, she would hold the ball, close her eyes, take a deep breath with her shoulders arcing upward, and exhale while opening her eyes, which were fixed on the hoop until the moment she released the ball. Following every deep breath, Hortência found the basket. I started to copy this breathing routine before taking penalties.

On meeting high-performance athletes, I realized the idea of seeking to learn from other sports was commonplace. Brazilian judoka Leandro Guilheiro, an Olympic and world medalist, told me that when he was in the armed forces, taking instructions with athletes from other disciplines, he took the opportunity to learn from them. "Talking to an athlete in the triple jump, I learned that they divided the jump into three phases, with each phase requiring a specific technique. When seeking to improve, they focused on just one phase at a time. I found that very interesting and thought maybe I could do the same for judo. I started to view my training in a new light, identifying phases of the fight that I could subdivide and practice with much more focus on each move," he said.

Maintaining a beginner's mind and developing all the dimensions of curiosity allows us not only to deepen specific knowledge and skills but also to broaden our base of knowledge. Through this approach, we develop a wider range of options when it comes to possible actions and become more adaptable in facing new challenges in sport and in life.

When he described his coaching style, Rudić told me, "I think anyone who wants to become a good player should open up mentally and learn more about everything. I gave the athletes books, took them to art exhibitions, and sought to provide moments for them to enrich themselves personally and culturally." Experiences that allow us to broaden our horizons make us better people.

When we decided to move to the United States, my husband, Luis, and I spoke with our daughters. I said, "We're going to stay there for a year initially, and if we don't like it, we can review the plans. But I want to agree on something with you: let's really make the most of this experience! We are not going to put our values to one side, but we are going to be open to new ones." With this openness in mind, despite the natural difficulties of undergoing change, we ended up adapting well and have now been in the United States for six years.

Immersion in a New Culture

The soccer player Raí is a legend of Brazilian soccer. He helped the national team get through a challenging qualify campaign for the 1994 World Cup and captained the team in the first round of the tournament, which resulted in the long-awaited crowning of Brazil as four-time champions.

Raí made history at São Paulo Futebol Clube, where he led the team to two Copa Libertadores da América titles, in 1992 and 1993, being the star of both campaigns, and to a first world club championship trophy, scoring both goals in a victory over the mighty Barcelona. In 1993, he accepted a transfer to Paris Saint-Germain (PSG). In his first season, when PSG won the 1993–1994 French championship, he was substituted in most games and came to spend many games on the bench. However, through persistence and dedication, he became one of the leading players as the side won the European Cup Winners Cup in 1996 (at the time the club's only international trophy), the French Championship, and the French Cup. In 2020, Raí was honored as the greatest player in PSG's history.

When I asked him how he managed to adapt to French soccer, he told me, "It all comes down to culture, both on and off the field. I realized that there were other ways of playing and of relating. It was a bit awkward at first. When I got there, the training sessions were shorter and more intense than in Brazil. My body was not used to it, and I had to adapt. European soccer was more pragmatic, more objective, working less with the ball, while in Brazilian soccer, we developed more touch."

His initial approach was to observe and focus on adapting to the intensity of training and the local style of play. He told me, "I adapted to them and then managed to add my own touch. That's the beauty of adapting successfully. People recognize you have made an effort and managed to be effective even using a style that wasn't natural to you. From there, you gain space, start to contribute, and others also begin to adopt your style of play." In adapting, he did not focus solely on training but sought to immerse himself in the local culture, making friends, learning the language, attending exhibitions, and listening to French music.

Water polo player Felipe Perrone, the current captain of the Spanish team, who has also played in Croatia, Italy, and Brazil, says that in order to adapt, he has always used this same strategy of immersion: "I seek to observe and to understand how the sports culture and the country work. I played for two years in Croatia and learned to speak Croatian. I went to restaurants, bars, and public spaces. I wanted to get to know the people and the history of the country. I even learned about the wars they suffered. Before we propose any change, we need to understand the current reality, to know why people think the way they do and act the way they act."

For many multinational companies, this is a valid lesson. I worked for many years at Itaú Unibanco and always prided myself on understanding corporate culture and, especially, the culture of the company I was working with. But when I moved to the United States and worked for the bank's American arm, I had to make an effort to adapt to the local culture, which was comprised of professionals from different countries. Observing interactions, the decision-making process, and how local employees interpret demands from the top offers valuable tips. The challenge goes far beyond mastering a new language, extending to the understanding of social interactions, the motivation for change, and the communications between a team and its leadership group.

Speed to Adapt

The International Judo Federation has implemented changes to the sport's rules in time for the 2020 Tokyo Olympics cycle. Among other changes, penalties are to be applied differently. Previously, a judoka would be eliminated after receiving four penalties. The limit has now been reduced to three. The rigor with which fouls are awarded has also increased. "Back when I was fighting, it took time for penalties to be issued. Today they are being applied more rigidly. There are fights that end inside a minute because of this. The justification for these new rules is that they make the fight more dynamic and encourage the athlete to attack. You have to adapt, look for new ways to surprise your opponent, and rethink your style of fighting, which often means taking two steps back in training and rebuilding," Leandro Guilheiro told me.

In sport, rule changes are not the only situations in which it is essential to adapt. We often need to take up a different position than we are used to playing or adapt a move to deal with an unexpected situation. Our ability to adapt stems from several factors. Continued and intensive practice in a range of different contexts, using approaches such as talent rotation, as discussed in chapter 2, is one way to increase our versatility. Knowing our strengths and potential limiters is also essential to adaptability. When we are clear about our greatest strengths and those of each member of our team, we can tweak the variables in our favor, delegate tasks, and count on the support of other members of the team.

When we seek high performance, there is no room for inflexibility or resistance. On the contrary, we should reflect on the situation and find strategic ways to act more flexibly. This holds true with other areas of our lives, such as family life or the corporate environment.

A rigid or resistant stance can paralyze us or cause us to waste energy on fighting something that is beyond our influence. This does not mean we must accept any and every situation. It is important to allow our goals and values to guide our actions and to recognize when we need to persist and have the courage to change the status quo.

When Change Is Worth It

My mother was not content with just launching a competitive Brazilian team. She wanted to go further, as she could not accept that the women's game was excluded from the Olympics, while men's water polo had been the first team sport, along with soccer, to debut at the Paris Olympics in 1900.

Many just accepted the idea that contact sports, such as water polo, by their very nature, precluded women from playing. My mother, together with progressive managers and coaches from other countries, acted to change the situation. It was not an easy path, but the obstacles did not deter them.

To disseminate the sport across the Americas, and thus attract support from other countries to the Olympic cause, we faced a challenge: to hold the South American championships in Medellín, Colombia. Everything was still improvised. We even had to play in a thirty-meter pool used for the men's game rather than the twenty-five-meter one used by women. My mother invited the official representative of US women's water polo,

Becky Shaw, to the championship as an observer, so as to make the event official.

We raised sponsorship and increased our participation in tournaments around the world. Our director was tireless, faxing the main media organizations with sports editors, informing them of the tournaments we were participating in and capturing significant column width in their publications. Later, we were invited onto popular national TV talk shows on the back of our pioneering spirit and increasing success. We also gave interviews for ESPN Brasil. Thus, the sport grew and became more widely known.

When the Brazilian team qualified for its second World Swimming Championship at Rome in 1994, we teamed up with other countries to further strengthen the campaign for women's polo to become an Olympic sport. In a meeting of the heads of all the countries, my mother suggested T-shirts be made showing a water polo ball and the words *Women for Olympics*. At first, only fifty shirts were produced, but production soon had to be increased, as all the teams wanted to promote this campaign for Olympic status. Every nationality—Americans, Hungarians, Russians, Australians, Dutch, Italians, Canadians, Brazilians—wore the shirt when they watched the games or were part of the competition environment. It created a bond among the players never seen before. We were all united and committed to a common dream.

A few months later, at the junior championship in Prague, the athletes, wearing swimming caps in five different colors, joined together and formed Olympic rings in the pool at the opening ceremony. This also made an impact in the media, but resistance remained. The federations of Eastern European countries, which were traditional powerhouses of the men's game, refused to accept the inclusion of women in the Olympic Games.

Then came the 1996 Atlanta Olympics. My parents attended as guests of one of the sponsors. In the hotel, leafing through *USA Today*, my mother read an article that described the progress of women in the Olympic Games but also highlighted the ongoing lack of equality. The report cited sports that included only the male version, but water polo was not on their list.

Once again, my mom sprang into action. She wrote a letter to the newspaper, as the Brazilian sport's director, praising the article but noting that women's water polo, which was already present in more than forty-eight countries, was also excluded from the Olympics. She stressed that regulators "should open their minds to the new world order and accept the global call for the inclusion of women's water polo."

To her surprise, the letter to the newspaper was not only published four days later but also featured prominently on the editorial page of *USA Today*. From that point on, the tone of the campaigns began to allege discrimination against women, and these sentiments grew ever louder. There was no longer any reason why women's water polo should not be an Olympic sport. This approach piled even more pressure on the international heads of the sport.

The long-awaited announcement came right after Atlanta. Even today, when we think back to the moment when, finally, the inclusion of women's water polo in the 2000 Sydney Olympics was approved, we cannot help but feel moved and delighted!

For all her work on behalf of sport and gender equality, Olga Pinciroli has been recognized with the Paragon Award from the Swimming Hall of Fame in the USA, an honor awarded to people who have made an extraordinary contribution to the development of sport on a worldwide level. She was also honored by the Brazilian Confederation of Water Sports (CBDA), who named the Brazilian water polo league's trophy after her, in recognition of her contribution to a sport she has done so much to bring into the light.

To challenge the status quo, there must be both the drive and inspiration to persist and the energy to act. The intense experience delivered by each step of the process generates the motivation needed to influence those around you to bring about a lasting change.

When she moved to Hawaii, Brazilian surfer Maya Gabeira fell in love with big-wave surfing. Most professional surfers tend to catch smaller waves, because to be a big rider, as surfers like Maya are known, requires a different set of skills. She knew the path would not be easy. "There were hardly any female big riders when I started, and I thought I needed to change that," she recalls.[3]

In 2013, he first time she decided to face the famous Praia do Norte, located in Vila de Nazaré, Portugal, where some of the biggest waves in the world can be found, she wiped out and ended up under the weight of a twenty-meter-high wave, a volume of water estimated to weigh 144 tons. The Brazilian was rescued by fellow surfer Carlos Burle and had to be resuscitated. Years of physical and mental recovery followed, but she decided to come back to face the monster that had brought her down.

In January 2018, she caught a wave at Praia do Norte, Portugal, that an independent expert measured at 20.7 meters high. It was the biggest wave ever ridden by a woman. She dreamed of joining the *Guinness Book of Records*, but at the time, there was only one category covering surfers of both sexes. However, that did not stop Maya. She gathered more than twenty thousand signatures on a petition and publicly pressured the surfing authorities. Months later, Guinness finally created a female category and recognized her achievement. On February 11, 2020, she broke her own record by surfing a 22.4-meter-high wave. One sign that things are changing, she joked, "is that this time I didn't need a petition for my record to be recognized."

Whether as an individual or a group, personally or as a family, in sport or in the corporate environment, to challenge the status quo, we need to identify the levers of change that will have the greatest impact on the system, keep practicing, and seek to take our development to new levels. It is important to keep in mind that you cannot bring about transformation by doing things the way they have always been done. By consistently adding small changes, you will ultimately transform the whole.

Courage and Vulnerability

Allyson Felix is an extremely talented American sprinter who competes in the hundred, two hundred, and four hundred meters. She has no fewer than twenty-five medals between Olympic Games and World Athletics Championships. By winning her tenth Olympic medal, after Tokyo in 2020, she equaled Carl Lewis as the top US Olympic medalist in track and field. In addition to being a woman who bettered the total of the fastest man in the world, she achieved this landmark total at the age of thirty-three, just ten months after becoming a mother following a complicated delivery in which the lives of both mother and child were at risk.

But it was not just on the track that she broke the mold. Following the birth of her daughter, her sponsor wanted to pay her only 70 percent of what she had been receiving previously. She refused to accept this and sought contractual guarantees that she would not be penalized in the event that her performance dipped in the months following the birth. Her stance bore fruit. The sponsor announced that it would not apply pay cuts to pregnant athletes for a period of twelve months. Later, it increased this period to eighteen months. All this was the result of the courage of an athlete who refused to accept what was being imposed on her.

As American researcher Brené Brown argues, to be brave, we need to have the courage to be vulnerable.[4] This means showing up and allowing yourself to be seen, airing your needs and not being afraid to ask, talking about how you feel, and having the difficult conversations that many people run away from. Courage is not the absence of fear but acting despite your fear. Accepting that we are human, embracing our vulnerability, and connecting with our sense of purpose is what strengthens us to act in support of our values and of something greater.

Allyson Felix used to be a private person, but in motherhood, she found the strength she needed to fight for a better future, not only for herself but also for all women, including her daughter. She has said, "All my experience in the sport has taught me to deal with failure, to surpass my limits and leave my comfort zone. Then came motherhood, which made me reflect on the *whys*. Why do I want to win? What fights do I want to fight?"[5] She also says that before becoming a mother, she had a very planned and structured life, but when her daughter was born, she learned to accept that she could not control everything, accept help, and go with the flow. "By opening up, becoming more vulnerable, talking about what I was going through and about my needs, as uncomfortable as it was, I realized it was worth it, as I was helping a lot of people."

Her concerns about the world her daughter was going to find also made her take up other battles. As she prepared for the Tokyo Olympics, Felix told a TV show that she had participated in a protest by the antiracism group Black Lives Matter. "I felt compelled to be there," she said, and she added, "I hope that, as Camryn [her daughter, who was one at the time] grows up, things change, but I'll have to give her the tools to be able to navigate through what is reality right now. It's a really sobering reality to have those talks and those conversations, but as soon as I became a mother, I knew that was going to happen."

Motherhood also opened my eyes to the need to act on behalf of women in the corporate environment. I noticed that it was hard to identify women who were equally dedicated and successful with both their careers and their families. When my first two daughters were born, I took four months' maternity leave—the period permitted by law in Brazil—and after my return to the workplace, my support network helped me to remain productive at work while also taking care of my family. When Olivia, my third child, was born, there was a new law in place that allowed some companies to extend maternity leave to six months. Those additional two months made a great difference to me, and knowing my baby was older, I returned to work much more emotionally prepared and better organized.

When the company gave me the opportunity to be head of human resources in the United States, maternity leave was set at a maximum of three months. I met with other team members to identify best practices in the market and discuss what it might take to change things. Our intention was not to benefit one group at the expense of another but, rather, to promote an environment that would benefit everyone, taking into account the particularities of each individual's situation. The outcome was that we sponsored extending the period of leave but also the right for parents to choose since, depending on each family's circumstances, the father might opt to take leave and care for the baby.

I have also always advocated a management perspective that values the quality of results rather than the number of hours put in. We were the first unit at the bank to introduce a remote working policy—long before the coronavirus pandemic made this a necessity—which challenged the beliefs and paradigms of many in senior management. At the time, we encountered a lot of resistance and skepticism, which is not unusual when trying to change the way things have always been done. The courage to act is related to being authentic and not being paralyzed when faced with criticism and challenges.

The twenty-sixth US president, Theodore Roosevelt, delivered a speech at the Sorbonne in Paris in 1910 that sums up well the importance of being authentic and having the courage to act. This speech is often referred to as "The Man in the Arena." He said,

> It is not the critic who counts; not the man who points out how the strong man stumbles, or where the doer of deeds could have done them better. The credit belongs to the man who is actually in the arena, whose face is marred by dust and sweat and blood; who strives valiantly; who errs, who comes short again and again, because there is no effort without error and shortcoming; but who does actually strive to do the deeds; who knows great enthusiasms, the great devotions; who spends himself in a worthy cause; who at the best knows in the end the triumph of high achievement, and who at the worst, if he fails, at least fails while daring greatly, so that his place shall never be with those cold and timid souls who neither know victory nor defeat.

Learn to Fail or Fail to Learn

The courage to experiment is innate to us all. When babies attempt to take their first steps, we see in them this resilience, in falling and getting up again for as long as it takes. It is interesting to watch, as they are undaunted by failure. They keep trying and even have fun in the process. This constant striving to overcome difficulties should not be driven by the parents. In fact, quite the contrary. "Don't do for children what they can do for themselves," said Maria Montessori, a woman who had outstanding interpersonal skills, which gave her great insights into others. Born in 1817, she was one of the first Italian doctors to specialize in education. By observing children in their interactions, she helped them to learn, progress, and blossom. Dr. Montessori's educational methods were guided by her belief that children learn best through direct experience—investigation, discovery, and individual attention. She argued that the learning environment should be an inspiring place that nurtures imagination.

Over time, we become more self-aware of our actions, and instead of channeling our energy into experimenting and taking risks—from which we learn—we focus on avoiding potential failure. This is the exact opposite of what we should be doing. That does not mean we should be hoping for mistakes or defeat, as they are best avoided where possible. But they are part of any journey that leads to learning and growth. Only those who never try do not fail.

Dean Simonton, professor of psychology at the University of California, Davis, and a great scholar of intelligence, creativity, and genius, conducted a series of studies on the most famous artists and scientists in human history, such as Pythagoras, Galileo Galilei, Descartes, Rembrandt, Tolstoy, and Mozart, and he found they all had something in common: how often they failed!

Michael Jordan attributes his success in becoming one of the greatest athletes of all time to his failures along the way. He once said, "I've missed more than nine thousand shots in my career. I've lost almost three hundred games. Twenty-six times, I've been trusted to take the game-winning shot and missed. I've failed over and over and over again in my life. And that is why I succeed." The biggest enemy of experimentation is the fear of failure. For athletes, fear manifests itself when they're faced with failing in front of family members, coaches, teammates, fans, or even an entire country.

The more intense our fear becomes, the more it limits our potential, as we avoid the risks necessary to learn and evolve. On the other hand, by giving ourselves permission to be human, we give ourselves permission to be imperfect and are better able to enjoy our journey through life. When we demand perfection, we can become defensive, which makes it harder to get up from a fall and takes us further from achieving our goals.

This also holds true for the business world. There are a number of examples of entrepreneurs whose résumés read like catalogs of failure before they finally began to reap the rewards of having the courage to act. Anita Roddick, founder of the Body Shop, an innovative cosmetics company that stands out for encouraging ethical consumerism, describes in her book *Business as Usual* several examples of mistakes and failures and how she got up from them.

Above all, failure and adversity teach us valuable lessons that can make us stronger. British writer J. K. Rowling gained worldwide fame for her Harry Potter series of books, which received multiple awards and sold more than five hundred million copies. However, before her sweeping success, she underwent a trying phase in her life.

Over a period of seven years, Rowling faced the death of her mother, the birth of her first child, divorce from her first husband, and severe financial difficulties, until, in 1997, she completed the first of seven books in the series: *Harry Potter and the Philosopher's Stone*. In 2008, she was invited to give the graduation speech at Harvard University, in which she shared some of the lessons she learned from those challenging times. She said,

> You might never fail on the scale I did, but some failure in life is inevitable. It is impossible to live without failing at something, unless you live so cautiously that you might as well not have lived at all—in which case you fail by default. Failure gave me an inner security that I had never attained by passing examinations. Failure taught me things about myself that I could have learned no other way. I discovered that I had a strong will, and more discipline than I had suspected ... The knowledge that you have emerged wiser and stronger from setbacks means that you are, ever after, secure in your ability to survive. You will never truly know yourself, or the strength of your relationships, until both have been tested by adversity. Such knowledge is a true gift, for all that it is painfully won, and it has been worth more than any qualification I ever earned.

Rodrigo Koxa is a Brazilian big rider who stood out from a young age for his dedication and passion for big-wave surfing. For many years, he led the Rhythm Bomb project, in which he would study forecasts of where to find the biggest waves around the world and travel to surf them. His career was trending up until he faced a traumatic situation at the end of 2014.

While he caught a wave in Nazaré, Portugal, his partner, who supported him from a Jet Ski, was unable to rescue him, and he feared for his life. Koxa was pounded by a number of huge waves and, being close to the lighthouse, was afraid of being thrown onto the rocks. Luckily, he made it out alive, but the terrifying episode shook him up psychologically.

He began to have recurring nightmares. Sponsors abandoned him, and he had to restructure financially, setting up a Jet Ski school. He returned to Nazaré and surfed some waves, but something was different. Then Koxa injured his shoulder, which led to surgery and physiotherapy. It was the worst phase of his life, in which he came to doubt whether he would ever go back to doing what he loved.

He turned to spirituality and dove deep into the search for self-knowledge, deciding to become a life coach. As part of the training for the program, he had to go through the process as a client. He said, "When the master coach asked me what my goal was, I replied, 'It's to surf the biggest wave in the world.' It was through this process that I reconnected with my passion and regained the courage to become that person with whom I most identified—a big rider."

The coaching course took place in September 2017. Two months later, he was back in Nazaré, surfing a wave 24.38 meters tall, the biggest wave ever surfed in the world. The feat earned him a Guinness world record. His story serves to reinforce the idea that self-knowledge is key to overcoming moments of failure and adversity.

The Hunger to Keep Improving

Thomas Edison, considered one of the most productive and innovative scientists of the modern era, who registered an astonishing 1,093 patents, was also one of the scientists who failed the most. There is a curious story in which, while Edison was carrying out one of his experiments, a colleague chided, "But you've already failed ten thousand times." Edison replied, "I have not failed ten thousand times—I've successfully found ten thousand ways that will not work." A few thousand experiments later, he invented the nickel-iron battery, which was more efficient than the lead-acid batteries used at the time and is still used today to store excess electricity from solar panels and wind turbines. This is a lovely example of how we can look at the same situation from the opposite perspective and how this different view can be crucial in our soldiering on or simply quitting.

Adam Krikorian, coach of the US women's water polo team, firmly believes that the way we view our mistakes and failures is critically important. He sees mistakes as opportunities for growth and improvement that drives our development. He encourages his players to adopt this view. He told me, "When we watch videos of our games and the mistakes we've made, I tell the athletes that there are two ways to look at them. We can think, *Oh my gosh, we are terrible!* or *Wow, look at how great we can be. Look at all the mistakes that we can work on.*"

He encourages all of his players to work on their strengths, but like a good coach, he is aware of the potential limiters each of them has, so those too get attention so they do not become obstacles to fulfilling the players' potential. Krikorian noticed that when he highlighted a weakness, many of his players took this as criticism. He always insists on reminding them, "We all have areas to work on. If we didn't, the process wouldn't be so much fun. View this failure as an opportunity for learning and growth."

With this mindset, failures and disappointments can be great motivators for our development, and without them, the challenge can be even greater. Krikorian told me that after taking the women's water polo gold medal at the 2012 London Olympics, most of the players on the US team retired. The following year, the coach had to practically build a new team from scratch with new young talent. Since then, this team has topped the podium in a number of major championships, such as the 2016 Rio Olympics, the world championships in 2015 and 2017, the Pan American Games in 2015, and several world water polo league titles. After so many victories, Krikorian revealed, "It's wonderful to win, obviously, but there's always the challenge of keeping everyone motivated to keep improving."

The hunger to keep improving is essential for the high-performance athlete. Scotsman Samuel Smiles wrote in his book *Self Help*, "It is doubtful whether any heavier curse could be imposed on man than the complete gratification of all his wishes without effort on his part, leaving nothing for his hopes, desires or struggles."

Krikorian's strategy to avoid this complacency is to create greater challenges in training by, for example, asking players to play out of position. But he confided in me, with his genuine smile, that with the team he was preparing for the 2020 Olympics in Tokyo, he was continually frustrated in his attempts to challenge them, as they always surprised him by coming up with ways to surpass themselves. It is no surprise they went on to give the United States its third consecutive Olympic gold medal in the sport.

Croatian Rudić has similar strategies for challenging his teams, promoting tournaments or training matches against stronger opposition when preparing for major competitions. He told me, "When we lost at the Olympics, there was a lot of pain, which we have to deal with if we are to evolve and remain focused, setting even more ambitious goals." A defeat during the run-up to a tournament can be an opportunity to motivate the team. "It is one time when losing can be good for the team, as it offers a chance to analyze things more deeply with the players and motivate them. Of course, we can also learn from winning and trying to understand what we did well in order to reproduce it. However, if the team has a run of wins before a tournament, there is a risk that the players will become complacent, believing that *I am the best and don't need to do any more*. But the sport teaches you differently. When you reach the top, you become a target to be taken down, so you should always seek to keep improving."

From Generation to Generation

In Super Bowl LV in 2021, Sara Thomas became the first woman to referee the game. ESPN even produced a video showing the impact this could have on children. Entitled *Making History*, the short video recognizes several women who have broken barriers and held positions that were once exclusively male, such as coaching baseball or an NBA basketball team, driving a Formula Indy car, or even becoming vice president of the USA. At the same time, a young girl was watching these women, imagining that one day she could join them. "Knowing the impact that

I'm having on not just my daughter, but young girls everywhere, women everywhere, … I'm probably gonna get a little teary-eyed," said Sara.[6]

I saw the power of this positive influence up close, in a microcosm, from generation to generation within my own family. My daughter Alissa, in her Stanford University admissions essay, summed up the entire process well:

> When my grandfather was nineteen, he had ten seconds to decide whether or not to snatch a photograph from the wall of a Tokyo train station. Ignoring the gazes of suspicious onlookers, he surreptitiously slipped the picture into his briefcase. To this day it is his most prized possession, displayed prominently in his São Paulo apartment. It was my companion, too; I saw it every Friday having lunch with my grandparents. In it, he is leading a throng of exuberant young men in suits and boater hats around an open-air stadium. They are smiling, laughing, and holding hands. Their excitement is still palpable sixty years later. I wondered why there were no women in this picture—only strapping young men. My grandfather is right in the first row, holding hands with total strangers. One Friday afternoon, my grandfather revealed that the picture showed the closing ceremony of the 1964 Olympic Games. He and his water polo team had practiced for years, endured disappointments, injuries, and enormous personal sacrifices. Their journey to Tokyo had taken seven days. But attending the Olympics had been worth every effort. "As Olympic athletes, we felt like citizens of an ideal nation without differences of creed, ideology, and race," he reminisced. Being immersed in this global community was the experience of a lifetime for him. Back then I often wondered if I'd ever have an opportunity to participate in something as remarkable.
>
> I have carried my grandfather's mantra—"be the first person in the pool, and the last one out"—with me at every water polo practice since sixth grade. I feel his

presence at 5 a.m.: "Shhhh … only those who want to be the best are awake now." Then his whisper is drowned out by the jarring sound of my alarm clock. The silence of these early morning hours is a cruel cheerleader. Only the "crazy ones" forsake sleep and the warmth of their bed for the shock of cold pool water! But I jolt into action like a machine, moving almost automatically: treading, sprinting, passing, shooting, dribbling. The world around me slows down and I feel as though I have slipped into a tiny crevasse separating past from present. My mind drifts to disappointments, rewards, and moments in which I have pushed past my physical limits. I have always heeded my grandfather's words: "Error doesn't limit, but fear does."

While I seek to follow in my grandfather's footsteps, I am also a product of my time and a lineage of strong women: my mother, a corporate executive, advocate for gender equity, and competitive water polo player, and my grandmother, a tireless champion of women in Olympic sports. The photograph on my dining room wall will have female Olympic athletes in it, and I will hopefully be one of them.

As we have seen, having the courage to act can not only change the result of a game or bring change to a company but also inspire social change and impact multiple generations. Learning, doing, reflecting, acting—this cycle leads to a path of growth and fulfillment that we are all capable of finding.

- There are no guarantees for success, but without the courage to act, success is not going to happen. To achieve excellence and happiness, we should have an attitude of curiosity, with openness to experimentation and courage to act.

- In order to fulfill our potential, we should engage in a cycle of reflection and change, which allows us to continually act and then learn from our actions, creating a positive spiral of growth and maturity.

- When we adopt a beginner's mind, exploiting our intrinsic curiosity, we deepen our learning and expand our base of knowledge, which broadens our range of options when it comes time for action.

- It is not easy to challenge the status quo. You need to have purpose, inspiration, courage to act, and persistence, as well as to accept that you are running the risk of failure and might be criticized along the way.

- Having courage does not mean you are not afraid; rather, it means you are willing to pursue your hopes and dreams.

- The main inhibitor of experimentation is fear of failure.

- Errors, mistakes, and failures are inevitable, but they can become our allies in the learning process, motivating us and forcing us to grow.

- The courage to act changes not only our own reality but also the realities of those around us, impacting an entire nation, the world, and generations to come.

Powerful Questions to Reflect Upon

- Do you set aside time to reflect on your experiences? Do you have the courage to step outside your comfort zone in pursuit of your goals?
- How do you deal with mistakes when trying to achieve your goals? Do you get frustrated? How much do your mistakes enable you to learn and evolve?
- How do you encourage yourself to experiment and learn from failure?

CHAPTER 8

───

TEAMWORK:
TOGETHER WE ALL ACHIEVE MORE

Talent wins games, but teamwork and
intelligence wins championships.
—Michael Jordan

There are five fundamental qualities that make every team great:
communication, trust, collective responsibility, caring and pride.
I like to think of each as a separate finger on the fist. Any one
individually is important. But all of them together are unbeatable.
—Mike "Coach K" Krzyzewski

It was winter in Catania, Sicily, and the icy wind whipped around our
faces. We waited with a mixture of excitement and doubt. The local
players from the city's water polo team added to our anxiety. "You will
witness something that will live with you forever," they told us. The
other players—Pita from Holland; Taryn from Australia; and Cristiana,
Monica, and Martina from Rome—and I had been together since the
early afternoon, ready to spend a sleepless night watching each stage of
the traditional Festa di Sant'Agata, the city's patron saint.

The end of the three-day celebration climaxed with a test of the
devotees' courage. We were all wrapped up in our caps, gloves, and

scarves, having earlier swapped our red carnations for white ones, which represent the saint's purity, and were ready for the long-awaited moment.

The night had already slipped into early morning by the time we reached the top of the San Giuliano slope, the most dangerous phase of the procession. The ceremonial litter—a kind of carriage with the bust of the saint and all the relics, weighing more than three tons—had to be carried up the hill. If this challenge went off smoothly, it would be taken as a divine sign that there was to be a good year ahead. A long rope was used to pull the litter, while the faithful, clad all in white, sang their praises in honor of the saint.

There was clear disagreement between the younger participants, who almost begged to be allowed to take the place of honor in pulling the litter up the hill, and the older ones, who were not yet ready to give up their station, which had no doubt taken them years to earn, and wished to honor the saint one more time before they retired from such physical exertion.

Amid the silence, a commanding voice rang out: *"Siamo tutti devotti tutti? Cittadini, viva Sant'Agata!"*[11] We took a deep breath and lent a hand while all of the devotees lined up before us, and in a coordinated explosion of effort, we pulled the rope, which slowly carried the litter up the hill. We were all as one, aligned with the goal.

Any failure not only risked bad news befalling the town the following year but also could have caused a disaster right there, with the carriage tumbling downhill into the worshippers accompanying the ceremony. More than a million people had taken to the streets to commemorate the Sicilian saint.

Breathing, coordination, and faith came together in a powerful display of collective energy, reinforced by the singing of the nuns of the Clarissa religious order, who appear only on that day to pay homage to Saint Agatha at the convent of Via dei Crociferi. In the end, everything went well, and at around six o'clock in the morning, the saint reached her destination in one piece to begin a well-earned rest at the altar of Chiesa di San Giuliano. Relieved and deeply touched by the ritual, we stopped at

---

[11] A rough translation would be "Are we all devoted? Citizens, long live Saint Agatha!"

a famous bakery for freshly baked bread and ate hot *panzerotti con crema bianca* and *al cacao catanesi* before heading home.

For us, in addition to the excitement and admiration we felt while watching the power of the collective in achieving a common goal, we now better understood the culture and history of that island so charming for its diversity and ancient rituals.

In Sicily, we forged a close bond—the foreign players, who were far from their families, and the home-grown players. We would gather on holidays or to celebrate after a game, try out a new pizzeria, or share Sunday lunches. We would come together to enjoy all the traditional foods, including the delicious seafood fresh from the fish market.

We loved it when we explored the wonderful local sights, such as Taormina and Siracusa, with its ruins and Greco-Roman theaters, some of which still operated with theatrical and musical performances, and Mount Etna, the highest active volcano in Europe, which is still active. Our local friends told us that the last time Etna erupted and the lava almost reached Catania, the townspeople put on the clothes of Saint Agatha, who protects the city, and successfully stopped the danger, which explains their devotion to the saint.

Against the incredible azure shades of the Mediterranean, we would set up the polo field right in front of the little town of Aci Castello, the meeting place for the water polo players. Then we would have a *mandorla macchiata al caffè granita* (an exquisite almond granita with a touch of coffee) inside a freshly baked brioche in the traditional bar Viscuso, which had been in existence since the early 1900s. We then finally headed off contentedly to our games in the sea.

This socializing between the foreign and local players and between the eldest and the youngest, together with the diversity of having players from different continents and cultures, forged a bond built of intimacy, respect, empathy, and understanding that would be one of the main factors in our remarkable achievement of defeating the best teams on the continent. That year, 1993–94, our club won the LEN Champions League[12] for the first time.

---

[12] The main European club tournament for women's water polo, known as the LEN Euro League Women since 2013.

Building a Team Means Investing in Relationships

There is an African proverb that says, "Alone we go faster; together we go farther." The quality of relationships is the number-one predictor of happiness according to Robert Waldinger, the director of Harvard's longest study on adult development. When we are part of a team, we can go faster and farther, and more happily. We can celebrate achievements and receive support and encouragement when we are suffering. Building a team requires time, persistence, and a focus on the relationships among its members.

All-star teams, made up of the best or most famous athletes in a particular sport, do not necessarily make the best teams. Why? Because a team is much more than the sum of the individual talent. It is a group of people who work as a unit, with shared purpose and goals.

Forming a sports team creates a space for people to develop, learn, grow, and pursue their dreams. This environment enables an individual to develop his or her independence through the interdependence created among the team. In a team, you can see that the whole is greater than the sum of the parts. This means each interaction between different parts of the system adds value beyond what might be measured by merely adding the individual contributions. I like the analogy of a picture puzzle, where the parts come together and only then generate the beauty of the final image. One of the factors that makes a team strong is the quality of interactions among players. For these to develop, it is necessary to invest a quantity of time but also to have quality time. Players on the same team need to spend time together in different contexts, engaging in different activities, creating interdependencies and shared meanings.

Hours of training, collective experiences, and teamwork are essential. The more we act collaboratively in dealing with a variety of situations, the more we expand our repertoire of moves and tactics, making the team increasingly harmonious in working together to maximize performance.

However, it is not enough to bring people together inside the pool, on the basketball court, or in an office and just hope that a team automatically forms. Sharing experiences outside the work environment is key. It is important that team members interact on a daily basis, go out for lunch or dinner, celebrate small achievements and birthdays, or even play other sports. This encourages a balance between work and leisure but also builds camaraderie and familiarity, which generate empathy.

Participating in one another's daily lives, living together like one family, and experiencing situations that invoke a range of emotions—whether sporting defeat or victory or something more akin to the Festa di Sant'Agata—allows intimacy to develop and relationships to mature. You get to know the history and values of people and what matters to them. This creates a bond of respect and understanding, which has a positive bearing when it comes to game time or a new project. I had teammates with whom I could communicate through just a glance, which helped with decision-making and improvisation.

These shared experiences do not have to be with all of the team all of the time. It is natural for subgroups to form and for people to have greater affinity with some colleagues than with others. The important thing is to discourage the formation of groups that do not embrace others or seek to exclude them. This, incidentally, should be a warning sign for a coach—or business leader in the corporate environment—to intervene.

Friendships Forged from Sport

Edson Arantes do Nascimento, known as Pelé, was named Athlete of the 20th Century by the French newspaper *L'Equipe*. Among his many notable achievements, he won the soccer World Cup in 1958, 1962, and 1970 with the Brazilian national team; was a two-time world club champion with Santos Futebol Clube; and is one of the leading goal scorers of all time. In a scene from the documentary *Pelé,* released by Netflix in 2021, the legendary player meets Mengálvio, Pepe, Lima, Edu, and Dorval, all friends of his from the successful Santos team in the 1960s. They eat beside the pool and share a good-humored conversation filled with affection and shared memories.

Pelé begins by commenting on the sunny day: "What a day! You really are the best, my friends, bringing this wonderful sun with you."

In recalling details of a game they played more than fifty years ago, Lima says, "You were the king. We knew that, so we focused on helping the king and on doing our part too."

Pelé interrupts him by humming a parody of Francisco Alves's song "Que Rei Sou Eu?" (What King Am I?). "Do you remember how I sang that song? What a king am I without a kingdom and without a crown, without a castle or a queen, wandering the world aimlessly?"

Some of them hum along with him, until Dorval jokes, "You've got a lot better musically, eh?" Everyone erupts with laughter.

At the end, Pelé tells his buddies, "Don't eat too much. You don't want to get fat, 'cause there's a game tomorrow!"

In the background, Mengálvio can be heard saying, "It was God who put this team together. We were a family." That is exactly how we feel when watching this scene—it is a nice, happy, relaxed family reunion.

Jesse Owens, an African American sprinter who won four gold medals at the 1936 Olympic Games in Berlin, said, "Friendships born on the field of athletic strife are the real gold of competition. Awards become corroded. Friends gather no dust."

Over the years, as I have participated in sport as the daughter of an Olympian, as a player, and as a mother of young athletes, I have witnessed the power of this environment in forging lasting friendships. When you are part of a team or sports community, you give your all, suffer, and enjoy what you do, chalking up victories, challenges, and disappointments while sharing a common dream. The shared experience is intense, formed through investing hours in or around swimming pools, sports courts, or playing fields. Then there are the trips, the so-called off-sites when, ahead of matches, we spend time away practicing but also enjoying activities together, creating stronger bonds. All of this wins a place in our hearts. No matter how much time passes, these friendships remain ever present in our lives.

Sometimes sport can throw together players from different teams and different eras. Pelé and Diego Maradona were often at the heart of heated discussions between Brazilians and Argentinians as to who was the greatest of all time. However, this country rivalry brought the two soccer geniuses together, and they became good friends. When Maradona passed away on November 25, 2020, Pelé paid him a beautiful tribute on his social media page:

It has been seven days since you left. Many people loved to spend their lives comparing us. You were a genius who enchanted the world. A magician with the ball at his feet. A true legend. But above all, to me, you will always be a big friend, with an even bigger heart.

Today, I realize the world would be a much better place if we spent less time comparing one another and more admiring each other. This is why I wish to say that you are incomparable.

Your journey stood out for its honesty. You always announced your loves and your dislikes to the four winds. And in your unique way, you have taught us that we need to love and say "I love you" much more often. Your sudden departure didn't give me a chance to say it, so I will just write: I love you, Diego.

My great friend, thank you so much for all our journey together. One day, up in heaven, we'll play on the same team. And it will be the first time that I'll punch the air without it being to celebrate a goal but rather because I can give you another hug.[1]

Relationships formed in the sporting environment are, above all, guided by the Olympic spirit, whose principles are ones of friendship, mutual understanding, equality, solidarity, and fair play. The ability of sport to cement relationships is not limited to the professionals. Recreational sport also promotes valuable qualities, such as trust, respect, effective communication, and camaraderie.

Thus, setting up opportunities for company employees to play team sports, for example, is a way to enhance relationships, forge bonds, and defuse conflicts. The spin-off benefit is that the employees become more productive and united in delivering results for the company.

During corporate induction programs or strategic planning events in my area, we often started the day with a game of basketball or finished the afternoon's activities with a game of soccer or volleyball. These sporting challenges get the inner energy flowing and give you an insight into people's physical and mental attributes in a new context, away from the day-to-day experience.

A team at work functions much like a sports team, with members cooperating with one another to achieve a common goal. Playing sports, in addition to making it easier for people to come together, can also be a fun way to instill the principles and values of teamwork.

Teams Are like Families

Venezuelan athlete Aníbal Sánchez played for sixteen years in US Major League Baseball. In 2019, when he was playing for the Washington Nationals, the coach called him up for a chat and said, "What I'm trying to do here is not just about building a team or producing winners. First and foremost, what I want is to create a family. Everyone here should feel like brothers and support one another." From that point on, at practice, they were constantly reminded of this, and it had a profound impact on the players. Aníbal said, "We all used to get along in practice and also hang out off the field. As with any family, we had conflicts, and we tried to solve them in the best way, with one-to-one or group conversations. The coach was not authoritarian, but he exercised his authority, as a father and mother need to do when mediating between their children. When the game started, no matter what, win or lose, we supported each other because we really saw each other as family."

Ubuntu means "I am what I am because of what we are." More than an African word, it represents a life philosophy. Glenn Anton "Doc" Rivers—who was named NBA Coach of the Year in 2000, when he was with the Orlando Magic, and later won the NBA title with the Boston Celtics in 2008—drew on this philosophy to inspire his teams and strengthen the bond among the players. In the Netflix series *The Playbook: A Coach's Rules for Life*, he states that putting the emphasis on the team as priority one was the essence of his success with the Celtics.

Essential to building a lasting, positive relationship is authenticity, in which all teammates feel they can be who they are in front of others and be respected. Respect has nothing to do with validation or the need for approval. When we are validated by others, we feel momentary pleasure, but in the long term, the relationship becomes superficial and dependent.

When we only reveal ourselves on the condition that we receive the approbation of others, we run the risk of diminishing who we are and not staying true to our values.

To resolve impasses and conflict, we need to be close to people and share an intimacy, whether it be in a romantic, family, or team relationship. Intimacy only occurs if you know who you are, open up your vulnerable side, allow people to get to know you, and show a genuine interest in others. This is no small thing. It takes courage to be vulnerable with others—to share desires, goals, fears, and dreams.

The emphasis is on genuinely expressing yourself (being real) and not looking to impress (presenting your best side). In order to get to know one another, it is essential to be both open and curious and to ask powerful questions that not only explore but also build on the answers. It is about truly listening and showing genuine interest, accepting the vulnerabilities of others, and acknowledging their virtues. This also extends to recognizing when they wish to be heard and when they would prefer to be left to themselves.

Intimacy is also built on empathy. It forms during real interactions, when facing difficulties, moments of sadness, or the struggle for something better, and also during moments of celebration. Unfortunately, levels of empathy are on the wane, as face-to-face interactions are becoming less frequent. This is especially a concern for the younger generations, who are growing up in an increasingly virtual environment, which is by no means a substitute for face-to-face contact. Given this reality, playing sport can be especially useful for developing this empathy, because during physical activity, we truly need to be living in the present moment and in synchrony with other players.

The Importance of Relationships

Maintaining high-quality relationships is not only key to our happiness and productivity but also vital to our well-being and survival. In recent years, the World Health Organization has highlighted the impact of loneliness, and several countries have been attempting to address the issue. In 2018, the United Kingdom appointed Tracey Crouch as minister for loneliness to help combat what has become a chronic issue for the country. Data from a British Red Cross survey the previous year suggested that one-fifth of the country's population felt lonely.[2]

Julianne Holt-Lunstad is a professor of psychology and neuroscience at Brigham Young University, Utah. She is a leading scholar with regard to the importance of social connection and the growing epidemic of loneliness, and she was the first US researcher to publish scientific evidence that loneliness increases the risk of premature mortality. In 2017, she copublished a study in the journal *American Psychologist* in which she presented the scientific basis for social connection to become a priority public health policy in the US.[3]

"It may sound a bit audacious, but just like we have consensus guidelines on nutrition, physical activity and sleep, and we have recommendations around what we eat and how much, and what kinds of exercise we should get, my recommendation would be to have similar guidelines for social connections," she said.[4] There is still a lack of studies trying to identify the best ways to measure this issue, but there is no shortage of evidence on the importance of cultivating relationships and belonging to a community.

There is an important difference between the concepts of isolation and loneliness. Isolation is defined by the actual size of the network of relationships someone has and the frequency of contact with people who are part of that network. Loneliness, however, is a subjective experience that derives from the individual's perception of isolation or from a discrepancy between his or her level of connection and his or her desire to connect. That is, some people can feel lonely even when they are not isolated, while others can be isolated yet not feel lonely.

The coronavirus pandemic has added a new layer of concern to the loneliness epidemic, as one of the most effective means to prevent the spread of the virus has been social distancing. Keeping in mind this difference between isolation and loneliness is crucial when dealing with a situation like the one imposed on us in 2020 and 2021. Keeping in touch with those close to us through social media and video calls was a positive option because even if it cannot replace physical contact, it keeps the relationship alive. When you form genuine, strong bonds, it is possible to feel connected to someone—and thus less lonely—merely through thinking about that person.

Cultivating relationships with friends, family, fellow workers, or sporting contacts is a powerful antidote to the devastating effects of loneliness. Even more casual contacts with neighbors or fellow shoppers at the supermarket can contribute to a sense of belonging and social support. We are social animals, and these more superficial relationships of greeting or smiling at someone on the street also provide important moments of connection. Any opportunity we have to improve the quality of our relationships and strengthen our bonds with others is not a luxury but a lifesaver.

Interdependence

In the book *Braving the Wilderness: The Quest for True Belonging and the Courage to Stand Alone*, vulnerability researcher Brené Brown suggests a mechanism by which the feeling of loneliness can lead us to further isolate ourselves: "When we feel isolated, disconnected and lonely, we try to protect ourselves. In that mode, we want to connect but our brain is attempting to override connection with self-protection. That means less empathy, more defensiveness, more numbing, and less sleeping."

One of the factors that causes many people to isolate themselves is difficulty in asking for, or accepting, support. Our Western culture values independence and views needing support as a sign of weakness. However, there is an important concept we learn when we are part of a sports team: interdependence.

When we are born, we are totally dependent, and our development is a step toward our independence. However, it is a sign of maturity when we reach independence and, later, interdependence, which is the idea that we can trust others, and they can trust us. The idea behind interdependence is that helping one another benefits both parties.

The Lebanese Khalil Gibran, who lived between 1883 and 1931, is one of the greatest poets in Arab literature. In an excerpt from a beautiful poem written in his most famous book, *The Prophet*, he illustrates the concept of interdependence: "Go to your fields and your gardens, and you shall learn that it is the pleasure of the bee to gather honey of the flower. But it is also the pleasure of the flower to yield its honey to the bee. For to the bee a flower is a fountain of life, and to the flower a bee is a messenger of love. And to both, bee and flower, the giving and the receiving of pleasure is a need and an ecstasy."

The starting point for every healthy relationship with others is having a healthy relationship with oneself. We create a virtuous circle when we help ourselves and others. That is, the more generous we are, the better we feel, and the better we feel, the more generous we wish to be. A clear example of this is the instruction on airplanes "If you need to use the oxygen mask, put it on yourself before helping whoever is in the seat beside you."

Empathy is the feeling that facilitates this virtuous circle of generosity. Without our feeling gratified at pleasing others, the system would not be sustainable. When we enter a win-win relationship with other members of the community, we gain satisfaction from doing good and, as a result, wish to do more of what gives us pleasure.

Happiness is only possible when we have some interdependence with others. Just as the flower would die without the presence and generosity of the bee and vice versa, we would not survive without the presence and generosity of others.

An alumnus of Stanford University, Brenda Villa is the world's most decorated female water polo player, having won four Olympic medals with team USA. When I asked her for some tips for my daughter Alissa, who was about to begin her studies at Stanford, Brenda replied, "I would tell her to mix in, make friends, and develop a support network, both within and away from the water polo team. It took me a while to do this, and I later realized that I could have made a lot more of my experience there."

From a family of first-generation Mexican Americans, Brenda told me she often had the sense that people thought she did not belong in certain places. She said, "This made me clam up and stop asking for help. I could have done more group work and learned much more from the beginning."

The tip she would offer any young athlete who wants to pursue a successful career like hers includes fomenting interdependence and the courage to face vulnerability: "Dream big, and share your dreams. Say them out loud; talk about them. There are those who keep dreams a secret to themselves, but there are many people in the world who will be able to support and guide you on your journey. However, how will people know about your dreams if you don't discuss them?"

Others can help us achieve our goals in a variety of ways: by being part of our support network, as discussed in chapter 1; through teamwork; or by becoming so-called accountability partners. An accountability partner is someone who helps us maintain discipline and commitment to our long-term goals. If you have a good friend who listens to you, celebrates the good times with you, and supports you through the difficult times, you can select him or her to be your accountability partner. This means that when you share your dreams, this person will support you and help you to stay focused on your goals.

Conflict and Adversity

When I asked Coach Adam Krikorian about how he organized his time in preparing the American women's water polo team, he told me, "I focus 20 percent on the technical and tactical side and the other 80 percent on relationships, as this aspect requires going deep into expanding both self-awareness and the awareness of others. Even the technical and tactical aspects take the perspective of how to improve the relationship."

He explained to me that building relationships is not as straightforward as it sounds, as it involves creating opportunities for people to feel comfortable in being vulnerable with one another. His strategy, in addition to promoting different shared experiences and working on communication, involves simulating adverse situations for the team to deal with as a collective.

He told me, "As a coach, one of the ways to get the group to connect and draw closer is to create challenges that they can only solve as a team, such as setting an extremely tough week of endurance training. It's the type of situation that if you try it on your own, you will fail. The only way to get through it is to trust the person beside you, be it in the pool or in agreeing energy-recovery periods. The greater that initial feeling of not being able to handle the challenge on your own, the deeper the connection you get when you all pull through together."

For Krikorian, conflict is also a catalyst for relationships to mature within a team. "To deal with conflict, the first step is to accept that it will happen and view it as an opportunity for growth. Then the focus is to work on open, honest, effective communication, and in most cases, the player will come out the other side better than she entered, and the relationships will be tighter," he said.

Disagreements and arguments often arise from the diversity of perspectives within a team and can be a great opportunity to learn— both about ourselves and about others. They are a chance to reflect on our own worldview and how it might be different from those of others. The best relationships are those in which problems are not ignored but confronted, so they do not become more serious. Conflict is a natural part of the process in which relationships mature over time.

John Gottman is an American psychologist and author who has gained worldwide renown for his research on romantic relationships, but his observations apply equally to other types of relationships, such as those between family members and team members. One of his main contributions to the field is the observation that it is not the presence of conflict that predicts whether a relationship will be happy and long-lasting; rather, it is the way a couple behaves and reacts during and after an argument.

According to Gottman, couples whose relationships thrive enter conflict differently than those who ultimately break up. They begin the disagreement more evenly and intersperse positive interactions throughout and after the exchanges. Healthy relationships are not about avoiding conflict and being a yes-person, but for the relationship to thrive, the balance needs to lean toward the positive.

Positive interactions include showing interest, truly wanting to listen to understand why the other person is upset, making eye contact, nodding, offering physical or verbal reassurance during a difficult conversation, showing empathy, and demonstrating that the other person is important to you, even though you might disagree with him or her on a specific point.

In addition to watching our behavior, it is necessary to filter our thoughts and make a conscious effort to remember the other person's positive features. In the heat of conflict, the tendency is to focus on people's negative aspects, and this often influences how we pursue the discussion, causing us to ignore opportunities to reach agreement and other positive interactions.

Collective Resilience

At the 1994 soccer World Cup finals in the United States, Brazil was crowned a four-time champion, defeating Italy in the final. In getting there, that year's team proved extremely resilient. Twenty-four years on from the previous title, the pressure on the players and coaching staff was enormous, especially during the qualifying games, when the team was in danger of missing out on the finals. But the more the pressure increased, the more united the team became. Facing Bolivia after a run of poor results, the team, led by Carlos Alberto Parreira, decided to take the field hand in hand. Brazil went on to win comfortably, 6–0, which set them on the way to qualification, and the hand-holding entry onto the field became a trademark they stuck with all the way to the final.

The resilience of a team refers to the processes by which team members use both their individual and collective resources to deal with adversity. Resilience is developed through the shared experience of challenging and sometimes stressful situations. At the critical moment, it is as if we are saying to the team, "We've been through so many difficult situations together that we know it's possible to overcome them. Keep believing, because we can get through this!"

Some research carried out by Loughborough University in England, which for five years has been ranked the world's best university for sports-related subjects,[5] analyzed the experiences of players who were part of the 2003 Rugby Union World Cup winning team and identified five factors that help to develop a resilient team.[6]

At first, especially in the early stages of team building, it is important to have leaders who create an environment that inspires and promotes greater self-confidence among the team members, something they named *transformational leadership*.

Raí, who captained Brazil in the first phase of the 1994 World Cup, agrees. "It is essential for the coach to be an inspiring leader, for him to transmit his passion for the sport to the players, and for him to instill the concept that the collective is more important than the individual," he said.

The intense fraternization among team members—both during training and matches and away from the game—supported by motivating leadership, encourages players to identify with the team. The second factor identified in the study relates to the moment when *I* gives way to *we*, and all the players recognize that the team represents part of their identity as individuals.

As the group matures, other members of the team start to emerge as leaders, and this drives the third factor: the need for shared leadership in order to create more role models for players.

A shared, diverse group of leaders was, in Raí's opinion, one of the factors that added steel to the team in 1994. "We had three leaders on the field—Dunga, Romário, and I, each with our own style. Dunga was more aggressive, the one who shouted and pumped up the team. I was more measured, leading by example. Romário displayed self-confidence. We complemented each other," he said.

The fourth factor in developing resilience is referred to as team learning, which relates to engagement in a process of self-awareness and the awareness of others gained through collective experience. This enables players to anticipate one another's actions and to coordinate their response to the in-game challenges.

Finally, the fifth factor relates to the importance of experiencing positive emotions. The idea is that moments of laughter, relaxation, and fun as a group act as shock absorbers, making the team more resistant to stress factors and moments of frustration.

A Shared Purpose

The term *ombudsman* refers to a person, entity, or sector of a company assigned to listen to the customer. The ombudsman's focus is to resolve the client's issue and identify which aspects of the organization need to be improved from a customer perspective. Our goal at Itaú Unibanco was to enhance the relationship with clients and to increase first-contact resolution using channels such as the internet, branches, and call centers.

When I took over the ombudsman at Itaú Unibanco, I knew I would need motivated and engaged employees to deal with the challenges the area represents. The first step was to reframe what it meant to work in that sector of the bank. We could view a customer's feedback as a complaint or choose to see it as an opportunity for the company to improve.

Each day, we practiced active, empathetic listening with customers in order to identify the best solutions and leverage points that, once improved, might elevate the entire customer relationship mechanism.

Through sharing the same purpose in seeking service excellence, the team members developed a strong bond, and this commitment translated into the way we communicated with customers and into the suggestions we came up with for improving the way the bank operated. When we are genuine and transparent, have integrity, and show love and respect for what we do, we form relationships built on trust, whether within a team, between areas, with customers, or with the wider communities around us. The entire chain of interaction gets a boost.

A company's most important asset is its people, who, when motivated, generate more intense levels of energy for action, which produces better results for the organization. The engagement of the team is an important factor for success, as the team members start to work in a natural flow, pursuing the same goals but more motivated by the customer's call, carrying out the task with the sense that it is more than just an obligation.

Within a group of people, whether a team, a company, a group at school, or a family, everyone has his or her own preferences, interests, and tastes and sometimes a different origin and background, which can generate a conflict of ideas or values among the group.

In 1958, Turkish American social psychologist Muzafer Sherif developed the superordinate goals method as a way of facilitating groups who are in conflict to work together. The idea stemmed from the principle that putting people together to spend time in dialogue and get to know one another would help them overcome any disagreements or prejudices. However, in many cases, the outcome was the complete opposite.

Sherif's aim was to develop a common goal, which can only be achieved if everyone works collaboratively, contributing his or her own skills and experiences. In other words, when the group seeks a greater meaning and all the participants feel integral to achieving success, interdependence and integration among the group members is created, which is essential for achieving the desired result. In cases of disagreement, the participants join together, setting aside their differences, as they know that cooperation is key to the project's survival.

In the different teams of which I was a part, I saw that the team members not only related well to one another but also supported one another in the pursuit of their dreams, sharing their aspirations, values, and a common sense of purpose.

Olympic champion sailors Martine Grael and Kahena Kunze are different people in many ways. "I am an Aquarius, perfectionist, methodical. Kahena is Pisces, optimistic, more flexible, and has a good relationship with everyone," Martine told me. She believes the partnership worked because they had a lot in common, in particular characteristics such as grit, determination, and ambition, which led them always to focus on the main task at hand, which was to give their best. "If you're sailing with someone who is not as ambitious, then you won't get very far."

After the 2004 Athens Olympic Games, sailor Robert Scheidt switched from the Laser class, with one sailor, to the Star class, which has two. Used to doing everything on his own, he found himself as part of a team in the new category, when he was joined by Bruno Prada, also from São Paulo. "This was a big change in my career. Before, I was in charge of my routine, but as part of a duo, everything became a compromise between the two of us," Robert said. Bruno was dreaming of going to the Olympics when he received an offer from Scheidt to sail together. "His eyes shone," Robert recalled. Even with the natural strain inherent in any relationship in spending many hours each day with the same person, with all the ups and downs of training, both had a shared commitment and a common goal: the Olympic podium. They qualified for Beijing in 2008 and London in 2012, gaining silver and bronze, respectively, and won three world titles.

A Team Is a Puzzle

In June 2003, soccer giant Real Madrid announced the hiring of Manchester United star David Beckham, who had shone as one of the best playmakers in the English game. Beckham was seen as one of the final pieces who came to be known as the *galacticos* on the Madrid side, along with Ronaldo, Zinedine Zidane, Luis Figo, Roberto Carlos, Raul, and others. The team included three players who had won the FIFA World Player of the Year Award, something no other team has achieved since.

On paper, the team seemed unbeatable, but in practice, it was not. The team lost games and missed out on championships to opponents whose budgets were much smaller. In the 2003–2004 season, it finished only third in the Spanish League (behind Deportivo La Coruña and Barcelona), while in the UEFA Champions League, it was eliminated in the quarterfinal stage by Monaco. Meanwhile, in the Copa del Rey, the domestic cup, it was defeated at home to Real Zaragoza after taking the lead.

Looking back at that period, the team's goalkeeper at the time, Iker Casillas, a World Cup winner with Spain in 2010, said, "It's not just the names that win a game. It's necessary to form a team, and we didn't have one … This phase is one I don't like to think about."[7]

If selecting the best players in the world is not a good formula for building a winning team, what is the solution? Legendary Croatian coach Ratko Rudić told me about his selection philosophy: "To call up a player, I had to be convinced that he could slot in and help the team in some way, even if he wasn't the best technically." Further, in order to build a winning team, he did not content himself with merely selecting players. He also went after professionals who could add value to the work that went into preparing the team. "Since the beginning of my career, I have always called on a group of support specialists to help players become elite-level athletes. It is necessary to have a good team of professionals to work on the physical, technical, tactical, and psychological aspects of training."

The coach of the American women's water polo team, Adam Krikorian, understands that the key to this selection dilemma is to discover how resilient an athlete is and to assess her ability to keep going when things get tough. "As a coach, you shouldn't select the best players but the best team. You have to consider the individuals who will handle those moments of pressure and those who connect best with each other," he explained to me before adding, "There are very talented players who weren't part of our team not because they lacked talent but because they weren't able to stick with the process."

This thought process must be followed for all members of the team: those who begin the game, the starters, and those who begin on the bench. Former coach of the US and Brazilian women's water polo teams, Sandy Nitta, told me, "The quality of a team is only as good as the last player on the bench." In other words, all the players—starters and reserves—have an important role within the group, contributing with technical aspects and in enhancing relations within the team. She also believes the needs of the group should prevail over individual talent. She said, "It's important to pull players out when they start to harm the team. Priority one is that it needs to be a team. This is more important than shooting, scoring, defending, and knowing how to play."

The Best of Each Player

After creating a team, the challenge is for each player individually to be able to give as much as possible for the team. The coach needs to be able to know the strengths and potential limiters of each athlete and of the team as a whole, so he or she can choose the style of play that allows the team to flourish.

In our conversation, soccer player Raí recalled how important it was for São Paulo's coach, two-time world champion Telê Santana, to be able to get a young Cafu to play at right-back, a position that needed to be filled in the star-studded squad being put together in the early 1990s. Raí said, "He came from a humble background and played in midfield, but he had everything to be a good fullback. He could get up and down, good stamina, could dribble, but he couldn't cross the ball or shoot well." Telê, seeing potential in the boy, made Cafu practice crossing and shooting endlessly, until he improved the basics. Slotting in this piece was so successful that it helped produce a winning team and transformed Cafu personally into one of the greatest fullbacks in the history of Brazilian football.

Sandy Nitta, when she took over as coach of the Brazilian national team, was able to bring out the best in each of us individually in contributing to the team. She always stressed that she was coaching not who we were but who we might become. At the time, there was a pattern to our performances that we noticed during the international championships. We would play very well—on par with any team in the world—in the first, second, and fourth quarters of games. But in the third quarter, our levels dropped off. Realizing this, the coach worked on maintaining greater consistency and also adapted our playing style to counter the strengths of the opposition.

A team is made up of people with different features and abilities, and learning to exploit these differences is a key factor in the search for excellence. In the early 1970s, psychologist Elliot Aronson created the jigsaw-puzzle method, which was successfully tested on students at the University of Texas and the University of California.

Aronson's idea was to divide the class into small groups, each of which was ethnically and racially diverse and contained a mix of skills and gender. The groups had to have a leader, usually the most mature student, and each leader had to specialize in one aspect of the lesson presented by the teacher. These specialists could discuss with the other specialists and then bring the lessons learned back to their own group. From then on, they worked together to achieve their common goal.

This method was innovative in that it introduced a technique based on cooperative learning, which is capable of reducing the conflict of ideas among students. Thus, it promotes more efficient learning, greater motivation in the group, and the pleasure of working as a team, generating more effective results.

The agile methodology, which has been widely used in organizations to deliver quick wins on projects related to innovation, for example, has a lot in common with Aronson's method. A team of managers is formed, each with his or her own expertise that contributes to delivering a given project. After they complete their mission, the team is dissolved, and each manager starts to put together a new team for a new project, which enables the continual exchange of experiences with the new team members and the use of each individual's strengths to achieve the goal.

The Values of Teamwork

Brazilian surfer Rodrigo Koxa began his sports career at the age of four, playing soccer. Thus, at a young age, he had the opportunity to learn about the values associated with teamwork and to experience the benefits of being part of a team. "We shared the good and the bad times. There's nothing better than celebrating victories with your team," he told me. Still a child, he fell in love with surfing, and he won his first regional championship at age twelve. Then he discovered big-wave surfing, which became his great passion. Tremendously focused and determined, he battled throughout his career before reaping the rewards of his perseverance. He broke the world record for the biggest wave and, in April 2018, won the coveted Quiksilver XXL Biggest Wave award at the Big Wave Awards of the World Surf League.

When it came to the acceptance speech, Koxa remembered how football had taught him the importance of the team. He made a point of sharing the award with Portuguese Sérgio Cosme, known as the guardian angel of Nazaré, Portugal, which is known for its huge waves. Serginho, as Koxa calls him, is a professional Jet Ski rescue pilot responsible for dragging him out to the waves and coming to rescue him when it is time. Koxa said, "I have always questioned why the event doesn't give an award to the pilot too. For those of us who surf the giant waves, there's always a rescue team behind us. It's a job that takes trust—that takes a team! I held the trophy, but the prize was shared, and whenever I have the opportunity, I publicly thank Serginho so that he can share in the glory too."

For athletes who are starting their sporting careers, coaches and referees have a fundamental role in teaching these concepts. Sandy Nitta has always said that when refereeing matches for younger players, referees should apply the rules more rigorously, as this is also a time of training, when the players are still learning the rules of the game. For more experienced players, there is more room to be flexible and let the game flow. Following the same logic, an important objective when training younger teams is to pass on Olympic values and educate them about what is expected when working as a team.

When my father was starting out in water polo, his coach, Hungarian Emeric Szasz, made a brave but principled decision in which he risked losing a championship in the name of teaching the values of teamwork. My father's team, Tietê, was playing in the final of the Brazilian championship against Fluminense. There was only a minute and a half remaining in the game, when my father, despite tight marking, shook off the Rio defenders, took a shot, and scored to tie the game. The rest of the team all went over to hug him.

However, once the celebration had died down, the coach switched him out of the game. "You should have passed the ball!" Emeric said, as another player had been much better positioned, and my father had opted for the more difficult individual play to achieve the target. From the bench, he then had to watch as Fluminense scored the game-winning goal, and his own side missed out on the title.

Although he felt frustrated at the time, it was a lesson that lived with him: it's not the good player who wins; it's the team. That decision, although it might have hurt the team at the time, strengthened the group for the future. A good coach identifies the best way, and the right moment, to teach each player the lesson he or she needs.

Being part of a sports team, in which goals and strategies are aligned, teaches us the fundamental need to cooperate if we are to reach a common goal. Sometimes you take up the slack for your colleague, and sometimes it is the other way around.

These lessons last a lifetime. My father took Emeric's lesson into his executive career. At Grupo Folha, he always championed the value of working together. "We had a weekly brainstorm. We encouraged the free exchange of opinions, with everyone given space to speak. Initially, what happened was that the newsroom—responsible for the company's most important asset, the content—monopolized airtime, proposing ideas or changes in the other units of the company. Although they came up with good suggestions, we placed a time limit on each unit leader to speak. While we may have had a drop-off in the quality of ideas initially, after a few weeks, the contribution to the company was infinitely greater," he told me.

Like my father, I also carried over lessons from sport into my executive career. When I played in Italy, being a striker, I had a financial incentive for every goal I scored. However, I thought the correct incentive should be for the team to win. After all, if I focused purely on attacking, I might leave the defense exposed or shoot when I should have passed. In other words, the best incentive is one that encourages teamwork.

In the search for excellence, a united team with solid core values and people committed to the success of the group is more powerful than individual talent working alone in isolation. Therefore, when slotting together the puzzle to create a winning team, this spirit of commitment should take center stage. Through the time spent together in both training and relaxing, the team becomes a family, one that—despite the occasional tensions present in any family—is willing to fight for each other and conquer. Out of this process, each member emerges wiser, more independent, and with friendships that last a lifetime.

- A team is a group of people who function as a unit, with shared purpose.
- Therefore, being part of a team, whether in sport, in the family, or at work, is an opportunity to grow, evolve, learn, and pursue a dream.
- Building a team is about building relationships, which requires both a qualitative and a quantitative investment of time. Shared experience reinforces emotional bonds, while the sharing of values and dreams increases empathy among team members.
- Cultivating relationships with friends, family, colleagues, or teammates is a powerful antidote to the detrimental effects of loneliness on mental and physical health.
- Interdependent relationships help in developing mature, independent, self-assured individuals.
- How we manage conflict is more important than conflict avoidance. Misunderstandings are part of any relationship and represent an opportunity for us to grow and mature.
- In addition to individual resilience, it is possible to develop team resilience, in which collective resources are used to adapt the team to adverse situations.
- A team is like a puzzle, in which each piece is important for achieving the common goal. The composition of the team should look beyond individual talents and abilities.
- The leader should be able to identify the strengths and potential limiters of each team member, so everyone can fully contribute to maximizing the performance of the group.

Powerful Questions to Reflect Upon

- How have you cultivated your relationships with family, friends, colleagues, and teammates?
- What priority have you given to getting along with people you care about and who care about you?
- What kind of people have you chosen to share the key moments of your day?
- How do you handle conflicts with people you love? What have you learned from these situations?
- Do you ask for and accept help as much as you offer to help others?

CHAPTER 9

———

THE POWER OF **COMMUNICATION**

Good leaders ask great questions that inspire others to dream
more, to think more, learn more, do more and become more.
—John Maxwell

Empathy: the art of emptying our mind and
listening with our whole being.
—Marshall B. Rosenberg

William Urizzi de Lima was a swimming coach for the first team at
Pinheiros Club in São Paulo. In addition to having a degree in physical
education, he studied psychology and edited three books on swimming
and gym training. Just before I left with the national team for an
international competition in 1993, I sought him out to talk with him
and better understand the work he was doing with high-performance
swimmers. I mentioned that my team members and I were becoming
stronger and more confident with each tournament, but we needed
to improve our performance as a team. I asked him, "What do you
suggest? Is there anything I can do, especially as captain, to enhance our
performance?"

He then told me about one of his strategies for uniting the swim team
during major championships, a simple routine he suggested we apply

consistently. The idea was for the players to meet for an hour each day to talk. The rule was simple. Everyone had the right to express herself uninterrupted. If a discussion ran on and we all agreed, we could extend the time, but the key part was that only the players took part, and what was said stayed in the meeting.

This practice significantly improved the degree of connection among the players. We talked about everything! Each player shared her joys and frustrations while the others listened attentively. The meeting was a place where we knew we could be genuine, let our guards down, and speak freely about what was happening inside and outside the pool.

The dynamic of the conversation allowed us to get to know one another on a deeper level and strengthened the intuitive understanding among us, which is key during the most challenging periods of games. We often discovered a side to one another that we had not seen. For example, there was a player who, during games, was very tough, but in the meetings, a new personality trait was revealed, as she showed herself to be sweet-natured, empathetic, and good at helping us focus on the key takeaways to strengthen our team.

During a game at one tournament, I had a bad headache. As usual, I did all I could to summon my reserves of energy and push through it, driving the team to victory to the last. When we sat down to talk that night, one of the players asked me, "Cris, were you OK today?"

My immediate response was "Of course." But a few seconds later, I came clean about the pounding headache and how I was trying to ignore it.

I was so used to playing through pain that I had not realized that was what my teammate was talking about. Our connection was such that they had noticed the subtleties in my facial expressions during the game. One of them told me, "It's important that we know someone is not feeling right, as we can look to cover her and take up the slack. You can tell us if you're not feeling well. Count on us! You don't want to do everything on your own."

Another added, "We're in this together. It's a team game. When you're not well, we'll help you out, just as we know you will do the same for us."

It was a key moment for me. I felt relieved from a responsibility I had put on my own shoulders. From that point on, I allowed myself to let my guard down more often.

Of course, during these meetings, conflicts arose. Some players did not like the aggressive manner in which they were being called out during the heat of the game, and they needed others to take a step back. For the most part, both sides got to explain how they felt, and there was a genuine effort to clear the air. The more we faced our disagreements head-on, the tighter our interpersonal bonds became. Resolving conflicts requires intimacy. The results were evident in the pool too. Our communication became more instinctive—often, just a look was needed—and we began to trust one another more.

These meetings were also opportunities for us to share stories or significant things that happened to us, which helped spread a sense of purpose among us. Purpose, of course, is contagious. Each of us inspires others through our commitment to our dreams.

In these moments, I discovered that good communication had the power not only to make a team stronger and more united but also to give greater meaning to our own journey. We continued with this routine until I retired from the national team. I was grateful to have learned this practice from a swimming coach I admired, who was kind enough to share his practices with us.

Creating a Safe Environment

In the first part of this book, I talked about the aspects that ensure a good foundation for a life of excellence and happiness. Next, I went deeper into how we can connect with our inner strength to overcome challenges and obstacles along the way. However, to reap the rewards, we need to be curious, keep an open mind, and have the courage to act. Furthermore, our network of relationships—in which we support and are supported by people who are important to us—helps us to go further.

Throughout our development and evolution, we become more independent, which is an essential step toward maturity, but interdependence—people mutually helping one another—contributes to unlocking our potential. In chapter 8, I talked about teamwork and how we can build and nurture positive, lasting, and authentic relationships. Now I am going to discuss a fundamental aspect that underlies interdependence and collaboration: the ability to communicate effectively and with intent.

Amy Edmondson, professor and researcher at Harvard Business School, developed the concept of team psychological safety.[1] It relates to how much the members of a team feel free to express their opinions, ask questions, ask for help, and risk making a mistake in front of their teammates. The team's emotional security is key to creativity, innovation, growth, and development, which are all essential for individuals and organizations to thrive in today's world of rapid technological innovation, in which constant change is a certainty. To develop psychological safety, we need to consider tasks to be a learning process, recognize our fallibility, and establish a climate of openness and curiosity in which questions are welcome.

In any collective structure—such as a sports team, company, family, or community—communication is crucial to building a healthy environment: a space with curiosity and openness to learn and innovate; with tolerance and even appreciation of differences; and with the freedom to express opinions and identify solutions for the common good. This is easier said than done. So how do we go about creating such an environment?

The way we communicate can have a positive or negative effect on our relationships and our lives as a whole. Communication can inspire, engage, collaborate, and build bridges. Communication failures, however, can cause harm, impact both the rapport and the results of a team, and undermine the harmony of the collective.

Good communication involves far more than articulation or the choice of words appropriate to the context. We can often communicate more efficiently through silence. Barack Obama, one of the best speakers of our time, is considered a master of the pause.[2] An effective technique, the pause can become five seconds of deafening silence, often used to give weight to the idea just expressed, while you look into the eyes of the listeners. The pause conveys confidence and dignity while sending a clear message that you care about your listeners.

It is important to think about not only the message you wish to pass on but also how best to deliver it, when, and why. Nonverbal aspects, such as our comportment, body language, tone of voice, eye contact, pauses, and facial expression, contribute to this process.

Effective communication should also consider the way in which we receive messages and respond to other people's words or actions. To do this, we need to work on our self-awareness and active listening. American writer Stephen Covey, author of the best-selling *The 7 Habits of Highly Effective People*, once said that most people listen not with the intention of understanding but with the intention of responding, while it should be the opposite. Active listening means being fully in the present moment, focused not only on what others are saying but also on what they are not saying explicitly—such as their motivations, feelings, and needs—while avoiding prejudice or prejudgments. Listening to someone is an act of respect and of showing genuine interest in the other person.

The art of communicating therefore involves emotional intelligence, which involves self-awareness, respect, empathy, and awareness of others. Good relationships take time, effort, and dedication. Shared experience and interactions or conversations that empower—like the meetings my teammates and I held on the Brazilian national team—can help develop these communication skills. Thus, it is possible to improve communication skills through making a conscious effort to do so.

When I spoke with sailors Martine Grael and Kahena Kunze, both were emphatic that communication between them was essential to their landing the long-awaited Olympic gold medal. "The training situations led to communication becoming something that is automatic during competition, because during the race, communication can come down to a single glance or sound, where one of us already knows what the other wishes to say," said Martine.

The Art of Humble Inquiry

When attending an important work meeting, my father would prepare for it as if it were a game of water polo. "For a competition, you have to know your team, the opponent, the referee, the competition environment, and the details of the situation, such as the weather, temperature, altitude, … and the same applies for any other situation," he told me. He was always on time and meticulously prepared. Having studied the agenda and the participants and having armed himself with all the information he needed, he would arrive at the meeting and fire off his trademark request: "Tell me a little about yourself and your story to get here."

This was not just an icebreaker but also his way of showing genuine interest in others and opening the door to make a connection. "People feel valued and at ease to talk because you are asking them about something they have complete control over. From then on, the conversation flows naturally," he told me.

This is an example of what Edgar Schein, professor emeritus at the Sloan School of Management at MIT, calls humble inquiry. Schein is considered an authority in the field of organizational psychology due to his work on the culture of organizations. In his book *Humble Inquiry: The Gentle Art of Asking Instead of Telling*, he advocates showing curiosity and genuine interest in others as a means to building positive, lasting relationships that allow for true interdependence.

Humble inquiry is the art of connecting with someone by demonstrating your willingness and desire to get to know him or her. This can be done through both what you say—e.g., "Tell me more about yourself" or "Tell me more about what you just said"—and how you receive what the other person says, indicating that you were truly listening. Sharing a story or personal anecdote is also a way of showing your interest. It is as if you are saying, "I'm sharing this because you matter to me. I'm open to hearing more about you too."

When we created the Client Forum at Unibanco—which was comprised of client representatives who worked with us for one year to share their experiences and suggestions for enhancing their relationship with the bank—I made a point of receiving all clients in person and taking every opportunity during this initial reception to get to know and understand a little about them. As manager of the quality area, I proudly presented our team's mission as wanting to listen to them and gain their perspective on our customer processes, from the sale of the products through to customer services in both the physical and virtual domains. Customers felt welcomed, valued, and confident they were being listened to. They knew their time was contributing to improving the service for all the bank's customers.

Having established this connection, we were able to collaborate on finding the best solutions. Customers were active in this process. These face-to-face experiences helped us to discern issues that affected individual customers from those that impacted many and thus necessitated improvements to our processes. When one customer adviser highlighted something he or she cared about in his or her relationship with the bank, others would often chime in, and this allowed us to understand the key points for improving customer satisfaction. One time, a client arrived at one of our sessions irate. He raged and talked nonstop, so I invited him to talk in private and listened to what he had to say, showing genuine interest in understanding what had happened. Finally, I asked, "What can I do for you?"

He paused, took a deep breath, and said, "No one has really listened to me till now. I want an apology!" In other words, he needed to feel heard and validated.

The basis to humble inquiry is interest and curiosity. The idea is not merely to ask but also to be ready to adapt your response and reaction to what you hear. Brazilian footballer Raí told me an interesting story about this.

Raí's father had humble origins, was self-taught, and only managed to complete his studies when he was around fifty years old. He fought to give his children better opportunities and always encouraged them to study and to play sport. As soon as he became more financially stable, his first investment was to purchase the titles to a club in the interior of São Paulo state—such was the importance he placed, intuitively, on playing sport.

Raí's father's encouragement worked. The six children graduated from good colleges in programs such as medicine and engineering. Raí and two of his brothers became professional athletes. One of them, Raimar, was a professional basketball player in the interior of São Paulo. The other was soccer legend Sócrates, who captained Brazil at the 1982 World Cup and became one of the great names in the history of the game.

Although five of the six brothers played soccer or basketball from a young age, one of the boys did not seem interested in playing sport. His father pulled him to one side for a chat. "I see your brothers all play sport, but you don't seem interested. Is there anything I can do to help?"

His son replied, "I would like to play tennis, but I know you can't afford this for me."

It was true that their financial situation was tight, but his father found the means to get his son a racket so he could try to find a sport to his liking. "And he still plays today!" Raí told me. "He didn't turn professional, but the sport is part of his life. If my father hadn't thought to stop and ask—and listened—my brother might have missed out on sport and all the benefits that we know it brings to our lives."

Humble inquiry allows us to get to know others and ourselves and to deepen the relationship. In a moment of sharing with my two eldest daughters, I asked them, "Who is your biggest critic?"

Giorgia, the middle daughter, replied a little pensively, "I am my biggest critic. I am always judging myself on the inside," which led her to reflect on the consequences of being so demanding on herself.

Alissa, the eldest, had a different answer. "My biggest critic is you, Mom."

Her answer took me by surprise. I asked about my behavior that led her to see me this way, and the conversation turned into a wonderful opportunity to reflect and rethink the way I communicated with her. Conversations like these bring us closer to the people who matter to us and give us a chance to realign key aspects of the relationship. The same message can be understood in two completely different ways by two different people. We should always, therefore, take account of each other's personal characteristics and adjust our communications accordingly.

Effective Communication

Lewis Senior began his career in the oil industry, where he rose to the position of worldwide manager of health, safety, and environment. His main mission was to reduce the number of accidents that occurred among employees on oil platforms. It was a dangerous environment, in which incidents were often fatal. Lewis began to realize the value of good communication skills.

He said, "We had rules, guidelines, and safety protocols. Everyone knew what to do and how to do it, but it wasn't enough. It was not simply a matter of recording the information and sharing it but of thinking about how to make this information impact each employee." He began to study the different personalities and think about how best to communicate with each of them.

To simplify theories of behavior, he identified four different personality types and assigned a color to each of them. The color green was associated with those who are analytical, detail-driven, and curious about the mechanics of things. They are active listeners, and their natural way of communicating is to focus on explaining and asking about the *how*.

Yellow was assigned to people who like to engage in conversation and interact with others and appreciate human connection. They like to know the *who* in a given situation. They are more selective listeners, paying attention to what falls in their field of interest and waiting for the right moment to add their point of view.

Red was for the doers, those more interested in the *what*—what needs doing, the goals and objectives. They quickly identify the aspects relevant to them (which differ from those of the other groups) and want to get started in taking action.

Finally, the color blue represented empathetic listeners, those who relate easily to a situation or to others and who want to know the *why* of things before engaging in something new.

Each of us has a little of each of these colors, but there are usually two that predominate. By being able to recognize and distinguish among different personalities and behavioral reactions, we improve the effectiveness of our communication with others and also our self-management by responding rather than reacting to unexpected situations.

Responding and *reacting* may seem like similar words in terms of meaning, but there is an important difference between them. When we react, we are on autopilot, saying or doing things without thinking about the consequences. Responding, on the other hand, involves making an intentional choice about what, how, why, and when we wish to act. To respond effectively and intentionally, it is necessary to focus on what is most important at that moment.

Personality differences are often overlooked, which generates doubts, lack of engagement, and even discord in interpersonal relationships. Imagine a person whose personality is related to the colors red and yellow—that is, he is more focused on hitting targets, getting things done, making speedy decisions, and connecting easily with people in meeting environments. When interacting with someone who operates in the blue and green colors, he may not understand why the other person is asking so many questions about the details of the execution and might interpret this behavior as a lack of confidence. In such situations, we find the challenges in communication.

The key to effective communication is to identify the type of information each personality values. Leaders, parents, and teachers can use this simple mechanism to establish distinct, more comprehensive ways to communicate and, thus, achieve more effective results.

There are other important aspects that influence human behavior, such as origin, cultural background, education, values, and previous experience. These aspects influence the conscious decisions we make and allow us to respond to situations. We all have biases that stem from our personalities, so when we manage to break from our natural instincts and align our communications to the needs of others, we take an important step in the relationship.

Lewis realized that for the safety guidelines and protocols to work, an analysis of the personalities of the employees would be needed in order to adapt the message. "Often, protocols and guidelines focus on saying who should do what and how it should be done, but there is rarely an explanation of why things should be done in a certain manner. And this is not exclusive to the oil industry. It is common in the corporate world in general. If you think about it, you'll notice that we're ignoring a portion of the population that needs to know the *why* in order to engage with the communication," he told me.

By tweaking the communications, Lewis was successful in reducing fatalities. During his tenure, he encouraged each employee to invest in self-awareness and in the awareness of team members. Leaders need to be aware of the different personality types on the team in order to adapt their message to each of them. Only in so doing was it possible to adapt the safety guidelines such that everyone was disposed to follow them.

In 2004, he founded Equilibria, a consulting and coaching company that specialized in improving communication skills by using a self-awareness tool.[3]

Knowing yourself goes beyond the study of personality. It depends on courage and a constant immersion in our emotions, thoughts, and actions, as I will discuss in chapter 10. To get to know each other, we need to be authentically curious and persistent in our relationships.

When we invest in these aspects, communication flows more effectively, leading to productive results for everyone. It's a win-win. This is true for both verbal and nonverbal communication. A pass of the ball in water polo, for example, is pure communication, even if conversation is not involved. To make a great pass, we need to know ourselves, know the other player, and read the situation quickly.

In 2021, Marcelinho Huertas got the most assists in a single season in the history of his current basketball team, Lenovo Tenerife in Spain. As point guard, his main role on court is to lead the offense, creating chances for his teammates to score and being the first line of defense.

To do this effectively, he needs spontaneous and nonverbal communication with his teammates in carrying out the moves they've practiced, adapting to the opponents' tactics, and improvising. "I know the players. I know their strengths and skills, and my focus is on leveraging the best from each of them on the court," he told me.

Collaborative Communication

People, in general, do not wake up with the desire to hurt or harm someone, but if we fail to create empathy, this can end up happening. Genuine relationships are critical to the development of empathy, which is the foundation of morality, the cement that keeps us together and prevents society from falling apart.

To develop empathy and a sense of morality in our social connections, we need to be immersed in relationships that are genuine, interacting with flesh and blood. Nowadays, social media often takes the place of face-to-face interactions, which leads to a divorce from reality, increased loneliness, and impaired development of socioemotional skills.

In the 1960s, American doctor of psychology Marshall Rosenberg developed the concept of nonviolent communication (NVC), also known as compassionate or collaborative communication. For those who are not familiar with the term, it is easy to assume this type of communication is based on being passive and not expressing our wishes, but it is quite the opposite. It is a method designed to promote self-awareness and active listening before we engage in the search for solutions that serve both sides, even if it means compromising. The focus is on interpersonal harmony and creating space for cooperation, thus avoiding an impasse.

One of the key aspects of NVC is the difference between need and strategy. We have basic needs, which are associated with our survival, such as air, food, shelter, movement, rest, and a sense of belonging, for example, and with our most important values, such as autonomy, freedom, integrity, cooperation, and care. These needs are inherent in all human beings. However, the means or strategies used to achieve them vary from person to person. While for some, receiving attention from a loved one is a way to satisfy the need for love, others need more, such as the touch of a hug, to feel loved.

Being aware of these differences allows us to be flexible in the way we attempt to meet our own needs and fulfill those of others. Conflicts often arise from a disagreement regarding strategy, and the key is to look at the underlying needs on each side.

Imagine a disagreement between two members of a team, in which one complains that the other offers help all the time, hampering her learning process and making her feel incompetent. The other replies that she is just trying to help.

In this example, the first person needs autonomy, and her strategy to achieve it is to attempt to do the work on her own. The second person has a need to care, and her strategy to achieve this is to offer help frequently. While team members argue over behaviors, the discussion will not move forward. But if they each make an effort to understand the other's underlying values, they can reach a solution that will work for both of them.

The first might say, "Autonomy is important to me. I like to do things for myself. I understand that it is important for you to be helpful and take care of others. How can we work together so that we both have our needs met?" From then on, the person who values caring could find an alternative way to provide care or understand that allowing her colleague to work alone is also a form of caring, as it allows her to learn.

When listening is directed to the needs behind the behaviors, a range of possible solutions opens up, as everyone connects with what really matters to each of the parties, and all can work toward a common goal— even if the goal is simply the harmony of the relationship.

Another important aspect to Rosenberg's model is that people are encouraged to observe facts and avoid judging the attitudes of others. Judgment creates defensiveness and drives people away, while observation promotes connection. If, for example, you call a teammate selfish for shooting when the better option would have been to pass, you are judging her attitude, and she will tend to become defensive in response. But if you are genuinely curious and ask, "When you took the shot instead of passing to me, what was your thinking there?" then you will connect with your teammate and give her the chance to recognize and learn from her mistake. Or she might surprise you with her answer, suggesting a motivation different from the one you imagined.

Curiosity in others is the key. Questions allow us to gain new insights that inspire our own actions and behavior. We will not always get it right, and the other person will not always get it right. Faced with a mistake, it is important to have the sensitivity to apologize and, as mentioned in chapter 7, take it as an opportunity to learn about the relationship.

Dealing with Your Own Emotions

Investing in nonviolent communication is not an easy task, especially when we are overwhelmed by the heat of emotion, but it is precisely at these times when we should connect with our inner strength to regain control over our behavior and respond, instead of simply reacting, to each other.

When my teammates and I were on our way to compete for the bronze medal at the Pan American Championship in Winnipeg in 1999, our Cuban opponents' bus broke down. The Brazilian team kindly offered them a ride, and the two teams shared a bus to the aquatic complex. Along the way, the Cuban women turned toward us and started singing provocatively about how they would win the game. We could easily have reacted, which would have taken our focus off the game ahead. But we were not to be swayed and said nothing. Our response came a while later in the pool, with victory and the bronze medal. Mastering communication does not always mean giving a response. Silence can be worth a thousand words.

When, in the middle of a game, something truly got me mad, I took a deep breath to calm down and connect with the present moment and my deepest values. My father always told me, "The best way to respond to provocation during the game, be it physical or emotional, is to score a goal," encouraging me to channel the energy from my anger to my advantage.

In a contact sport, tempers often run high, and it takes discipline to master and channel those feelings toward achieving the main goal. This also applies to meetings in a corporate or family setting. As team captain, my father developed strategies to help other players with this process. If he sensed that one of his teammates was about to lose control, he would pull him to one side. "When you remove the audience, whether it be the crowd itself, the opponent, or anyone else who's around, you give the person a chance to connect with himself and with you and, thus, to calm down," he told me.

To get the teammate's attention, he would begin the conversation by highlighting something positive the person had done or reminding him of his strengths. This opened the channel of communication. Only then did he offer criticism, which was then followed by returning the focus to the shared goal: "Come on; if you can do this, we'll all get the benefit."

"Praise in public; criticize in private" was something my father always applied to sports, work, and family life.

In chapter 4, I talked about giving ourselves permission to be human and about the importance of accepting emotions and letting them flow through us without resisting. However, this does not mean we should allow our emotions to take over. It is essential that we learn control and keep our response in line with our goals and values.

Everyone should become familiar with his or her pressure-release valves and how to trigger them when the natural instinctive reaction is to explode. The more adversity we undergo, the more we build resilience and learn how to deal with these moments. This is why I push the importance of playing sport as a stage for life, as it allows us to continually practice self-control and, as a consequence, improve our communication skills. Constant practice and repetition allow us to evolve.

Leadership Roles

With the Brazilian national team, I noticed different reactions when the national anthem was played before the games. Players' different approaches to this dramatic point in proceedings have always been a subject of interest to me. For some, it was galvanizing. For others, it was such an emotional moment that it took their focus off the start of the game. Another key moment was when players made a mistake and got called out by their teammates. Some remained focused and did their best to make up for the goal conceded. Others got angry and reacted defensively, seeking to justify themselves.

Both as a team captain and as an executive, I developed my ability to recognize these individual differences, customizing communication to generate the best results. I paid close attention to each person's behavior in order to identify how to extract the best from everyone and encourage cohesion as a team. This was a full-time job, and there was always something to learn. I followed the same process with family relationships.

Adam Krikorian told me, "The best leader is the one who adapts his communication style. You need to be able to read a situation and provide what the group needs at that time. There are occasions when I am extremely vocal, with a commanding tone. At other times, I keep quiet and just watch the exchange between the players. Occasionally, I give directions, but I usually rely on asking questions, which make the players think and draw their own conclusions." He concluded, "This doesn't mean that I make the right decision every time, but I try to continually improve and learn from my experiences."

Leaders do not need to behave as if they know it all. Often, saying, "I don't know," is the best answer, as it allows for learning. When leaders have the courage to be vulnerable, they inspire their team to be curious and keep an open mind, which encourages a growth mentality.

Daniel Goleman is an internationally renowned psychologist and writer and a great scholar of emotional intelligence. He argues that a leader needs to develop three types of focus: inner, other, and outer. Inner focus is based on self-awareness and self-knowledge. Focusing on others is associated with the development of empathy at three levels: cognitive empathy, which involves understanding others' mental models (how they see the world and what they think about it); emotional empathy, which is associated with knowing what is going on with others (how they are feeling); and empathic concern, which is the ability to detect others' needs and have the genuine desire to help them. Finally, there is the focus on the outer, which refers to looking at the big picture and reconnecting with the objectives and goals underlying the behaviors and actions.

The leader should be someone who cares about others and the common cause of the group and who lives the role in an authentic and transparent manner. When I asked two-time Olympic bronze medalist judoka Leandro Guilheiro about his relationship with Coach João Gonçalves, he told me, "He was a real leader! He set an example for his discipline and dedication and for all his achievements both as an athlete [five Olympics, two as a swimmer and three in water polo] and coach [two Olympics as a judo coach]. He was also passionate about what he did, sharing fundamental truths through his actions and words. He was an inspiring leader who demonstrated his authority without being overbearing or arbitrary. He would read the situation and measure his words, either encouraging you or calling you out, as the situation required. I had great conversations with him. He was the first person I went to when I was thinking of changing division. He gave me his full attention and encouraged me to proceed with this new challenge."

In the 1994 soccer World Cup, Raí started the competition as team captain. He started three of the seven games. After the first phase, he was replaced by Mazinho and passed the captain's armband to Dunga, who went on to lift the trophy. He told me, "Many expected me to have a negative reaction, but I kept encouraging the team and continued to support the player who replaced me. I knew I had a leadership role on that team, which I had captained for three years. I've always preferred to lead through example."

When he returned from the World Cup, he was asked by a fellow player, "Raí, how did you manage to remain positive? I'll admit to you that when the coach switches me out, I feel so wronged that as much as I might want to, I can't support the team anymore."

Raí replied, smiling, "I'd rather have been the player who played in the first three games of a winning team than the one who exited a team that lost."

He told me this story while reinforcing what he considers the most important aspect of a leader: "understanding that the collective is more important than the individual."

Coaches, Parents, and Athletes

Families and coaches are important parts of the support network helping young sports players become high-performance athletes. The ideal situation is one in which coaches and parents work as a team, helping each child or adolescent to fulfill his or her potential.

It is important for parents to get involved in their children's sporting lives, but care is needed not to get too involved such that their involvement becomes an obstacle to the children's development. Parents often react to their children's reactions. Some get upset because they think the coach is being too hard on the children or because they disagree with the coach's decisions, such as not giving their children enough playing time.

The problem here is not necessarily the disagreements themselves but the way in which the disagreements are expressed and communicated. As I mentioned in chapter 4, helping children through adversity does not mean resolving everything for them but keeping an eye out and ensuring the children have the ways and means to deal with, and learn from, the situation by themselves.

Except in extreme cases, parents can usually encourage the young athletes to have their own conversations with the coach, so the children can hear for themselves what they need to do to improve. At the same time, when parents have an honest interaction with the coach and are fully open to hearing the bad as well as the good, they demonstrate a sense of partnership and trust in the process that is developing their children physically and mentally.

Coaches, on the other hand, can get the parents involved so that they feel like an integral part of the team leading their children along the path to excellence. Frank Steel, the head at Gulliver Schools, which has been named the Overall Best Sports Program by the *Miami Herald*

Athletic no fewer than nineteen times,[4] suggests that one way to achieve this is to engage parents in activities that are important but parallel to the technical side of the game. For example, the parents might help with transportation, food preparation, organization of the supporters, and events to raise money for road trips to other locations.

When I talked to Lewis Senior, he asked, "How often do parents and coaches, before the start of each season or cycle, align their goals and agree on responsibilities regarding the athletes' development?" These meetings could be productive in gaining mutual agreement among the parties, as happens in the corporate world when two departments set a joint target together. The success of this initiative depends on a joint effort, with the objectives and activities fully aligned.

Conflict between parents and coaches often arises from a lack of familiarity with the training process; the inherent demands of competitive sport; and the motivations behind the behavior of both parties, as highlighted above. These interactions at the beginning of a cycle serve to clarify different roles and share objectives. Coaches and family members are role models for youngsters, and this extends to the way the role models behave, communicate, and resolve conflicts among themselves.

The word *educate* has its etymological origin in Latin and comes from the word *ducere*, which means "to guide, conduct, or lead." In other words, educating people means guiding their development and leading them to fulfill their potential. When thinking about the key characteristics of mentors I had along my journey, I remember well the late Mauro Maugeri, coach of Orizzonte Catania. He used to communicate passionately, pushing me to my limits even during training, where I had the best time of my life, challenging me in a fun way. Maugeri contributed to my technical development by showing me different defensive positions for my body in the water and by asking about my dreams and motivations, with both the Italian and the Brazilian teams, which helped me to structure my thoughts and actions. He also shared his dreams and ambitions with the team, so we felt like partners and accomplices on a journey that required us to surpass the limits of body and mind. And we found joy in the process. This was one of the phases of my life when I trained the hardest, while also enjoying the team's company on unforgettable occasions, such as the Sant'Agata festival mentioned previously. This was how we developed a great connection out of the water, a level of intimacy that certainly was reflected in the performance in the water.

Communication should be appropriate to the athlete's stage of development, as mentioned in chapter 1. With adult athletes, the coach holds the leadership role and expresses confidence in the integrity of the communication, which facilitates teamwork. As communication is a two-way street, athletes play an active role in building the relationship among the entire team.

With his vast experience in basketball, having played for the Brazilian national team, European teams, and a stint in the NBA, Marcelinho Huertas has worked with many coaches with different styles. "The way to make demands, berate, train, or motivate, varies from one coach to the other, and the player needs to learn to adapt," he told me, suggesting we should not take things personally but should reflect on the message the coach wants to pass on, because the coach is just as keen to succeed as the player. "The idea is to stop and think. *What did he mean by that? Was he right? Maybe I should talk to him to clarify or talk to the technical assistant,* for example."

Marcelinho is an example of how an athlete with a solid background, one who has invested in gaining self-knowledge and developing his communication skills, has been able to adapt to any situation. "I have fond memories of all the coaches I have worked with. With all of them, I created a strong bond," he concluded.

Praise and Expectations

Carol Dweck, professor of psychology at Stanford University, found in her research that students who believed their intelligence could be developed performed better than those who believed intelligence was fixed. She referred to these two ways of thinking as the growth mindset and the fixed mindset, respectively, as discussed in chapter 1.

How parents, coaches, and teachers communicate with children and young people is crucial to the development of the growth mindset. The way they are praised—for example, in praising the effort to achieve a result rather than merely the intelligence and results—can stimulate one or the other way of thinking.

Her book *Mindset: The New Psychology of Success* is considered a classic of psychology that has influenced a whole generation of educators. However, in watching her theory being put into practice, Dweck observed some distortions to the way it was applied.

"Perhaps the most common misconception is simply equating the growth mindset with effort. Certainly, effort is key for students' achievement, but it's not the only thing. Students need to try new strategies and seek input from others when they're stuck. They need this repertoire of approaches—not just sheer effort—to learn and improve," she said in a recent review about the impact of her theory on education.[5]

Effort is a means of achieving the objectives of learning, improving at something, and getting results. Praising this effort when students are failing to learn should not be a way of comforting them. On the contrary, the idea is for the students to learn to direct their attention to what they need to do to develop their skills and overcome the challenges and obstacles that lie in their path.

In situations like this, instead of simply praising the effort, the adult can suggest, "Why don't we talk about what you've tried so far and what you can do differently next time?" The ability to develop a growth mindset and the confidence that we can learn something new is not only about how we are praised but also about the questions we ask, which focus us on the most important aspects of the situation.

Faced with a child who says, "I can't do this math. Math is not for me," the educator might say, "You're not able to do this math yet." *Yet* is a simple word, but it can be powerful, as it conveys the possibility of success. It reinforces the idea that we don't need to get everything right the first time but can accumulate knowledge step by step.

Tal Ben-Shahar, a professor at Harvard University who is a reference for positive psychology and leadership, told me how he stimulates the growth mentality in his children: "I don't usually look at their grades unless they decide to suddenly produce them, as I always tell them that it only matters to me that they work hard, regardless of the outcome. For example, when my youngest son was proud and pleased that he had got high marks for most subjects but was disappointed with a low score for one subject, I told him, 'Son, do you know what made me really happy? It wasn't your grades but the fact that you put in all that effort, spending your time doing something that is important and meaningful to you. That's what really matters to me.'"

When the external environment does not follow the same approach we believe in, such as, for example, when the school only focuses on achievements, Ben-Shahar suggests that parents emphasize the other extreme even more, by valuing the process. This way, children experience both aspects. "We shouldn't value purely the means or the processes, as the end results are also important. It is about getting a balance between the two, like a pendulum that sometimes swings to one side and sometimes to the other," he said.

All of this is true when we communicate with adults too—the conversation between coaches and athletes applies to that between corporate leaders and their teams. It is important that praise be genuine and feedback be truly based on the process and results of each person. Praise that is not borne out by reality can have an adverse effect, impacting people's self-esteem. When there is a difficulty, the focus should be on reviewing individuals' learning processes and helping them find the points of leverage that will enable them to develop.

In the 1960s, Robert Rosenthal, at the time a Harvard University professor, and Lenore Jacobson, the principal of an elementary school in San Francisco, conducted some research they called "Pygmalion in the Classroom."[6]

According to Greek mythology, Pygmalion was king of the island of Cyprus and a gifted sculptor. He once made a sculpture of a woman and became so enchanted with it that he fell in love with the statue. The goddess of love and beauty, Aphrodite, was so moved that she gave life to the statue, which became his beloved, Galatea. Among many interpretations, this myth represents the power our expectations can have on the behavior of other people, so that they end up becoming our preconceived image of them.

The researchers told the elementary school teachers that they had assessed all the children in a group and identified those with the greatest potential for learning, using an intelligence test. However, in fact, the choice had been random. At the end of the year, all the children were reassessed, and a significant improvement was recorded in the performances of those previously considered the best. In other words, the teachers' expectations had been self-fulfilling.

The way each educator communicates what he or she believes to a student or athlete creates fertile ground for new possibilities. It carries the same impact as having a mentor who believes in us, unveiling the potential for greatness in every human being. A great example of this was the North American educator Marva Collins. She used her own retirement fund to create a private elementary school in a poor neighborhood of Chicago. She assumed all students could be taught and were capable of overcoming their learning difficulties if she believed in them. "There is a brilliant child locked inside every student," she often said.

Her initiative was successful, with all her students graduating from elementary school, moving on to high school, and then entering college. In addition, Collins gained national recognition by being invited by US presidents Ronald Reagan and George W. Bush to become secretary of education. Collins declined, preferring to pursue her mission of helping each child to develop and fulfill his or her potential.

Two prominent scholars in leadership, Bruce Avolio and Fred Luthans, have demonstrated that the Pygmalion effect also occurs in the corporate environment. In *The High Impact Leader: Moments Matter in Accelerating Authentic Leadership Development*, they suggest that the expectations that managers place on employees, believing in their potential, translate into performance improvement at the level of both the individual and the organization.

The Impact of Positivity in Communication

The way we behave when hearing good news or about something that has gone well, whether from a spouse, friend, family member, or team member, is an important indicator of the success of the relationship.

According to research led by Shelly Gable, a psychologist and professor at the University of California, Santa Barbara, when someone tells us something important and positive—for example, that he or she received a promotion or won an important championship—we can react in four different ways: a destructive passive response (listening without eye contact, not paying attention, changing the subject, or talking about your own day or work); a destructive active response (highlighting negative aspects regarding the person's good news, such as "This new position will bring you more responsibilities. Can you handle it?" or "Now we are going to spend less time together"); a constructive passive response (nodding, smiling, agreeing, and moving on); or a constructive active response (demonstrating real interest, asking more questions, showing enthusiasm, and reinforcing the positive aspects by saying, for example, "Tell me how it happened," or "Let's celebrate!").

Responding positively and constructively to the good news your partner receives—whether a spouse, friend, colleague, or teammate—by acknowledging the other's joy and genuinely empathizing with him or her increases the well-being of both parties while also cultivating the resilience of the relationship in the long term. In other words, this type of response not only brings you together momentarily but also expands the period of happiness, creating stronger bonds.

In addition, the constructive active response, when used regularly, creates a virtuous circle in the relationship, which becomes better able to handle negative moments and disagreements (which exist in all relationships).

As mentioned in chapter 8, conflicts are important and allow relationships to mature, but they should be accompanied by a strong dose of positivity. The key in these moments is to accentuate the positive points that bring greater unity and joy to the relationship, instead of seeking to eliminate the negatives, the areas of disagreement. That is, we may not agree, and the issue may be something we will need to work out between us, but focusing on the many other positive things at the heart of the relationship will bring us closer.

It is possible to exercise the constructive active response on a daily basis. The more we show interest in something, the more interested we become. Behavior induces attitude, which becomes a habit.

Simple acts of communication, such as expressing interest in others, listening to them carefully, and demonstrating that we really care, can help transform a relationship into something deeper and longer lasting.

Good communication promotes deep exchanges that lead us to learn more about one another and about ourselves and allow us not only to accept but also to appreciate diversity and the disparity of interpretations and personalities. Through interpersonal relationships, we develop empathy and learn to listen and understand each other. This ability creates space for us to search for better solutions that benefit all of us in fulfilling our potential.

Main Points Covered in This Chapter

- Communication is the basis of trust, connection, and building relationships.
- The art of communicating depends on good emotional intelligence, which involves self-knowledge, knowledge of others, and empathy.
- Curiosity and genuine interest in others are fundamental to building positive relationships.
- Collaborative communication encourages people to base their opinions on the observation of facts, genuinely investigate others' needs, and avoid judging the attitudes and behaviors of others.
- The development of self-knowledge is the first step toward self-management, which leads us to *respond* in different ways, instead of simply *reacting* to situations that take us out of our comfort zone.
- A leader needs to develop three types of focus: inner, other, and outer. This is done through self-knowledge, empathy, and a process of reflection, connecting behaviors and actions to goals.
- The way parents, educators, and coaches relate and form partnerships sets an example for young people to follow and strengthens the support network.
- Praising effort contributes to greater self-esteem and a growth mindset, since talent and abilities can be developed. In addition to the praise being authentic, it is important for the educator to ask questions that identify when a new method or practice needs to be changed or introduced in order to achieve a better result.
- How we respond to news of positive events that others share with us is important in strengthening bonds and deepening relationships.

Powerful Questions to Reflect Upon

- What has been the impact of your communication on family members, colleagues, and teammates? Are you achieving the expected result?
- Have you been able to exercise self-control and respond rather than react during times of pressure and conflict?
- How can you respond with greater tolerance to and appreciation of ideas and opinions different from your own?
- How can you understand, without judging, other people's motivations during a negotiation, so that a positive result is achieved?
- How can you be a better mentor, educator, or manager to the people around you?
- Have you allowed yourself the time to listen actively to those close to you and those whom you love?
- How have you responded during moments of sharing good news?

CONCLUSIONS FROM DIMENSION 3:
COURAGE AND COLLABORATION

In this third part of the book, we saw that after creating a good support structure and connecting with our inner energy, it is necessary to act and collaborate in order to achieve excellence and happiness.

For this, it is necessary to have the courage to exit the comfort zone, curiosity, time to reflect, and openness to new experiences. It is important to accept—and even celebrate—mistakes as an inherent part of the learning process that leads to success.

To unlock our potential, our interpersonal connections represent a great means to develop emotional intelligence by teaching about team building, effective communication, and how to strengthen relationships.

In the WeTeam method, the focus is on raising awareness of how action is essential if we are to become the best version of ourselves. Self-knowledge and a genuine interest in others—along with effective, meaningful communication—lead to stronger relationships and positive results.

DIMENSION 4

———

MEANING AND CHOICES

CHAPTER 10

SELF-KNOWLEDGE: A DIVE INTO YOURSELF

> Know thyself and thou shalt know God and the
> universe. For if thou find not what thou seeketh first
> within thyself, nor will thy find it beyond.
> —Maxim from the temple of Delphi, Greece

> Self-knowledge is no guarantee of happiness, but it is on the
> side of happiness and can supply the courage to fight for it.
> —Simone de Beauvoir

Campeche Beach in Florianópolis, Brazil, is known for its intense waves, and on that morning, the sea was especially rough. Running along the sand, from afar, I saw a woman struggling in the water who seemed to be drowning. As I had done in similar situations with my father, I focused on not losing sight of her. As the sea swallowed her, I swam out to meet her.

When I took her arm, my first step was to make sure her head was out of the water, so she could breathe among the waves. A few seconds later, which felt like minutes, scared, she asked me, "Are your feet touching the seabed?"

As I was trained to support myself in the water thanks to water polo, I was able to calm her by holding her securely. Her question told me she had caught her breath and was ready for the next step. "I'm here to help. Now we'll get you out of the water!" I told her.

It was not easy. With each wave, we took advantage of that moment of inertia when we could swim toward the beach and gain a few more meters. Keeping her always by my side and pointing up from the sea, I realized she was fading. We managed to get as close as possible to the sand, when others on the beach began to understand the situation and came out to meet us.

At the time, I was in Florianópolis to take a course in anthroposophy, and the person drowning was one of my colleagues. "You are my guardian angel. Thank you for saving my life," she said to me the morning after.

Introduced by Austrian philosopher Rudolf Steiner at the beginning of the twentieth century, anthroposophy is a field of knowledge applied to diverse areas, such as health, agriculture, education, and personal and organizational development. It unites the conventional scientific method with spiritual aspects and, in this way, seeks to understand the nature of *Homo sapiens* and the universe. The term *anthroposophy* has etymological origins in the Greek words *anthropos*, which means "man," and *sophia*, which means "wisdom."

I came across this philosophy when, at the age of thirty-seven, I had two daughters and was working full-on at the bank. In the search for a new paradigm to enhance my knowledge of human beings and to better balance my personal and professional lives, I became interested in the biographical method, which is based on anthroposophical medicine. With this approach, life cycles are divided into septennia—periods of seven years—which contain archetypal situations that most people face. In the first seven years of life, for example, we begin to develop the view we have of ourselves and the world, which will form the basis of our self-confidence. If the images formed are positive, children will feel disposed to explore who they are and to experience the pleasure of being alive, and this will stay with them throughout life.

When I entered the water to save my colleague, all the experiences I had had in my first septennium, such as the sea adventures with my father and his lessons about respecting nature, came back to me and made even more sense. I felt a tremendous sense of achievement on realizing that my previous experiences had culminated in my being able to help someone.

At that time, I was in the middle of my sixth septennium, which runs from ages thirty-five to forty-two. According to anthroposophy, this is the stage in which we connect with our essence and focus on what makes sense to us in living according to what we believe in. For me, it was a relentless quest to improve and develop as a person.

I decided to dive headlong into this new perspective on human beings. It was a time when I was rediscovering art, through paintings, pottery, and sculpture, and in which I explored concepts about spirituality, met different people, and embraced completely new experiences.

The biographical method encourages us to take an objective look back at our own experiences, tracing our path and distinguishing things that are common to others who go through the same phase (the archetypal) from those that are unique to us personally. For me, it was a great opportunity to deepen my self-knowledge by adding a different perspective.

Regardless of the approach chosen, I believe it is important that we use our past as a source to understand the present and plan the future. Guided by curiosity and seeking to learn from both our mistakes and our successes, we can identify our strengths and limitations, reframe experiences, and connect with our truth. This process increases our awareness of the power of the freedom of choice we have over our actions.

All the experiences we go through in life are opportunities to know ourselves better. There are times when we focus our attention on action and other times when we focus on reflection, and thus we build a virtuous circle for awakening our true potential.

There are several strategies we can use to engage in a more active process of self-awareness and self-knowledge, such as taking self-development courses, studying, reading, or seeking support from a professional. It is also positive when we allow ourselves time to reflect on situations that took place during the day, sharing them with a partner, family member, or friend or by keeping a diary. The important thing is to find the path that makes sense to each of us and to remain open to new experiences on our journey through life.

Life Is a Journey of Learning and Self-Knowledge

In the past, neuroscientists believed the brain's ability to be malleable and mold itself to new experiences was a phenomenon reserved exclusively for childhood. In other words, they assumed there was not much possibility of changing our abilities or general behavior after adulthood. However, during the past twenty years, neuroscience has identified that this brain plasticity is present throughout our lives until the day we die. The brain and the environment thus mold each other throughout our journey.

The starting point for being able to change the course of our lives at any moment is believing in the change. This concept, prominent in modern science, has been around for centuries in the philosophy of Buddhism, which talks about meditation as a basis for the temporary nature of things, as we see in the different seasons and changes to the trees and the scenery. By recognizing the impermanence of things with relation to ourselves, we develop our potential to learn and grow.

Mahatma Gandhi once said, "Men often become what they believe themselves to be. If I believe I cannot do something, it makes me incapable of doing it. But when I believe I can, then I acquire the ability to do it even if I didn't have it in the beginning."

These changes are not necessarily sudden, with major disruption, but can occur gradually and almost imperceptibly in everyday life. When we look at our past, we notice how much we have been able to change.

Self-knowledge is fundamental for rediscovering our essence during these natural transformations and for leading the changes toward fulfilling our potential. Moments of reflection on our experiences allow us to identify the points of leverage—the moments that proved the difference in promoting change—that allowed us to grow and evolve as a whole.

Water polo player Brenda Villa, voted Player of the Decade for 2000–2010 by the International Swimming Federation (FINA), climbed the podium at four Olympics with the American women's water polo team. Revisiting these experiences allowed her to take a dip into her self-knowledge.

She said, "At the first one, in Sydney 2000, I was so happy to be there that I only really dreamed of becoming an Olympic champion when I was on the podium, holding the silver medal. In Athens 2004, the situation was different. We had won the world championship and were the favorites, but things didn't turn out as we would have liked, as we lost the semifinal. And what was most beautiful about this experience is that we came back and fought for third place with the same determination! Our goal was to win it all, but when you realize you can't reach your goal, it's so easy to stop caring. But we didn't. We pulled ourselves together and fought until the end in the fight for bronze. I am very grateful for this lesson, which I have carried throughout my life."

In Beijing in 2008, the US team took silver, but Brenda says they were disappointed and did not celebrate finishing second. She felt the main lesson from the experience was that we should always honor our history, regardless of the results achieved. That was what motivated her to play on for another four years, culminating in her taking gold at the 2012 Olympics in London. She told me, "I didn't want my final experience to be negative—not because of the silver medal but for the fact this would not have allowed us to feel the pride of the whole journey to get there." After the gold, she was honored in her hometown when they named the pool at which she began her water polo training after her. There she experienced a sense of plenitude at fulfilling her dreams and receiving the gratitude of the community who had supported her from the beginning.

Brenda then decided to make a career transition. She became a coach, working to support inclusion and diversity in water sports. This decision followed some reflection during her final years of playing the sport she loved so much. Although she still loved to compete, the fun she used to get from training had faded.

When we stay alert, open, and curious, monitoring ourselves as we go, we have the chance to assess when the time is right to make changes and realign ourselves with new goals.

The Spiral Theory of Knowledge

American sprinter Allyson Felix was also a medalist in five Olympics. When she qualified for Athens in 2004, she was only eighteen years old. She said, "I took all I could from that wonderful experience—the opening ceremony, being in the Olympic village, watching athletes I admired in the cafeteria. At race time, there wasn't that much pressure on me.

I craved the gold but ended up taking the silver. I remember talking to my coach and he said, 'To achieve something great, in the right way and with integrity, takes time and patience.' That was my greatest lesson. I took the decision right there that I would dedicate myself even more to my dream."[1]

Over the next four years, Felix committed to putting in the extra work needed to win. At the 2008 Beijing Olympics, there was a greater burden of expectation on her to win. She said, "I had sponsors, I was the favorite, and I wanted to show the world that I was much faster." She took the silver medal again and was extremely disappointed not to land the gold. "I was devastated. I thought I had done everything I needed to do to be champion. How could this have gone so wrong?" The lesson she took from this experience was to pay more attention to the details. "As soon as I got my bearings, I started looking at the aspects that I could improve, such as diet, and my choice of team. We made all the changes necessary to improve for the next cycle."

In London in 2012, she became an individual Olympic champion, winning gold in her favorite event: the two hundred meters. In that same Olympics, she won two more gold medals, in the 4×100-meter and 4×400-meter relays. In addition to consistent training and the extra care she took in preparing to reach her third Olympics, she deployed a different strategy for her stay at the event. In London, she decided to create an environment that made her feel at home, as that was important to her. "I didn't stay in the Olympic village but in an apartment nearby, while my parents stayed in a house a few blocks away. It was my mother who prepared my food. I had my family there, and some friends came to watch me too. We created a relaxing atmosphere," she said.

Amid the celebration of her victories in 2012, Felix realized the magic really had happened along the way. "Those eight years it took me to get there were the ones in which I grew up and became the person I wanted to be."

Two months before qualifying for Rio in 2016, she suffered an ankle injury, which meant she missed out on the two hundred meters. However, even hurt, she achieved the qualifying time to compete in the four hundred meters. She said, "From that moment on, I didn't have time to feel bad or regret it. I made just one decision—to give it my all and see it through." The lesson in 2016 was about coping with adversity. The past year had been difficult in her personal life too, as she had lost not only her grandparents but also her dog. "I wasn't 100 percent. It was far from ideal. And what I learned is that we must keep fighting. We cannot give up." Felix took silver in the four hundred meters and won two more gold medals in the 4×100-meter and 4×400-meter relays.

At thirty-five, and after becoming a mother for the first time with Camryn, who was born prematurely via a risky cesarean in November 2018, Felix excelled again. At the Olympics in Tokyo in 2020, she took bronze in the four hundred meters and won gold in the 4×400-meter relay, becoming the athlete who has won the most track-and-field gold medals in Olympic history, surpassing even the great Carl Lewis. "This one is very different, and it's very special. And it just took a lot to get here," she said, referring to, among other factors, the public's own distrust. "I think people thought it was a long shot for me to even be on the US team. And then I wasn't a pick for the medals. But you know, just give me a shot," she added.

The process of self-knowledge does not follow a linear path but one that is more like a spiral, in the shape of a coil. We follow the spiral around until at some point, we learn the same thing but to a greater depth of understanding. The accounts of Brenda Villa and Allyson Felix are examples of this, even though they describe participating in the same event, the Olympics. Each experience was unique, and with each new experience, followed by a period of reflection, the athletes gained an extra layer of knowledge and self-awareness.

The structure of this book and of the work methodology—the WeTeam method—have been designed in this spiral format. I did not collect several theories randomly, because that would not have built a concept that could easily be put into practice. Each chapter and theme is part of building the spiral of knowledge. Everything is connected.

The spiral theory of knowledge is related to engagement in profound learning, which applies lessons from scientific and philosophical research, teachings of the great masters and popular wisdom, and the knowledge we acquire through *mesearch*, research we carry out on ourselves, in identifying what works for us.

Research involving statistical data gathered on the average of a population allows us to learn how to achieve a better quality of life, for example, by reading about the importance of nutrition, sleep, and exercise. Mesearch, on the other hand, allows us to identify what we should spend more time doing in our lives, how we should do it, and for how long. It is the tool that tells us which element we need to prioritize in order to improve our health and well-being.

I am currently experimenting with removing gluten from my diet. I feel more energy and enthusiasm. Whenever I hear about an interesting study, I will sit and think about trialing it, put it into practice, check the results, and then reflect on whether to incorporate the change into my routine. For years now, I have been using breathing exercises as a means of boosting and accessing my energy reservoirs, but after watching a documentary about Wim Hof, mentioned in chapter 6, and having studied his training methods, which involve cold therapy and breathing, I appreciate daily cold showers and dips in icy waters whenever I get the opportunity.

I have also had some experiences in which I did not adapt well, such as intermittent fasting, in which prolonged periods of fasting are interspersed with periods of eating. I know many people have benefitted from this dietary strategy, but for me, it did not work out at this point in my life. The important thing, as in any learning process, is to be curious enough to explore a new idea and, if it makes sense to you, to be open to trying it and identifying the lessons learned.

When we grow comfortable, we often stop experimenting and, thus, stop challenging ourselves to explore our limits and our potential. By investing in self-knowledge, we become more aware and deliberate in our choices and can reap the benefits as we pursue our purpose and happiness.

The Power of Questions

Once, as part of a group dynamic focused on the players' self-awareness, our coach, Sandy, asked all of us to write down what our main strengths and potential limiters were. Sandy watched as I scribbled down what I considered my best qualities: focusing on learning, pursuing self-improvement, building a high-performance team, and being a perfectionist. She then asked me, "Do you think being a perfectionist is always something positive?"

My eyes widened, and I swallowed hard, confused. She did not say another word but smiled and left to look at the other players' notes. I was speechless. Up to then, I had always prided myself on my perfectionism, but I had never stopped to think about the pros and cons of relentlessly pursuing perfection. Was achieving perfection really possible? Did we need to attempt perfection in everything we did? And at what cost?

Today I am aware that I need to pay attention to my perfectionism and my tendency to place excessive demands on myself and those around me. Because of that simple question raised many years ago, I have had the chance to reflect on how this characteristic has impacted myself, my daughters, my husband, teammates, employees, and colleagues. This has freed me to stay alert and focus my energy on what really matters, to the appropriate degree, without losing sight of the circumstances and limitations of each person involved.

The following saying is attributed to physicist Albert Einstein: "If I had an hour to solve a problem and my life depended on the solution, I would spend the first fifty-five minutes determining the right question to ask, because once I found it, I could solve the problem in less than five minutes." Asking the right questions is much more important than providing an answer. My coach could have given her opinion on perfectionism but instead chose a simple question, which led me to reconsider my views on a subject, to the extent that it still influences my actions today.

It is not a process of simple interrogation but, rather, one of inquiry that provokes reflection and directs attention to the key aspects to be explored, thus promoting learning. Probing questions open the doors to dialogue and discovery, inviting creativity and innovation and leading to action. They can trigger small changes that bring profound results. In addition, they are powerful tools for developing self-knowledge and help establish good communication and deeper relationships. Thus, it is important we also ask probing questions of ourselves.

Arno Penzias, who, like Einstein, won the Nobel Prize for physics, told a conference on innovation, "When I get up in the morning, the first thing I ask myself is *Why do I still believe so firmly in what I believe?*"

His statement reflected the importance of questioning ourselves and our convictions in keeping creativity alive.[2]

Our attention is directed by the things we choose to ask ourselves and those around us. The questions we ask create our reality. They work like a spotlight illuminating a single corner. The essence of self-knowledge is in learning about ourselves and which situations, mental states, and behaviors are associated with our best performance and the awakening of our potential.

How can we discover what works for us? Through probing questions that focus our attention on these aspects: *What is going well in my life? What gives me energy? What inspires me? What am I doing well? What am I evolving into? What am I grateful for?* This type of self-analysis also functions at the group or organizational level. *What are we doing as a team that is working?*

The questions we ask ourselves and each other may initially be more generic but become more specific as we gather information about a particular topic. Thus, our knowledge evolves as we climb the spiral.

When I talked to Tal Ben-Shahar, he mentioned that he is also a perfectionist, but he pointed out that there are two types of perfectionism: adaptive and dysfunctional. The first leads us to be responsible, reliable, and dedicated to constantly improving in order to achieve our goals. The second is related to an intense and obsessive fear of failure, such that we become afraid to try anything and end up living under the precept of "All or nothing." In the second situation, people hide behind a mask, which makes it hard for them to really connect with others, as they are too focused on the need to maintain an image of perfection.

Then he said, "In the past, when people said I needed to work on my perfectionism, I thought, *But I don't want to lose it.* I think a lot of my perfectionist traits lie behind my success. When I understood that there was this difference, it became clearer to me that I could identify the specific aspects that I would need to change." After our conversation, I was able to ask myself more specific questions, which have taken me to another level of self-knowledge: *Which points in my perfectionism have been positive?*

Irrational Thoughts

According to cognitive therapy, developed by American psychiatrist Aaron Beck, the way we think or interpret situations impacts our emotions and, thus, our behavior when we act. Imagine two athletes with the same levels of skill and preparation for a given competition. When they arrive, they can see that the weather conditions are not good. Athlete A thinks, *I hate this sort of weather. I can't do my best today.* Athlete B, on the other hand, thinks, *I'm glad I've trained in different conditions. I'm prepared for this.*

Despite being equally prepared, the athletes will feel very different during the competition. A's thoughts will likely cause him to feel anxious, while B will feel encouraged and excited. How they think and feel will affect their behavior and performance.

The principle of cognitive therapy is to recognize that it is not necessarily the events themselves that impact us but, rather, how we interpret them. If you start looking at things from different perspectives, reflecting on your interpretation, you can change the way you feel and act.

What causes one person to feel fear and anxiety, while the other feels excited and encouraged? Why does one feel threatened, while the other feels challenged?

When we talk about something as complex as human behavior, our thoughts are like points of leverage that offer us tips on how and where to act. They are a little piece of a whole, and if we make a tiny change, we generate a significant transformation to the entire system. It is not about eliminating negative emotions, because these feelings are legitimate. It is about restoring rationality. After all, most of the time, our interpretation of a situation happens automatically, and we do not always realize how irrational it can be.

Among the most common irrational interpretations is the tendency to maximize negative experiences, minimize positive ones, or invent an explanation that seems plausible for dealing with a challenging situation. Ben-Shahar refers to them as the three Ms: *magnify*, *minimize*, and *make up*.

Magnifying refers to exaggerating the significance of a situation or seeing it as a harbinger of catastrophe. For example, when a player misses a penalty, he might think, *I will never score a penalty. I am terrible at shooting.* Minimizing relates to the tendency to ignore the bigger picture and focus on just one aspect. Imagine a player scores five goals in a match but gives the ball away for a goal on the counterattack. He might think, *How could I give that ball away? I'm not good enough*, ignoring his performance in the rest of the game. For the third *M*, we invent some rationalization or make up our own version of reality in order to alleviate the stress of a difficult situation or, alternatively, to punish ourselves. For example, a player might think, *It is my fault the team lost*, when we know that in reality, there are many factors involved in a loss.

The antidote to these tendencies is to be aware of them and to challenge these thoughts as to whether they represent an objective interpretation of reality. To do this, we need to gain a broader perspective of the situation. Some questions we might ask ourselves in this process include the following: *Does my conclusion represent reality? Is it rational? Am I missing something important? What other factors should be taken into account?* Act like your own lawyer, looking for evidence to build your case. Questions create our reality.

This is an exercise that requires practice, but the more we do it, the better we become. We can even teach our children to do this from an early age. Karen Reivich, a psychologist at the University of Pennsylvania, demonstrated the positive effects in a study teaching teenagers to recognize and distinguish rational from irrational thoughts. The result was a 50 percent reduction in the chance of developing depression in later years compared to other teenagers in the study.

Rational thinking is associated with expansion, with looking at the big picture and seeing reality as it is. This process of reframing our thoughts is related to the language and words we use to describe an event. By changing the words with which we assess or interpret a situation, we can change our emotional state and, consequently, our actions.

Educators and parents can help young people reframe experiences with simple observations, such as one Tal Ben-Shahar told me: "I was watching my oldest son's basketball practice, when a younger boy came over and started ragging on him. I could see my son getting upset. He came over to me, and I said, 'Son, this boy is here to help you deal with the distractions.' And then his attitude changed completely. He knew that developing his ability to focus would be essential for the upcoming tournaments." With this one observation, he helped give his son a different meaning to the situation.

Listening to the Emotions

John Gottman, one of the leading lights in the study of emotional intelligence, puts it thusly: "In the last decade, science has made many discoveries and advances regarding the role that emotions play in our lives. Researchers have found that more than IQ (intelligence quotient), emotional awareness and our ability to deal with emotions are determinants of success and happiness in all walks of life."[3]

Emotions are not indicative of who we are and do not necessarily lead us to the truth. The point is to listen to what they are telling us rather than to do exactly what they are telling us.

Take fear as an example. When we feel fear at the top of a cliff, our emotion is a wake-up call to be careful. When we feel fear before making a public presentation or before a match, this signals that we are about to do something of great importance to us. Listening to and interpreting what our emotions are telling us is essential for us to be able to interpret and reframe our experiences. We can do this through having internal dialogue, keeping a journal, or talking to a friend. Painful emotions lead us to limit our scope so we can focus and overcome the challenge ahead as quickly as possible. This is a survival mechanism, because if we are facing an imminent threat, we should be focusing on the threat and nothing else. Joyful emotions, on the other hand, broaden our perspective of situations, making us more open to forming new connections, to appreciating the moment, and to interacting with other tribes. By experiencing and learning to interpret our emotions, we increase our abilities and self-awareness.

Zooming In and Zooming Out

In order to make important decisions in our lives, we need to gain different perspectives so as to get a complete picture and analyze the best alternatives. How should we do this?

Benita Willis is an Australian long-distance runner who participated in four Olympics—between 2000 and 2012—and was a gold medalist at the World Athletics Cross Country Championship held in Brussels in 2004. While conducting self-analysis of her career in an interview, she talked up the importance of working on the mental aspects of what she did: "When we talk about the top-level marathon-runners, the physical capabilities are very similar. The person who wins is the one who gets it right on the day mentally. I would say that in big races the mental component outweighs the physical component."[4]

She attributes the coach as having an important role in this regard: "He's there to make sure you stay in shape, to prepare you mentally for tough races, to hear how you feel day after day, and to help you make decisions about skipping training if you're feeling tired. This was essential when I was training for a marathon, as I ran an average of 180km per week. With such intense training you feel tired almost every day, but we need to differentiate between normal tiredness and fatigue that stems from overtraining. A good trainer can help you with that!"

As an athlete, even though you are engaged on the athletic field, you still need to be able to observe the race or game as a whole. Harvard University professor Ronald Heifetz uses a metaphor to highlight the importance of these two perspectives, which he suggests are key to adaptive leadership, referring to them as the dance floor and the balcony. When we are on the dance floor, we are in the middle of the action, and our focus is on what we are doing, as we perceive only what is immediately around us. When we go up to the balcony and observe things from above, we get the bigger picture.

Examples of when we are on the dance floor are moments when we are connected with the here and now, or are in the flow state—meditation in action. When we are in the balcony, we observe the bigger picture and reflect on the best operating strategy, which allows us to make decisions that increase our chance of success.

Finding the balance between these two perspectives is important. Taking a step back—like zooming out of a scene in a movie—allows us to reflect strategically on the situation. Zooming in, focusing on the present moment and practicing mindfulness, allows us to act at the correct time for the situation we are facing.

Switching to the balcony is not always an easy task. Benita Willis emphasizes the importance of her coach in helping her to get an overview of the situation and her place in it and in figuring out what is to be done. This role does not necessarily have to be carried out by a coach; it could be anyone close to you. But it can be essential in helping you get another point of view.

We can develop this ability of navigating between the dance floor and the balcony through practice and maturity. Psychological maturity stems precisely from our ability to change perspective freely and deliberately, choosing between engaging in the here and now and projecting ourselves in time and space in order to take in the big picture.

Complementary to this concept is some famous research carried out in the 1960s by renowned professor and psychologist Walter Mischel,[13] who studied the effect of delayed gratification and self-control. In the study, Mischel analyzed the responses of young children who were offered either a single marshmallow at that moment or the promise of two marshmallows if they waited ten to twenty minutes.

Some of the little ones were able to wait, while others succumbed to temptation and chose the immediate reward. The research followed up by investigating how the participants were faring thirty years on. The indications were that children who had waited to receive the bonus marshmallow were more successful in life as adults across a range of domains: they performed better at school and at work; were more likely to have overcome personal and professional challenges; and had better health and lower body fat.

That is, those who, from an early age, displayed an ability to base their choice on a wider context rather than on immediate reward also displayed a range of positive attributes in later life. This does not necessarily mean we should always push back immediate pleasures into the longer term, as we may never get to enjoy them. Rather, the idea is to make choices that consider the bigger picture, even if it means delaying the rewards for a while. Important in concluding Mischel's study is how we can teach greater self-control and analysis of the decision-making process.

---

[13] Walter Mischel lectured at the University of Colorado (1956–1958), at Harvard University (1958–1962), and at Stanford University (1962–1983). Since 1983, he has been with the Department of Psychology at Columbia University.

What Adversity Teaches Us about Ourselves

Leandro Guilheiro, a Brazilian judoka who was a medalist in two Olympics, told me that the way he responded to moments of frustration and defeat throughout his career changed. He said, "When I was younger, I dealt very badly with defeat. I kept looking for someone else to blame, abdicating responsibility. As I matured, I accepted responsibility, started to deal better with frustrations, and became a more balanced individual. However, as part of this process, I noticed that I—who was used to being a fighter in every sense—was losing some momentum, some of that outrage in defeat, and that wasn't good either. So I found a balance. The best way to handle defeat is to feel the outrage but channel it so that you do your best to keep improving."

Morgan McCall, professor emeritus at the University of South California and author of the book *High Flyers: Developing the Next Generation of Leaders*, identified a common element among successful leaders: the kind of experiences they underwent before reaching their present position. All of them had endured hardship, difficulties, and challenges before assuming leadership roles. He argues that personal development is accelerated when we persist in the face of difficulties.

An athlete practices every day so he or she can hone or develop a new skill. Athletes often experience pain, which is part of their learning and hardening process. There is physical pain, such as when weight training, completing a long-distance swim in a given time, or doing shuttle runs in a beep test. When the sport being played is meaningful to the athlete, even if the physical pain remains, the mental pain can be transformed. There is satisfaction in having made progress, in having completed the training, or in having put in the additional physical effort until the end. There is a process in which the physical pain is redefined and becomes a challenge to be overcome—one for which there is great motivation.

Throughout this book, we have reflected on how adversity can be viewed as an opportunity for learning and growth. Adversity shapes us while also teaching us a great deal.

Putting this subject into a family context, it is important that parents allow their children, within limits, to experience the challenging situations and emotions that arise in their lives—such as sadness, anxiety, frustration, and fear—in order to grow and flourish. Without these difficulties, it is the equivalent of going to a gym where all the weights are set close to zero. Psychological muscles need hardship, challenges, and obstacles if they are to develop. Learning the theory of swimming cannot replace the need to swim.

It is hard for parents to watch their children suffer, but it serves the all-important function of helping the children to develop the skills needed to overcome the inherent ups and downs in life. Allowing children to deal with adversity is also a way of enabling them to experience the feeling of achievement and success that comes from overcoming the odds and pulling through with all they learned along the way. Such experiences, and the emotions that come with them, live on in the memory and engender a positive self-image, self-esteem, and courage to face future challenges.

Parents, like educators and managers, need to be involved in the process of promoting and supporting change when needed. Every individual, even those in the same family, has different development needs. The focus should be on identifying what is important—that is, the point of leverage for developing potential. Some may need greater encouragement in achieving their goals, others may need clearer boundaries, and others may need love and understanding. It is always worth remembering that the way parents, leaders, and other authority figures deal with different situations sets an example and is an inspiration to those watching.

As Tal Ben-Shahar illustrated well in our conversation, "When we cry, we also stop crying. We learn to overcome sadness. But if we don't cry, we don't learn how to stop crying or how to overcome sadness."

Be Authentic

When I won the best player award and was top scorer in a championship, I was bursting with happiness. I could not wait to celebrate with my teammates. But I noticed that one person in particular, a great friend and part of my team, did not come to celebrate with me. That made me profoundly sad. I still remember my father's words: "Cris, don't feel guilty for being happy! There are times when people celebrate with you, but it does not always work out that way. We cannot control the reactions of others, so we should not try to leave our celebrations and dreams in the hands of others in the hope that they will validate us."

To this day, I carry this lesson about the importance of being authentic. Each day, we should practice trying to set aside who we think we are supposed to be in order to enjoy being who we are. Being authentic does not necessarily come naturally but often depends on making the conscious decision to live the way we want to live and be who we want to be, no matter how vulnerable we may feel at times.

To be authentic is to be connected to our essence, acting in a manner that is consistent with our goals and values. To get there, the first step is self-knowledge.

Self-knowledge and continuous learning are vital concepts that cut across all spheres in the pursuit of a full and fulfilling life. The process of learning about ourselves runs throughout our journey. And this process involves continually interspersing moments of action and experimentation with moments of reflection and introspection, in which we broaden our self-awareness.

Main Points Covered in This Chapter

- Change is the only certainty in our lives. Self-knowledge is essential for us to find our essence and drive changes that lead to a fulfilling life.

- The process of self-knowledge is not linear but, rather, a spiral. As we advance toward mastering a skill, we build on previous lessons learned, reaching, at each stage, a greater level of depth and understanding.

- Probing questions are powerful tools for building self-knowledge and enabling others to learn more about you.

- By learning to challenge our own thoughts in terms of rationality and whether they represent an objective interpretation of reality, we can better regulate our emotions and actions.

- Living in the here and now interspersed with stepping back from situations—zooming in and zooming out—is essential for generating perspectives that guide better decisions.

- It is important for parents to allow their children to experience hardships and challenging situations that may cause painful emotions. Dealing with adversity contributes to self-awareness, self-esteem, and personal growth, strengthening our psychological muscles.

- To be authentic is to be connected to our essence, acting in a manner that is consistent with our goals and values.

- Self-knowledge and continuous learning are vital concepts that cut across all spheres in the pursuit of excellence and happiness.

- Have you found moments in your day to reflect on your experiences and responses to specific situations as a means to deepen your self-knowledge?
- What is going well in your life? What is working? What are you doing well?
- What are you doing as a team or family that has worked?
- Are the choices in your life aligned to your essence?
- What have moments of pleasure, joy, or success taught you? What about the moments of pain?
- Have you thought about how you interpreted reality during times of frustration? Have you been acting as your own defense attorney in order to identify different perspectives on the situations you have experienced? What other factors might you need to consider?

CHAPTER 11

A LIFE WITH **PURPOSE** ALIGNED TO YOUR **VALUES**

Life is never made unbearable by circumstances
but only by lack of meaning and purpose.
—Viktor Frankl

When one door of happiness closes, another opens;
but often we look so long at the closed door that we do
not see the one which has been opened for us.
—Helen Keller

"Japan, after fifteen days of traveling, was the first time I felt that extraordinary sensation. It was at the height of the Cold War. In Brazil, there was a military dictatorship. The threat of nuclear war was real. When we arrived in Tokyo to compete in the 1964 Olympic Games, the reality check was intense. There were no borders. It felt like another world, where respect, solidarity, and diversity filled the air. When we were all stood together in that dark tunnel, side by side with athletes from so many other sports and nationalities, we had no idea of the emotion we would feel when we entered the stadium and received the ovation from the fans. The rumbling, the waving of scarves, the swirl of the Japanese umbrellas distributed to the crowd—it all made everything perfect. The Olympic flame was lit by Yoshinori Sakai, an athlete born on the day the atomic bomb landed on Hiroshima. Emperor Showa watched over this symbolic gesture of peace."

I remember my father, who participated in the Olympics in Tokyo in 1964 and Mexico City in 1968, telling these stories to my brothers and me on our way to watch the sunrise at the beach, in the afternoons by the pool, or especially at Sunday lunch. He was inspiring. He told us stories that brought to life the Olympic values and how they helped his dreams to crystallize, placing excellence center stage in the pursuit of his goals. The Olympic ideal brought him a sense of purpose. He gave us all the details, from the social occasions and sporting traditions of each country to becoming a high-performance athlete, struggling for the podium, and constantly striving to reach beyond what he thought possible. Every time I heard him describe the Olympic village, I was instantly transported there, imagining myself amid the excitement and color.

"It was an environment totally free from any political, racial, or religious doctrine. Everyone was happy for what they represented. Some were more passionate in their dealings, while others were more relaxed, but more than anything, they all knew they were experiencing one of the greatest ideals of youth," he said.

My brothers and I were thrilled with these stories, which shaped our values for life. My father was always good at telling stories, making them fun, and he oozed passion for sport and the Olympic spirit. From his recounting his experiences, we started to form our own dreams and think about how we might get there. That is not to say everything was easy or without trial-and-error and some twists along the way.

When I started playing as a pioneer in a sport my parents and grandparents knew and loved, they would automatically come to support me. I felt as if I were living in a movie my father had described to me many times. This family involvement—all of us together with the goal of building a new sport—gave the experience a great a sense of meaning.

In 1992, our family attended the Barcelona Olympics. I got to experience firsthand much of what my father had described. We would get up at seven in the morning so we could follow as many different events as possible. We watched the American basketball Dream Team and the heats and semifinals of the best athletes in athletics, volleyball, swimming, water polo, and judo. We watched only a few finals, as tickets were much more expensive, but we got to savor the athletes' ultimate struggles and the thrill of seeing them climb the podium after many years of dedication. Just by being there, they were all winners in our eyes. We admired every detail and ritual, trying to interpret the meaning of every expression each athlete made. My parents discussed and pointed out the details of every sport to us: the uniforms, the presentation of the teams and their national anthems, the different ways they gathered themselves before a race, the explosion of energy that launched them into peak performance, and more. I felt the joy of being among the best in the world while also taking in the cultural and historical side of an Olympic Games. At the time, I was already a professional athlete, playing in Italy. But women's water polo was not yet an Olympic sport, which just made my dream burn more fiercely within me.

At the opening ceremony, when we saw the torch on the big screen, passing from hand to hand through the streets of Barcelona before finally entering the stadium, the thrill was so great that we were as breathless as the many participants actually taking part in the symbolic ceremony. At the point the Olympic flame was to be lit by archer Antonio Rebollo, my brothers and I held hands. Suddenly, all the stories we had heard made sense, and we were ready to live these values through our own journeys. The ceremony ended with soprano Montserrat Caballé singing in Catalan "Amics per Sempre" (Friends Forever), a song written for the 1992 Summer Olympics.

The experience left a deep impression on me, and the Olympic paradigm still guides my family in whatever we may be doing, professionally or otherwise.

Years later, I went with my three daughters to watch the games in Rio in 2016, and they too had a chance to experience those same feelings and meaning. Whether it be in sport or in the dreams they choose to follow, these lessons will help them build relationships, pursue a cause, and overcome the challenges in their path.

Inspiring Purpose

Once people identify their purpose, which varies according to their stage in life, they have a greater chance of working autonomously toward their goal. How can we encourage people to find meaning in what they do?

William Damon, a professor at Stanford University and director of the Stanford Center on Adolescence, is one of the world's leading scholars in human development. In his book *The Path to Purpose: How Young People Find Their Calling in Life*, he reports that young people have shown increasing levels of anxiety compared to previous generations. Only one-fifth are actually engaged in activities they describe as productive and pleasurable, and this proportion has been declining over the years. Damon found that the main ingredient for young adults is to have a clear sense of purpose in their lives that motivates them and gives them direction.

A sense of purpose is not something that develops through explicit instruction or that can be imposed. It arises from inspiration. It is not enough to tell children or students that they need to find meaning in what they do. The parent or educator needs to shine the light. The young need to be able to see those they admire striving passionately to achieve their goals.

I used to see how dedicated my father was in managing Grupo Folha, which edits the *Folha de São Paulo* newspaper. He would be all over the technological challenges, debating us about well-written articles, teaching us the value of freedom of expression for the development of a country, and praising the efficiency of the new printing machines.

I was young when he finished his water polo career, but his passion for sport continued throughout his life, and we lived and breathed this passion on weekend trips and vacations. My brothers and I would note how animated he was in watching a game, no matter the sport, be it live or on television, and his contagious energy when we discussed the latest achievements or stories relating to high-performance athletes.

The idea is not for children to necessarily find meaning in the same things as their parents but to be encouraged to seek out what moves them and makes sense for them. Asking questions is one way to promote this voyage of discovery. Frank Steel told me about how his father opened his eyes by asking a simple but powerful question: "I had just been accepted at the University of Yale. I was very happy and went to share my achievement with my father, who replied, 'Why are you going to Yale?' At first, I thought the answer would be obvious, as it was a renowned university, but it took a while for me to find a really satisfactory answer to that question. It is always a good idea to understand why we want to do the things we want to do. Some will take a long time, others will stretch us beyond our limits, and if you are not clear why you have chosen that particular path, you may have more difficulty in facing the challenges."

Steel suggests that this self-reflection should be encouraged at school and says that as principal, his main objective is for students to identify their *whys*: "Why are you coming to our school? Why do we offer the classes that we offer, and why do they take the classes they take?" His aspirations strike a chord with those of William Damon, who believes schools that encourage their students to find purpose will create happier students who are curious about the world, interested in learning, resilient, and better able to deal with challenges and obstacles.

Other questions can be asked to encourage people of all ages to identify their purpose: "What do you really care about right now? What is important to you? Who is important to you?" These questions act as a compass in helping them find their own path.

It is also good to encourage answers to be shared with others, as purpose is contagious and has the power to positively influence everyone.

In addition to role models and probing questions, activities that bring us joy, a feeling of contentment, and satisfaction represent one of the most important ways to discover our strengths and passions. Experiences that make us feel whole and fulfilled help us to discover what has meaning in our lives. Having enjoyed a particular activity, we tend to repeat the activity and hone our skills until we have mastery. A positive spiral of growth and development is created.

Martine Grael is the daughter of Torben Grael, two-time Olympic champion (Los Angeles in 1984 and Seoul in 1988) and the niece of Lars, two-time Olympic bronze medalist (Seoul in 1988 and Atlanta in 1996). However, she never felt the weight of her surname or pressure from her parents. She said, "My parents worked hard to make sport fun. We did a lot of family outings together on the boat, and the important thing was always the joy we felt just being there. I remember that we—my mother, brother, and I—took boat trips around the island near our house. Each day, we had a different challenge. It was really fun."

Martine shared a story from her childhood that conveys this feeling well: "On one of these trips, as a tot, I fell into the water. Everything was fine, and there was no danger, but my mother was afraid I would be traumatized by the experience. So she immediately threw my brother into the water and said, 'When you get tired of playing in there, call me, and I'll fetch you.' My brother understood nothing. I thought it was all a big joke. And to this day, we laugh about it."

Along her journey, she came to find new meaning in sport. She told me, "The collective aspect of sport is wonderful. You feel that you belong to something bigger, and you all evolve together. Things start to take on new meaning. At the age of sixteen, my father asked me why I liked sailing. He didn't pressure me but questioned something that was like a pillar to me. It was then that I realized that I enjoyed the whole experience but that competing was what really got me going. So I started to pour myself into the sport until I became a professional."

A Sense of Belonging

One way leaders and managers can create a sense of purpose with their employees also involves inspiration and setting an example. Douglas Conant, who was CEO of Campbell Soup Company and is the author of *TouchPoints: Creating Powerful Leadership Connections in the Smallest of Moments*, wrote in an article for *Harvard Business Review*, "That is the real job of a true leader—to offer a vision that inspires and motivates. But as difficult as that is to achieve, it is not enough. People also need to know that you yourself, as a leader, are in touch with reality, that you are willing to roll-up your sleeves and engage in the hard work that execution entails."[1]

That is, what leaders communicate verbally is not enough; they should also demonstrate, through their actions, a real commitment to the cause.

The Gallup Organization, a research consultancy that helps global leaders and organizations with problem solving, interviewed more than eighty thousand managers from different companies worldwide, with the objective of identifying the best place to work—the companies that score most highly in areas such as profitability, customer satisfaction, and employee retention.

Among the key elements identified as leading to increased productivity and higher levels of engagement was the following statement: "The mission or purpose of my company makes me feel my work is important."

As Gallup's executives put it, "when employees of an organization feel they are an integral part of a larger whole, they are more likely to stay committed to that organization. It is natural for human beings to want to be part of something meaningful, to know they are making a difference and contributing to an important mission. The best workplaces give employees a sense of purpose, help them feel that they belong and that they are making a difference."[2]

It is not a matter of simply spelling out the company's mission, vision, and values in a broad sense. A company's leaders must translate the organizational intent into language that is accessible, walking the talk and aligning actions to the goal, so employees are able to connect with the company's values.

In Brazil, I was involved in the merger of two banking giants of the Brazilian market, Itaú and Unibanco, which created the largest financial group in the Southern Hemisphere. When we entered the conference room where the new vision for Itaú Unibanco would be presented, Pedro Moreira Salles, then chairman of the board of directors, whispered to me, "You will like what you see." And I certainly did. A few minutes later, I was introduced to the goals that would guide the bank's activities over the years ahead: leadership in customer satisfaction and sustainable results. It became even more evident to me that what had always motivated me in the corporate sphere was feeling I was an integral and active part of achieving the company's vision.

The words *clients* and *sustainability* were key, as this commitment translated into ethical decision-making. My area of expertise had a direct impact in this regard. I knew that this strategy would drive all investment decisions, priority-setting, and internal decision-making. Even ten years after the merger and all the changes in the financial market, this magnetic north remained a constant. Itaú Unibanco is one of the leading banks in Environmental, Social, and Governance (ESG), affirming the company's commitment to making a positive impact in relation to the environment and social causes.

The Power of Purpose

Aníbal Sánchez was just sixteen years old when he moved from Venezuela to the United States to play in Minor League Baseball, a pyramid of professional baseball leagues that supports the major leagues.

He said, "I barely knew how to speak English. People would ask me, 'Where are you from?' and I would reply with my name. It wasn't easy, but I had a rule in mind: *No matter the language, the game is the same. Do your best.* That's what mattered to me. I wanted to get to the Major League, and not only that, I wanted to stay in the Major League." And that is exactly how it played out. Sánchez has been among the best players and with the best teams since 2006.

The challenges have changed during his career, but they have remained nonetheless. He said, "In the minor league, in addition to the language barrier and being away from my family, who I only called once per week, conditions were more basic. We traveled to games by bus—more than fourteen hours sometimes; we shared rooms in the hotels and had to save for food, which ended up not being very healthy. In the Major League, you have a whole organized structure of hotels, rest, food, and air transport. The challenge then is to maintain that hunger to keep improving and innovating. In both situations, it was the love of baseball that helped me overcome any challenge."

When we have purpose, our decision-making process becomes more organic and natural. Everything makes more sense because it is aligned to that purpose. Purpose naturally leads us to prioritize what really matters to us. It allows us to view times of hardship and adversity as a choice rather than a sacrifice.

Like Aníbal Sánchez, I learned early on that a journey based on passion for what we do feeds a powerful inner strength to persevere, resist the pain of training, overcome frustrations, and seek daily evolution.

Having a *why* contributes to our physical and mental well-being and enhances our social and family ties. In 2019, the *Journal of the American Medical Association* published a study that attempted to measure the sense of purpose in approximately seven thousand people, who had an average age of sixty-eight. The researchers tracked these individuals over a period of five years and found that those who scored higher for purpose were half as likely to die as those who scored lower.[3] In other words, finding meaning in life presents physical and mental health benefits, in addition to increasing our longevity.

The number of centenarians living in the Blue Zones corroborates this idea. All of the communities studied shared a strong sense of purpose in their lives. "The residents of Okinawa, Japan, use the word *Ikigai* and those on the Nicoya Peninsula, Costa Rica, call it the *plan de vida*. In both cultures, the phrase essentially translates as 'the reason I wake up each morning,'" says Buettner.[4]

Purpose also lies behind longevity in sport. When, at forty-three, Tom Brady—who already had more Super Bowl rings than any other player in the history of the game—moved to the unfashionable Tampa Bay Buccaneers, many doubted he would win his seventh Super Bowl. He had won the previous six with the New England Patriots, for whom he played for twenty years. Seeing a decrease in the player's physical prowess in recent seasons, the Patriots decided to let Brady leave rather than meet his contractual demands. Few teams seemed interested in his services, but that only served as extra motivation for Brady to excel.

The doubts centered on his age and the fact that the Buccaneers had not really shone in recent seasons. After a campaign of ups and downs, they secured a wild-card spot for the playoffs before upsetting the odds and going on to reach the final to face the reigning champions, the Kansas City Chiefs, who were led by superstar quarterback Patrick Mahomes, who, at twenty-five, was eighteen years younger than Brady. The result? Tampa Bay won 31–9, with an exquisite performance by Brady, who was voted the most valuable player of the match.

What motivated him to face that challenge at that point in his life, when he was already the best in his position in the history of the game? "I have things to prove to myself. The only way is through. If I don't go for it, I'll never know what I could have accomplished. Wanting to do something is different from actually doing it. If I stood at the bottom of a mountain and told myself I could scale the highest peak but then didn't do anything about it—what's the point of that?" Brady said, reinforcing the importance of acting upon our sense of purpose, when he accepted the invitation to join Tampa Bay. "I'm trying to do things that have never been done in my sport. That's actually fun for me, too, because I know I can do them. When a team gives you the opportunity to do those things with them, well … if not with them, then who? At some point you have to throw your whole body into what you're doing. You have to say, *Let's ride. Let's see what we got.*"[5]

Tom Brady responded to an internal challenge to try to make it once again to the top.

When I spoke with two-time Olympic champion and fifteen-time world yachting champion Robert Scheidt about what drove him as he prepared for his seventh Olympics in Tokyo in 2020, his sense of purpose and passion for the sport were evident. He said, "I like the adrenaline from competition, feeling the flag go up, starting the procedure to push off. I feel so alive when I'm in this situation. Being able to experience this is the ultimate. If my body is allowing it and if life is giving me this chance, it's the most beautiful thing I can do."

Overcoming Obstacles

Danny Crates played rugby and dreamed of turning professional when, at the age of twenty-one, a car accident changed his destiny. With his right arm amputated, everyone thought he would need to rethink his sporting ambitions, but his passion was such that in less than a year, he surprised everyone when he returned to training.

When one of his games was televised, his physique attracted attention, and he was invited to join the UK Paralympic athletics team. Crates seized the opportunity and developed a brilliant career, which led him to win the bronze medal in the four hundred meters at the Paralympics in Sydney in 2000 and the gold in the eight hundred meters in Athens in 2004, when he broke the world record for the distance. In 2008, he was honored to carry the British flag at the opening ceremony of the Beijing Paralympic Games.

One of the phrases Crates never tires of repeating, which appears on the cover of his autobiography, *Danny Boy*, is "No hurdle in life is impossible to overcome." His story shows how his love for the sport gave him the strength to deal with a crisis and pursue his dreams and aspirations.

What is your calling? Without purpose, it is hard to have a fulfilling life. When we identify our purpose, our journey is not easy, but there is satisfaction in working hard and overcoming difficulties. Having a *why* allows us to reframe the pain and setbacks we encounter on the way and view adversity as a challenge. It is as if we have found a spiritual dimension to what we are doing that connects us to some meaning in life.

It may sound as if we are talking about something radical or grandiose, but that is not the idea. Meaning is found much more in our daily journey than in any destiny associated with heroic acts.

The meaning we give to our lives and the situations we face is up to us. For example, in doing a job, we can understand it as a mere task, as a career, as a stepping-stone toward something greater, or as a calling.

Heeding the Call

Sports players and athletes are often seen pointing to the sky after scoring a goal, crossing the finish line, or making a basket. Many thank God or mention a higher power in postgame interviews. The connection between sports and God (or the gods) goes back to the ancient Greeks, if not before. In the year 776 BC, the Olympic Games were always played to appease or praise the gods.

It is difficult to know exactly what gave rise to these games. Mythology is entwined with history, and events that took place at that time are often explained as consequences of divine intervention.

Religiosity is not the only way to develop spirituality. Spirituality also grows when we have a strong sense of purpose in our lives. This meaning varies and can evolve as we pass through each phase of our journey. As an athlete, my purpose was tied to seeking high performance, constantly surpassing myself, representing my country, and dreaming of our team becoming one of best in the world and playing an Olympic sport.

In corporate life, what moved me was learning from the experience of clients and employees in trying to create a more harmonious and rewarding relationship for everyone. As a mother, I find great meaning in preparing my daughters for the pursuit of their dreams and for the reality that everything will not always work out the way we would like it to. Identifying our dreams and passions is key to developing our potential, our relationships, and our attributes, such as resilience, persistence, and continual learning.

Spirituality also manifests itself when we feel there is a greater power guiding us, are in contact with nature, or follow the faith we have in life and the paths we choose.

As a five-year-old, Brazilian judoka Leandro Guilheiro watched on television as judoka Aurélio Miguel took gold at the Olympic Games in Seoul in 1988. He told me, "My generation was driven by this victory. Because of Aurélio Miguel, our school started offering the children judo lessons. I fell in love with the sport. I'll never know how to explain my relationship with judo, because it's something bigger, like a calling. I felt the need to fight and to always give my best."

For Guilheiro, in addition to discipline and determination, a key aspect to becoming a champion is having patience with, and faith in, the process. He said, "As a five-year-old, I knew it would take me a long time to reach the Olympics. It takes patience, and a lot of faith in the path you have chosen, to be able to overcome the uncertainties and obstacles that arise. It's not a passive patience, obviously. It is about understanding that every barrier you face, every competition you lose, and every opponent you don't manage to defeat is an opportunity to evolve."

Freedom to Make the Most of the Here and Now

In his book *Happier: Learn the Secrets of Daily Joy and Lasting Fulfillment*, Tal Ben-Shahar tells the story of an American philosopher who joined a group of Buddhist monks to go climbing in the Himalayan Mountains. As he looked up to the peak of the mountain, the philosopher sensed the fatigue in his body and noted the great distance that still separated him from his goal—and this made him feel even more tired. He ended up losing his strength and desire to continue and, although he was the youngest on the expedition, became the only member of the group to give up halfway through the climb.

The monks, according to Ben-Shahar, also wanted to reach the summit and would keep an eye on it as they went, to make sure they were on the right path. Knowing they were heading in the right direction allowed them to focus their attention and enjoy every step, rather than be overwhelmed by the thought of what was still to come. The role of purpose is to give direction to our goals, and the role of our goals is to liberate us to enjoy the here and now.

Ben Shahar writes, "If we set off on a road trip with no destination in mind, the trip itself is unlikely to be much fun. If we do not know where we are going or even where we want to go, every fork in the road becomes a site of ambivalence—neither left nor right seems like a good choice, as we don't know if we want to go where this road takes us. So, instead of concentrating on the landscape, and on the scenery and flowers along the road, we are consumed with hesitation and uncertainty. What will happen if I go this way? Where will I end up if I turn down there? If we have a destination in mind and know which direction we are going, we are free to focus all our attention on making the most of wherever it is we are."[6]

Our happiness and sense of fulfillment derive not just from achieving our goals but also from enjoying the journey we take in pursuing them. To evolve in any skill and succeed—in sport, at work, or in our personal lives—we need both intrinsic and extrinsic motivation.

Extrinsic motivation is associated with external factors, such as gratification, recognition from others, and the harvesting of results. Intrinsic motivation, on the other hand, relates to why we want to achieve our goals. Here I emphasize the power of the *and*. We should not value one over the other.

When the journey is pleasant, failure has less of an impact on whether we continue. Robert Scheidt was disappointed to win "only" the silver medal at Sydney in 2000, but that just motivated him to go for gold at Athens in 2004. He said, "I always enjoyed not just the result but also the journey. It kept me highly motivated to get better every day, to keep evolving. I knew that for 2004, I could improve my sailing. Losing in 2000 became fuel for me to want a rematch."

Adam Krikorian, coach of the American women's water polo team, also believes in the power of the journey in acting as a great motivator. He told me, "For me, the reason I do what I do is not to win another gold medal but because I want to improve. There is nothing better than experiencing the highs and lows, successes and failures. Medals and trophies just gather dust by your headboard. The memories and the lessons stay with you all the way. The important thing is to enjoy the process, love the details, and—who knows?—in the end maybe have a gold medal around your neck."

The Quality Experience

American Joshua Waitzkin started playing chess at the age of six, becoming a child prodigy at the game.[14] At thirteen, he became a national master, and at sixteen, he became an international master, the second-highest rank for a chess player. At around twenty-three years of age, he turned his back on the game because he no longer felt any purpose in playing, or as he himself said, he fell out of love with the game. A few years later, he resurfaced as a world champion in tai chi and jujitsu.

Tal Ben-Shahar describes Waitzkin as a highly accomplished person both intellectually and physically, someone who believes that for children to thrive and flourish, they should experience quality in some of their activities. He ascribes the term *quality* to something they are dedicated to, are passionate about, and, ideally, can deploy their strengths in.

"Quality can be experienced in any area of life—sport, chess, math, history, cooking or even origami," Ben-Shahar says. The key point is that a profound childhood experience will enable someone to transpose quality into any other activity he or she may perform in life.

By experiencing something at a high level—such as playing sport—you learn to work hard, apply yourself, perform under pressure, and deal with failures and defeat. In so doing, you create the tools needed for success later in life. I followed this process closely with my daughters. I noticed how, from a young age, through talking to their coaches, they learned to listen to authority figures and communicate with confidence, assertiveness, and respect, including with their teachers and, more recently, with recruiters when seeking a university where they could pursue their dreams.

---

[14] The 1993 movie *Searching for Bobby Fischer* is based on his story, with Waitzkin himself making a cameo appearance.

One of my first coaches on the Brazilian national team was Eduardo Abla, known as Duda. He has always believed that when we act with a determination that borders on an obsession in pursuing our dreams, we change everything around us—from connections, habits, and choices to the practices that lead us to make an incremental improvement every day. He once beckoned me to come up onstage at the closing ceremony of a world tournament in Canada—after I had been nominated as one of the best players—to speak about our pioneering spirit and the rapid evolution of the women's game in Brazil. We received an ovation and much praise after sharing the recent progress we had made and results we had achieved. Duda took me completely by surprise, but I followed his instructions and asked for the microphone. At the end of the day, he hugged me and said, "This was your lesson for the day. It has helped to sow the seeds for our journey in world sport."

When I stopped playing water polo professionally and went to work in the corporate world, I incorporated many of the values I had gained from sport in finding new purpose. For example, I retained the determination I'd developed as an athlete to create a self-improvement mindset at the company.

If taught from an early age, these sporting values can bring future benefits beyond health and fitness. For teenagers, playing sport can improve self-esteem at the moment when they are developing their own identities and worries about the future, helping to smooth the way.

Nigerian Simidele Adeagbo played sports from a young age at school when her family lived in the United States. As a teenager, she tried various sports, such as hockey, volleyball, and basketball, but she identified most with athletics. She dreamed of becoming an Olympic triple-jump athlete and came close to qualifying for the US Olympic team.

After ten years, Simidele called an end to her sporting career and moved into corporate life, where she demonstrated the same quality in the sense described earlier and was hired by the largest sporting goods manufacturer in the world, Nike. While at Nike, she was offered a job in Johannesburg, South Africa, and realized there was a gap between the way people on other continents perceived Africa and the reality. The continent had an image of famine and war rather than of a vibrant, growing economy containing four hundred companies that earned more than $1 billion in revenue. Traveling through several African countries, she discovered beauties that she herself did not know. That was when she heard an inner call to change the narrative, and for this, she needed a transformation of her own.

She decided to become the first Nigerian to compete in the Winter Olympics, at Pyeongchang, South Korea, in 2018, and the first black African to compete in the women's skeleton event, one of the most challenging events at the games. For the skeleton, the athlete lies head-down on an open sled and descends a toboggan run at more than seventy-five miles per hour, with her face just a few centimeters from the ground, with no brake or seat belt.

Simidele was thirty-six years old and had not practiced a high-level sport for ten years. When she began at skeleton, feeling like a fish out of water and facing a whole new world of terms, equipment, and motions, she remembered her purpose: to change the image of African women around the world. She thus paid attention to her appearance, adding various symbols to her equipment that would remind people of her continent. Finally, she committed herself, body and soul, to her cause. She said, "After making history in Pyeongchang, I'm preparing for the 2022 Games, as narratives don't change overnight. It's an evolution and there's a lot of work to be done. ... I'm an ordinary person, the same as anybody else, but I made a choice to change a narrative. I thought about how I could do this and deliver on this commitment. Ultimately, I want to inspire the next generation to dream without limits. Through this humble experience, we all have power as change makers."[7]

Thus, Simidele was able to extrapolate her individual purpose, demonstrating that sport can also bring about social transformation.

Sport in Society

Kenyan Abel Mutai, bronze medalist in the three-thousand-meter steeplechase at the 2012 London Olympics, was on the verge of winning a cross-country event in Burlada, Navarra, Spain, in 2013. However, at the end of the race, he got confused by the signs, relaxed his pace, and started greeting members of the crowd—because he believed he had already crossed the finish line. In fact, there were still a few meters to go. Right behind him, in second place, Spaniard Iván Fernández Anaya, seeing his rival's mistake, decided he did not want to take the opportunity to pass him for the win. Instead, he drew the Kenyan's attention to his error and allowed him to finish the race in first place.

The journalists quizzed the Spaniard about his actions, asking, "Why did you do that?"

Surprised, Anaya replied, "Do what?" It had never even crossed his mind to win from a misunderstanding by his rival rather than from his own efforts.

"You let him win," said a journalist.

"I didn't let him. He won the race," replied Anaya.

Competitiveness, so important in driving the search for improvement, also calls for technical and moral magnanimity. It is called fair play and can be transferred to all areas of life. The term was created in 1896 by Baron Pierre de Coubertein of France, one of the founders of the modern Olympic Games, in the hope that loyalty and respect might go hand in hand with competition.

The Olympic spirit is a philosophy of life, a point of reference both inside and outside of sport. It encourages character development and awareness of good citizenship and is capable of translating from small nuclei, such as the family, to society at large. Sport helps to inspire and educate in building a fairer future for all.

My father, who participated in two Olympics, took these values, which he learned in sports, into corporate life. During his tenure at the Brazilian newspaper association, in 1992, he implemented a major project called Ler (Read), which proposed a coordinated action among all news media (with 85 percent of all the newspapers in circulation) to create an educational supplement. The objective was to reinforce the newspaper's social commitment; think about the reader of the future; contribute to the quality of education; and help develop critically minded, independent citizens. The initiative was well received by schools, teachers, students, parents, and commercial partners. The project helped to consolidate citizenship and democracy in the country.

Former football player Raí had not even finished his playing career when he also got involved in a social project. In 1998, he created the Gol de Letra foundation, which seeks to educate, through sport and culture, children, adolescents, and young adults about social protection across several states in Brazil. "What always moved me was working to positively impact the environment, be it at the micro level—the team—or at the macro level—the country and society—as I do at Gol de Letra," he told me.

The foundation's pedagogical project was based on a French methodology. Raí said, "We developed agents for the communities, who could promote sports activities in the neighborhood, organizing championships and other events."

The project was so successful that the São Paulo state government adapted it for a coaching program—that is, the foundation's methodology became public policy. Today this project is called Etec de Esportes, the first to develop young promoters of sport. The Gol de Letra foundation has certainly impacted the next generations and helped the development of society.

The family played an important role in reinforcing this social awareness in Raí. His father pointed out to him and his brothers the injustices and inequalities in the world. Raí told me, "As he came from poverty, he urged us to think about the subject." So much so that in addition to Gol de Letra, Raí also helped found the movement Atletas pela Cidadania (Athletes for Citizenship), which later became Atletas pelo Brasil (Athletes for Brazil). The NGO fights for changes in legislation and public policy that encourage participation in sport.

Brenda Villa, one of the most successful players in the world of water polo, also grew up supported by family values and always fought for social opportunities, inclusion, and diversity in sport. The daughter of Mexican immigrants, she was introduced to water polo at a young age. After a journey driven by dreams, values, and purpose—that included winning four Olympic medals—she was delighted when they named the aquatic center after her in her small hometown of Commerce. She said, "From family education, I learned that school came first, but with my dreams and competitiveness, I grabbed the chance to play sport. I was able to play water polo almost for free when I was growing up, and this stuck with me. I always thought about access and opportunity, and this was given to me. So when I retired from my sports career, I wanted to make sure I could give back."

After retiring, Villa started a nonprofit organization called Project 2020, which has benefitted hundreds of children in her local community. Recently, in an effort to serve underfunded communities across the United States, she founded the Brenda Villa Foundation.[8] She is also a member of the board of USA Water Polo, the national governing body for the sport, and other key committees. She told me, "My purpose today is to contribute to a more inclusive world, one that promotes understanding and tolerance and that transmits to children values such as integrity, loyalty, authenticity, diversity, and a strong connection with family members."

Career Transition

In parallel to participating on the Brazilian water polo team, my father always studied and worked. He was studying engineering when he participated in his first Olympiad in Tokyo in 1964. He graduated in 1966 and began working at Companhia Lithographica Ypiranga, a printing company. Two years later, he managed to juggle the Mexico City Olympics with his job. He played polo until 1974, and although the sport was not professional, his routine of training and competitions was just as intense as it is for professionals today. He trained before and after work, played on weekends, and traveled to competitions.

My father decided to quit water polo while at the top of his game, still with the Brazilian national team. "Just as it's important to know when to get in, it's equally important to know when to get out," he always told me. For his farewell, the Brazilian Confederation of Water Sports organized two championships, one in Rio de Janeiro and another in São Paulo, the two cities where water polo was most popular. As guest of honor, he played the first half of each game for his São Paulo club and the second half for the national team.

The stands were full. There were speeches from players, from directors at the confederation, and from members of the Brazilian Olympic committee. It was a ceremony that marked the end of a phase in the life of the then captain of the Brazilian team. In his own speech, my father declared, "This will be my last water polo match in my life." My paternal grandmother recounted this moment to me and, with tears of pride in her eyes, recalled the words used to thank her son and what it meant to watch him play for the last time the sport of which he had complete mastery, the product of many years of practice and dedication. After his farewell, my father kept his promise and never reentered the pool to play. He joined Grupo Folha, a Brazilian media conglomerate, where he had a successful career as an executive.

Only when I started playing and asked him to teach me water polo did he return to the pool, both to train with me and to be an active part of my network of support and encouragement in the new sport.

It was a planned transition that had been well thought through. However, it is not always possible to prepare the ground for a career change, be it in a sport or in professional life. The path is often not so smooth.

When it comes to soccer, the most popular sport in Brazil, the situation for players is complex. Many young players start out dreaming of a better life and a comfortable future. However, a recent study showed that 45 percent of professional players in Brazil earn no more than the minimum wage and sometimes less. Another 42 percent earn between one and two times the minimum wage, while 9 percent of players earn between two times and twenty times the minimum wage. Only 4 percent of professional players earn more than this—the most famous names at the clubs in the top two Brazilian leagues.[9]

In other words, the vast majority are unable to put aside any savings to facilitate a smooth career transition when they leave the sport. Meanwhile, the professional routine—with daily training, games on weekends, and few hours of leisure—is hardly conducive to studying and preparing for another profession.

I believe preparation for the end of a sporting career should start as soon as we pursue the dream. How should we go about this? By investing time in our education and seeking an area of specialization that matches our preferences.

During my sports career, I never ignored my development in other areas, and this came a lot from my parents, who always emphasized the importance of academic performance in addition to sport. In Brazil, I reconciled championships with college, while in Italy, I took the opportunity to do a postgraduate degree in economics. It was not always possible to schedule training and trips around the school calendar, but I always tried to reach a compromise with the teachers. Even during the closed season, I sought to build my knowledge by working in companies. When I returned from Italy, I joined an excellent trainee program in financial markets at Unibanco and was able to put into practice what I had studied.

The skills acquired in sport are never lost. The ability to organize and to manage time and energy; to adapt to different scenarios and setbacks; a sense of dedication, perseverance, and teamwork—these were skills recognized by my first manager in justifying my hiring at the bank. He later told me that the HR department had questioned why they should hire someone who would still have commitments with the Brazilian national team. His answer had been "Because an athlete is prepared to push back the boundaries and seek excellence, no matter whether it is on the sports field or in the work environment." The difference is in the approach and the level of dedication in working toward the goals.

Bruno Schmidt, Olympic champion in beach volleyball at Rio in 2016, told me, "The transition is the hardest part for every athlete, as we have dedicated our lives to that dream. In our early twenties, we think time will never pass, but once we are in our early thirties, we realize that it passes quickly. I, for example, am starting to prepare myself. Four years ago, I only played beach volleyball. Now I'm studying at night, going to law school. Every hour of my day is busy. It's tiring, but I know it will be worth it."

He still has not identified a precise date to retire: "I'm taking it one day at a time, living my passion for beach volleyball while at the same time planting a seed that I will reap in the future." Despite choosing not to continue working with volleyball, he said emphatically, "Without a doubt, I will use everything I learned from the sport in whatever I do. The most important lesson is that nothing comes easy. Everything takes a lot of dedication."

In addition to the athlete's own dedication, it is essential for public authorities and clubs to think of a structure that prepares athletes for the future. Along with his sports career, water polo player Felipe Perrone has completed a degree and postgraduate program in sports management. He has another degree as a coach. He said, "I know it's very difficult to go back and experience from other areas what I get now from water polo, but life doesn't end after sport."

He told me that Spain has programs focused on the future of athletes, called high-performance centers, which select talented young people from across the country. In addition to providing a structure for training and development in sport, they manage their students' academic education. The centers offer residential programs in soccer, handball, volleyball, hockey, tennis, swimming, gymnastics, tae kwon do, and others. The centers are also supported by a physiotherapist and doctor and have all the means for developing the youngsters both physically and academically.

In Spain, there are also quotas of university places reserved for these athletes in preparing them for the future. "Nowadays, in the Spanish water polo team, we have engineers and lawyers. They can't work now, but they're better prepared for the transition," Perrone explained to me.

In the United States, universities play a key role in educating and preparing athletes for life after their sports careers. Scholarships are always highly sought after. The key part is the incentive offered to the athlete to continue studying while simultaneously participating in the university's competitive sports teams. The student athlete gains by having a longer-lasting career in sport without abandoning his or her studies, while discussions are ongoing regarding ideas that might enhance the athlete's journey after his or her sporting career.

The Difficult Time to Stop

For me, one of the biggest signs that I needed to call time on my sporting career appeared when, ahead of a game against Russia, a team that is typically quite physical in the water, I felt tired at the thought of facing them. That had never happened to me before. It was a clear sign for me and a hard one to face up to, but the feeling led me to start thinking about the transition process.

It is not an easy time, be it in sport or in a corporate career. Staying alert to the fact that everything will end one day—in order for a new stage to begin—is an important aspect in facilitating the process of change and leaving our familiar comfort zone.

The process of preparing ourselves, when possible, allows us to reflect and have a greater understanding of the facts. When he was about to hang up his cleats at around thirty-four years of age, Raí invested in sessions with a psychologist. He said, "This was a key decision that helped me uncover things about myself that I might have learned anyway but would maybe have taken too long." Still a professional soccer player, he took courses and founded the Gol de Letra Foundation. "Many people, when they quit [the game], they think about taking a year out to decide what to do next. For me, it was good to already have an activity lined up, even if I wanted to do other things."

Tal Ben-Shahar was a squash player who, even from the age of sixteen, said to himself, "What will I do when I am thirty years old and I have to retire? The solution in my mind was to become a coach and continue in a career linked to the sport."

However, fate did not play along with his plans. At twenty-one, he had to change tack. "I got seriously hurt, and this ended my squash career. I remember going to the doctor. He said I needed some extremely delicate surgery on my spine—one in which he couldn't promise how it would turn out. 'Either you do the operation or give up on your professional sports aspirations.' So I gave up. It wasn't a very difficult choice, as I didn't want such risky surgery."

At that moment, Ben-Shahar faced a crisis. "What helped me a lot was something my squash coach—a true philosopher and intellectual—told me: 'You'll find something else to fall in love with, and you'll be able to continue being what you were as an athlete.' I heard him but didn't really believe it, because there was nothing on the horizon. But he was right. It took me almost two years to find something else I was passionate about—philosophy and psychology, which I am still committed to today."

With this experience, Ben-Shahar's message is this: when you know that what you care about will end, it is important to ask yourself how you can use the skills and strengths you have developed in other areas of life, so you can continue along the path to fulfillment. "Fulfillment is not defined by participating in the Olympics, nor by climbing the podium. Of course these things are good. They are important and motivational. Fulfillment is found on the road to the podium, or in the business you are starting or book you are writing," he concluded.

In that phase of my life, I rediscovered my purpose. But it was not easy. My exit from the bank did not play out as I had planned. Situations that take us by surprise leave us with no course of action and with uncertainty about the future.

By writing this book and creating a company focused on developing human potential, I have found a new path. I have brought together the values I have always held dear in my life—high performance and excellence in execution—to inspire and guide transformations in individuals, teams, and organizations. With the courage to experiment, I have discovered, in the science of happiness and positive psychology, a way to translate the concepts and pursue this work in a way that is both enjoyable and easy to apply in everyday life. I feel fulfilled every time I realize that I have helped someone to have a happier, healthier, and more harmonious journey.

Having a purpose guides our goals, decisions, and daily choices. It allows us to make the most of life's journey in the here and now, which is enriched when we align our actions to our deepest values. Therefore, it is always good to ask ourselves if we are prioritizing and acting upon what really fulfills us, because when we focus on what we love and are able to accomplish, we find happiness and fulfillment.

Main Points Covered in This Chapter

- A sense of purpose is developed through inspiration. It is contagious and has the power to positively influence those around you.

- Leaders, parents, and educators should be positive role models who inspire their charges through their ability to walk the talk.

- Having meaning in our lives gives us the strength to overcome obstacles, as persevering becomes a life choice rather than a sacrifice.

- To advance with any skill and succeed—be it in sport, work, or personal life—we need intrinsic and extrinsic motivation.

- Fair play epitomizes values such as loyalty and respect for competition. This concept can be expanded to all spheres of life.

- The Olympic spirit is a philosophy of life that encourages character development and builds awareness of what it means to be a good citizen. It is capable of translating from small nuclei, such as the family, to society at large.

- In many situations, we can reframe our work in ways that add a greater sense of meaning. Small changes can make a big difference.

- We should prepare for the transitional phase of our sporting or professional careers from the moment we begin them. Investing in education and intellectual development brings us greater security, self-esteem, and freedom of choice.

- Change is not easy. When you know that something central to you is going to end, it is important to think about how to use the skills and strengths you have gained in a new context.

Powerful Questions to Reflect Upon

- Have your choices and goals fit your passions, values, and sense of purpose?
- What do you really care about right now? What is meaningful to you? Who is important to you?
- What are you developing now that will support you in the next phase of life?
- Where have you made a difference? In what ways, large or small, are you contributing to others and the wider world?
- Have you been focusing on the meaningful elements of your life?
- What can you do to find more meaning and purpose in what you are doing currently, both in your personal life and at work?

CHAPTER 12

HAPPINESS, THE ULTIMATE CURRENCY

Happiness is the meaning and the purpose of
life, the whole aim of human existence.
—Aristotle

Many persons have a wrong idea of what constitutes true
happiness. It is not attained through self-gratification but
through fidelity to a worthy purpose. Happiness should be a
means of accomplishment, like health, not an end in itself.
—Helen Keller

We had spent the day together on the beach as a family, playing sports
and enjoying one another's company. I was now living in the United States
and had just arrived in Brazil with my husband and daughters for a few
days to visit my family. The sun had already set as I joined my father on
the sofa in our house in Ilhabela, on the São Paulo coast. I looked into
his eyes and said, "Dad, I have a proposal. I want to write a book about
life lessons we have gained from sport. I need you for this journey! How
about we do it together?"

At the time, I was going through a career transition. It was a time
filled with uncertainty, and that family vacation was a real oasis. The
previous night, I had flipped through some of my old diaries, which I had

found in a closet. One page in particular remained etched in my mind throughout that day. On it, the following was written in giant letters: "Cris, when will you finally heed the call to write a book?"

That question was a spotlight in the darkness, highlighting the answer I was seeking. My father's acquiescence only further illuminated the path before me.

Every conversation with him, from the very first exchanges to the first drafts to the meetings in which we debated the content for each section of the book, has been a meaningful journey for me. It excites me when I can relate a theory or empirical studies to something we have experienced in practice and, thus, enhance the way I work with the development of human potential. Having athletes and experts in the community share their experiences has greatly energized us.

The writing of this book has enabled me to examine both the external world and my internal world. The more I reflect on the methodology and the results obtained from the work I do with others, the more I learn about what works for me.

This journey has led to meaningful exchanges with my daughters, my husband, and my mother too as they read excerpts from these pages sharing memories and stories of grit and overcoming the odds from the athletes I interviewed. In addition to their valuable suggestions, we shared moments of deep connection during this year in which the world has been devastated by the coronavirus pandemic, which has greatly constrained social interactions.

During periods of change, in which we face emptiness or uncertainty, it is worth remembering the metaphor of a gardener. He plants the seed, ensuring there is enough light, and then promotes the conditions needed for the tree to flourish, patiently watering and adding nutrients when needed. The word *patience* has the same origin as the word *suffering*,[1] being derived from the Latin *patientia*, the idea that embedded within is the ability to accept painful emotions and allow them to flow through us. The key is to identify the seed we wish to plant and then to be patient and enjoy each step of the transformational journey to when it flourishes.

Coming now to the last chapter of this book, I appreciate the beauty of watching the flower bloom from that seed planted at the end of a sunny afternoon on the sofa of our beach house. It was even clearer to me that happiness derives from the choices we make in our daily lives, from where we choose to focus our attention, and from being deeply connected with our sense of purpose and the people who matter to us.

Universal Goals

All over the world, people pursue happiness as a universal goal. But what constitutes happiness? It is much more than simply the emotion of joy. It can be present even when we are undergoing hardship or suffering. In other words, enjoying a fulfilling life does not necessarily mean smiling and feeling pleasure all the time.

If we translate *happiness* to mean a life without sadness, we will end up frustrated and disappointed, as this is not a realistic goal. I might also aspire to reach a state of complete and constant serenity, but is this feasible? No, although I always try to create small islands of serenity in my day. The answer is in how we define *happiness* and in what we choose to pursue.

I have been able to surprise some of my interviewees with the question "What is happiness to you?" And they have surprised me, in turn, with some of the inspiring answers presented in this book.

Elite yachtsman Robert Scheidt associates happiness with living with his children and the possibility of continuing to do what he loves. "Today, for me, happiness is seeing my children smiling and in good health. It's about enjoying their company, enjoying life, and doing everything I am able to do in the sport I love," he replied.

Kahena Kunze, Olympic and world yachting champion, took a similar line: "Happiness is being with the people you like, doing what you like. When this happens, even a nonhappy day is a happy day."

For our journey to be a happy one, we need to be clear about our purpose and future goals. This is not to say that achieving our goals will bring us happiness. It is true that when we reach a goal, we might experience a rush of elation, but that feeling may quickly disappear. Happiness comes from the process of pursuing a goal that is meaningful to us.

I echo the words of water polo player Felipe Perrone, who participated in four Olympics: three for Spain and one for Brazil. He told me,

"Happiness is living in the now, being present, truly experiencing what we are doing."

It is common to believe that the relationship between success and happiness is one-way—that success brings happiness. But scientific studies have shown that the opposite is also true and that the effect is much longer lasting. Studies led by Stanford University researcher and doctor of psychology Sonja Lyubomirsky identified that people who are happy on their journey are more successful with regard to various aspects of life. They have better relationships, are more likely to thrive at work, lead a better quality of life, and live longer.[2] They are also more creative, productive, and resilient, tending to better withstand the moments of pain we all undergo.[2] Therefore, happiness is a means to achieving excellence and the results desired.

David Boudia is an American diver. As a seven-year-old, he watched the 1996 Atlanta Olympics on TV and got hooked on the dream of becoming an Olympian. He said, "I spent seven hours in the pool every day. My only focus was on winning an Olympic medal, and what motivated me was the idea of the fame and success that would come from this victory."[3] At just nineteen, he qualified for the 2008 Beijing Olympics, and he believed that would be his big chance. He placed tenth and, not having reached his goal, suffered a deep depression.

At that point, Boudia realized that focusing solely on results was not enough and was, in fact, undermining his chance of success. "I started to look around me and concentrate on the present moment and value the journey," he said, describing how he slowly returned to training while developing this new mindset. His focus was no longer on external recognition but on the satisfaction that comes from giving your best and enjoying the journey toward your goals. In London in 2012, he won the gold medal on the ten-meter platform and took the bronze on the ten-meter synchronized platform. His story of learning and development is an example of how to associate the elements that create happiness with the pursuit of excellence. Otherwise, the obstacles can become unbearable.

The Paradox in the Search for Happiness

Naturally, we aim to be happy. However, people who make the pursuit of happiness their goal in life tend to feel unhappy. Why is this? How can we resolve this paradox that the more we pursue happiness, the less happy we become?

"Happiness is like sunlight. If you look at it directly, you won't be able to see it, and it will even hurt your eyes. But if you look at it through a prism, all that energy gets dispersed into the colors of the rainbow. So you are then seeing the sunlight indirectly. We should look for the elements that will lead us to happiness rather than look for happiness itself. Happiness is not the end of the journey but, rather, something to be cultivated in our daily lives," says Tal Ben-Shahar, PhD, specialist in positive psychology and the science of happiness.

He suggests that in order to live a fulfilling life, we need to work on five main aspects, which he has given the acronym SPIRE: spiritual, physical, intellectual, relational, and emotional. Ben-Shahar stresses that these are the dimensions he has identified but that each of us could identify one or other additional aspect in our lives not covered in his model. He challenges us to reflect on the main aspects of our lives that, for us, bring happiness.

The spiritual dimension does not relate simply to religion but to aligning ourselves to some purpose and thus finding meaning in our actions and experiences. Whether it be waking up in the morning and immersing myself in writing a chapter of my book or focusing on a rewarding conversation with one of my daughters, these activities hold great meaning to me, related to my sense of purpose in life and my spiritual well-being.

The physical dimension relates to the mind-body connection. Everything we do—or do not do—with our body influences our mind and vice versa. If I exercise regularly, manage the quantity and quality of my sleep, and eat healthily, I am cultivating physical well-being.

The intellectual dimension comprises a thirst for learning, in seeking to discover more about the world or topics of interest to us, such as art, music, philosophy, religion, other people, or our own selves. By having the courage to experiment and learn about new things and then reflect on the experiences, we contribute to our intellectual well-being.

The relational dimension is about connecting with others in an authentic manner and evolving through the interdependence of a group. We are relational beings. As discussed in previous chapters, the quality of our relationships affects our well-being, mental health, and longevity. It is not surprising that the number-one generator of happiness is time spent with people we care about and who care about us. If I decide to spend more time with them, I am investing in relational well-being.

Finally, the emotional dimension is related to giving ourselves permission to be human and accepting all of our emotions as legitimate. By letting painful emotions flow through us and exploring what they are telling us, we are able to reframe experiences and learn from them, building emotional well-being.

My experience in sport fits this model well, of viewing happiness through the lens of these five dimensions, analogous to the light of a rainbow. I felt a passion and desire to represent my country, to evolve, and to perfect my performance (the spiritual dimension). I kept myself in great shape, managing my body, sleep, and meals, and I also created space for recovery by doing something I enjoyed, such as swimming in the ocean (the physical dimension). I practiced intensely and learned the technical, tactical, and strategic aspects of the sport in depth while also investing in mental toughness and gathering knowledge on human performance and effective teams (the intellectual dimension). I was part of a community, forming intense, lasting, and authentic bonds with my teammates and coaches—bonds I still cultivate today—and felt the strength of my family's support (the relational dimension). Finally, I sought to learn from the range of emotions I experienced, from the most painful to the most joyful, with all the levels of intensity in between (the emotional dimension). This is a lifelong journey.

There is a connection among the five dimensions of SPIRE. It is not necessary to invest the same level of energy in each of them simultaneously. How we find a balance depends on *mesearch*, which means looking within to identify which element to prioritize at a given moment in our lives. Mesearch also allows us to identify what works better for us at a given moment and how to improve.

We also do not need to exercise all five dimensions in one activity; rather, we focus on the dimensions that are most needed to fulfill our routine. While with the bank, I found meaning in my work (spiritual dimension), as I was dedicated to finding the best customer solutions and creating an inclusive, engaging environment for employees with diverse backgrounds (intellectual dimension).

At the same time, I experienced the joy of being a mother, in which I learned about unconditional love and the intense connection among our family (relational dimension). I learned that I needed to continue to play sport in order to gather calm during the day and be able to focus on my intellectual activities (physical dimension). I also continued to invest in self-knowledge and meditation, which helps me to interpret my emotions (emotional dimension). This does not mean I was always in balance—far from it. Yet I did my best to return to these activities whenever I felt the need.

Changes of direction, be they macro or micro, are important in helping us find what works for us—often through trial-and-error and mesearch—and thus develop our full potential.

The ideas discussed in this book are derived from systemic thinking, which starts from the principle that all parts of our reality are connected. That is, each part impacts the whole, and the whole impacts each part. The key point to systemic thinking is that once we understand the interconnectedness of the different elements, we can identify the levers of change that will, in turn, have the greatest impact on the whole.

Our happiness functions like a system in which all the elements of SPIRE are interconnected. Introducing changes to any of the elements may positively impact all the others. This form of holistic thinking is the path that leads to realizing our potential and finding happiness and fulfillment.

The Example of Helen Keller

American Helen Keller, one of the writers (and people) I most admire, graduated with a BA in philosophy in 1904 and went on to become a world-famous speaker—all after turning permanently deaf and blind at the age of nineteen months, following an unknown disease diagnosed as cerebral fever.

She lived in darkness, solitude, and silence for five years. Then her parents called in a twenty-year-old visually impaired teacher named Anne Sullivan. In just one month, Anne helped Helen relate to the world through the palm of her hand. In one of the first lessons, she placed her pupil's hand in cold water, and over the other hand, she traced out the word *water*, first slowly and then more quickly. With this method, the signs touched Helen's consciousness, now with new meaning (of something cool and fresh that trickled between her fingers). Soon she understood the concept of language and was able to spell by using her fingers, which, in her words, opened up the world outside.

In 1933, Keller wrote an essay entitled "Three Days to See" in the cultural magazine the *Atlantic Monthly*, describing what she would do if her hearing and eyesight were restored, even for just a little while. She ended by creating a recipe for a happy life. She wrote, "We should live each day with gentleness, vigor, and a keenness of appreciation which are often lost when time stretches before us in the constant panorama of more days and months and years to come."

Through her own way of dealing with life, the writer put SPIRE into practice. On the spiritual side, she believed that because we do not see life, or our own senses, as finite, we end up taking things for granted. If we lived each day as if it were our last, we would have more appreciation for the meaning of life. Finding sense in what we do and experience is key to her philosophy, as is finding beauty in different places, such as in art, for example. Keller said in her essay that on her second day of sight, she would visit the Metropolitan Museum in New York to take in the paintings by artists such as Leonardo da Vinci, Raphael Sanzio, and Rembrandt.

Keller, in addition to being known for her intellectual side, was also active physically. She took long hikes in the mountains, exploring the physical world through touch and smell. She also attached great importance to relationships. When she described what she would do on her first day with sight, she said, "I should want to see the people whose kindness and gentleness and companionship have made my life worth living. ... I should call to me all my dear friends and look long into their faces, imprinting upon my mind the outward evidences of the beauty that is within them.'⁴

The emotional part comes through in how she described the joy of living. She even proposed a hypothetical university course on "How to use your eyes," in which the professor would show students how they could add joy to their lives by really seeing what was going unnoticed in front of them.

She wrote, "I who am blind can give one hint to those who see—one admonition to those who would make full use of the gift of sight: Use your eyes as if tomorrow you would be stricken blind. And the same method can be applied to the other senses. Hear the music of voices, the song of a bird, the mighty strains of an orchestra, as if you would be stricken deaf tomorrow. Touch each object you want to touch as if tomorrow your tactile sense would fail. Smell the perfume of flowers, taste with relish each morsel, as if tomorrow you could never smell and taste again."

The Science of Happiness

Happiness is the great leveler when it comes to privilege, as it is everyone's right. It does not discriminate. Importantly, the science of happiness is not a panacea. If our basic needs—such as food, water, shelter, sleep, and safety—are not met, it is unlikely we will be talking about the meaning of life.

However, that is not to say that findings from this science cannot also benefit those who are undergoing even the worst of situations. Even if we are mired in activities and situations, if we find time for at least one activity in our day or week in which we find deep meaning—such as playing with children, caring for a loved one, or walking in a park—even for a few minutes, this will relieve moments of stress and increase well-being.

We can also increase our happiness if we focus on the present and appreciate the good in our lives. We tend to relive negative experiences over and over while not taking in the positive experiences we had during the day.

One of the most powerful ways to increase our levels of happiness and resilience is generosity. Robert Greenleaf, a renowned writer and consultant in the field of leadership, conducted a study in the 1970s to identify the essential characteristic of extraordinary leaders in times of extreme hardship. The finding was related not to charisma, oratory skills, strategic vision, or intellectual brilliance but to the fact that they were servant leaders. The primary role of servant leaders is to serve the people they lead, while the ability to listen is their main tool. Listening is a way of giving, in which we are donating our time and our attention. This is the type of donation we most need today.

By devoting myself to my role as a high-performance and happiness mentor, my goal is to support individuals and teams in realizing their potential and becoming the best version of themselves for that given point in time. In this, the power of choice is key. When we choose to align ourselves to our values and beliefs and exercise the muscles of the elements described for each of them, we will have a foundation that supports and inspires better choices and continuous evolution.

Where to Focus Our Gaze

Raí practiced and loved sports from a young age. In his late teens, he dreamed of traveling the world and was still unclear about the path he would take professionally. When, at the age of seventeen, his girlfriend became pregnant, he did not hesitate to take responsibility, get married, and start working. He told me, "I was already playing soccer for an amateur side, Botafogo de Ribeirão Preto. It was in my own hands to become a professional. So I started to take the sport more seriously, and that became my path."

He started his career at Botafogo, in the interior of São Paulo, which had a pregame routine of forming a prayer circle before games. He said, "There was always one of the players who would say a few words and lead the ceremony, until one day—I was about nineteen years old—I don't know why, but they asked me to speak. I was taken aback and let my message come from the heart: 'I would like to say that it is a privilege that we enjoy, doing what we love and getting paid for it. Our job is to take care of our body and our mind. There is no greater privilege than that.' Without intending to, I moved everyone. There are players who still tell me today, 'I have never forgotten what you said that day. You were so young, and yet you touched us deeply.'"

Our level of well-being is determined by what we choose to focus our attention on and how we interpret the events that happen to us. Raí could have been paralyzed by the news of early fatherhood but chose to focus on the present and face the situation in keeping with his values, rerouting his life. In so doing, he opened a path in which he chose to become a professional.

The verb *appreciate* is noteworthy and special. It has two meanings. The first is to admire, enjoy, or contemplate. It can be anything from a conversation with, or hug from, a loved one to intensely following each player's moves in the final of an Olympic event. It can be watching your daughter discover something new when playing in the garden or admiring the sunset over the ocean. To appreciate also means to increase in value. A well-managed financial investment, for example, appreciates. A work of art can appreciate over time.

The two concepts are interconnected. When we appreciate the good and the beautiful around us, life appreciates, increasing in value, becoming even more special. If we practice this habit of learning to pick out the positives, it becomes natural to us. On the other hand, when we take things for granted and do not appreciate their value, we compromise our potential for happiness and success, as there is a devaluation of what is good and beautiful.

In an article published in the *Journal of Personality and Social Psychology*, American psychologists Robert Emmons and Michael McCullough studied the effects of gratitude. They gave the following instruction to the volunteers in the study: "There are many things in life, large and small, for which we can be grateful. Think back over the past week and write down on the lines below up to five things in your life that you are grateful or thankful for." The events recorded varied, from waking up in the morning to the existence of a favorite band, a certain TV show, or an act of generosity by a friend.

Regardless of what they wrote down, the daily exercise in gratitude brought numerous benefits. Participants felt happier, more optimistic, more likely to work toward their goals, more generous, and physically healthier.[5]

Complementing this study, in 2014, Israeli researchers Hadassah Littman-Ovadia and Dina Nir demonstrated that in addition to exercises in gratitude and appreciation for past events, appreciating future events also brings benefits. They instructed the participants as follows: "Think of three good things (items, people or events) waiting for you tomorrow and write them down. Choose one of them and try to experience and maintain the sincere heart-felt feelings associated with it for five minutes." They repeated the exercise every day for a week, and the results showed that participants felt more optimistic and experienced fewer painful emotions, with a lower level of emotional exhaustion.[6]

My family and I have adapted these exercises for our family. We start the day by visualizing things we are looking forward to—for example, an upcoming meeting, practicing a skill, playing a game, or preparing for an encounter. Then, at the end of the day, we express our gratitude for the three most meaningful things that happened to us. My youngest daughter still enjoys doing this with me after her prayers. This simple exercise has a powerful effect in changing our perspective on events and encouraging us to live in the present. It exercises our positivity muscle, as we practice viewing the glass as half full rather than half empty.

If we focus on our actions, appreciating what has worked out successfully in the past, the benefits extend to further enhancing our performance, as we identify the aspects we should reinforce in order to form habits.

Whichever way you intend to carry out your exercise in gratitude—such as using a journal or talking over dinner, during team meetings, or before bedtime—it is important that it is done regularly and consistently until it becomes a habit. We should truly experience what we are grateful for and are looking for and perform this exercise with intent. This process triggers a virtuous circle of growth and well-being, making us more aware and open to positive experiences, which reinforces our strengths, self-knowledge, and confidence.

Call It Well-Being, Happiness, or Mental Health

In the book *How Full Is Your Bucket? Positive Strategies for Life and Work*, authors Donald Clifton, PhD, professor of educational psychology at the University of Nebraska, and Tom Rath, an expert on strengths and well-being, explain that we all have an "invisible bucket," which continually fills or empties, depending on what others say or do to us. When our bucket is full, our well-being increases; but when it is empty, we feel frustrated, sad, or drained. Interestingly, in addition to the bucket, we have an "invisible dipper." Whenever we use it to fill other people's buckets, saying or doing something that reinforces their positive emotions, we end up filling our own bucket as well. On the other hand, every time we use this dipper to empty someone's bucket, weakening his or her positive emotions, we also end up emptying our own bucket.

With this metaphor, the authors posit that the way we treat other people has a direct influence not only on the well-being, productivity, health, and longevity of others but also on our own. Authentic expressions of gratitude and appreciation can transform our relationships at work, in the family, and with everyone around us and, thus, should be encouraged.

Google is a multibillion-dollar enterprise regularly recognized as one of the best companies to work for.[7] Its head offices are known for their distinctive architectural features, which also support sustainability by respecting the community and the environment. Workplaces are spacious and have leisure areas and activities. The company encourages employees to move about more, stay physically active, and eat healthily. There is an organizational culture that values physical and mental health and well-being. Though Google is a giant in the technology field, most of the initiatives that set it apart could be applied in companies of any size that wish to make employee well-being a priority.[8]

This is an example of systemic thinking, in which, by focusing on the different aspects of SPIRE, the system as a whole benefits—the employees are happier at work, and the organization enjoys greater productivity and profitability.

Why invest in employee satisfaction? As employees become more fulfilled, they automatically become more creative, productive, resilient, motivated, engaged, and effective at working in teams.

Until recently, the prevailing thinking in the field of organizational behavior was a mindset that originated during the Industrial Revolution in the eighteenth century, which focused on making employees more efficient, as if they were machines on an assembly line. Currently, with the evolution of technology and the constant demand for innovation, organizational needs have changed, and there is a greater need for people who can think outside the box, apply their skills, and work as a team. Often, agile squads are created—multidisciplinary teams formed for a short period to deliver a specific project before being reassigned to new ones.

The metaphor of the company as a machine has given way to that of a garden, as described at the beginning of this chapter, in which we seek to create conditions for employees to flourish, develop their skills, build their knowledge, and realize their potential. Thus, the individuality of each person combines with the interdependence of all so that the whole garden can thrive and benefit.

The Genius of the *And*

The motto of the Olympic Games is *"Citius, Altius, Fortius"* (Faster, Higher, Stronger). It represents the aspirations behind the Olympics and is an invitation to push ourselves further, both as athletes and as a society. During the 2020 Olympic games in Tokyo, the International Olympic Committee added the Latin word *Communiter* (Together) to emphasize solidarity during tough times, such as the pandemic. The motto now reads, "Faster, Higher, Stronger—Together."

The secret to a full life lies in the genius of the *and*, rather than the tyranny of the *or*, as discussed previously. This means that an alternative motto of "Slower, Deeper, and Kinder" should be deemed not to oppose the original Olympic slogan but, rather, to complement it.

In life, there are situations in which we truly need to be more efficient, do more, and climb higher, and there are others in which it is good to slow down and examine the details in gaining a better understanding of what we are doing. There are times when we need to be strong and times when we need to connect to our more vulnerable side.

In some motorsports, the driver must decide when to make a pit stop to refuel and change tires. This is a strategic decision, the outcome of which could mean winning or losing the race. The idea of leaving the track may seem like a waste of precious seconds at first, but there have been several instances when drivers ignored the request to make a pit stop and regretted it afterward.

Grit and perseverance are crucial characteristics for achieving excellence, but it is essential to know when to persist and when to review our goals. We need to be alert as to whether our persistence is affecting our health or causing us to burn out and whether we are being true to ourselves. There are times when reviewing our expectations and changing course is the smartest, most strategic, and most courageous thing to do. We realize our potential when grit and perseverance serve our values and our goals.

There is a lot to be learned from the outside world and the many stimuli that bombard us, but there is also much to learn from our inner world and from silence. Today we often see people at the point of burnout because they are constantly pushing that bit harder, ignoring the pit stops in life, until the situation becomes unsustainable and often irreversible.

Since the coronavirus pandemic began in 2020, remote work has become a reality for a significant number of people. One of the starkest challenges to working from home is the lack of boundaries between work, leisure, household chores, and childcare.

Lewis Senior, CEO and cofounder of Equilibria, a consulting company, suggests that it is important to establish these boundaries. He told me, "We often need an external reminder to make this distinction, such as taking a walk around the block after the working day is over or even taping a sign to the door that reads, 'Office,' which is removed at the end of work-related activities."

When we carry out one task at a time, in an era when multitasking tends to dominate our day, we focus our attention and connect with the present moment, which makes us more productive, improves the quality of what we are doing, and enhances our level of engagement. In addition, setting boundaries gives us clarity about the time allocated to different aspects of our lives and helps us identify opportunities for breaks—which allow us to replenish our energy reserves, as discussed in chapter 6.

We also need moments of recollection, to take time to be alone and enter a more introspective state. Introspection refers to becoming aware of, and reflecting on, our inner experiences, such as our thoughts and feelings. Making a habit of this promotes a significant increase in self-knowledge and empowers us to deal with day-to-day challenges.

The social-distancing measures introduced during the COVID-19 pandemic led some people to feel isolated, while others had the day-to-day experience of living with family members magnified. It is interesting to note that the sensation of loneliness was not necessarily assuaged by this intense interaction, as sharing a living space does not necessarily mean, de facto, connecting and relating to those around you.

For those who have spent more time with family, the incidents of conflict may have increased, which is only natural. The difficulty in resolving these conflicts, however, may have been exacerbated by those involved being unable to experience moments of recollection. It takes a conscious effort to establish these breaks in our daily routines.

It also falls to us to prioritize time with the people we care about. It may sound strange to schedule dinner with your family, with whom you have spent entire days for months, but the point here is about the quality of the time spent. It is about breaking out from auto mode and truly connecting with the people you love. Whether during or outside of a pandemic, creating opportunities and routines for nurturing relationships, with ourselves and with those who matter to us, is an important contributor to our mental health and happiness.

Tal Ben-Shahar told me he has an agreement with his family—his wife and three children—that they have a movie night once a week. However, one week, during the pandemic, he had a tough day. As much as he wanted, he knew he would not be entirely there. He said, "At seven o'clock, I told them I wasn't feeling well and needed a few moments alone. I went to my room, opened a book, cried a little over what had happened that day, and went to sleep. The next morning, I was feeling better."

In addition to illustrating the importance of balancing moments alone with those connecting with the family, his example also demonstrates how he was able to identify his own needs and take the initiative to meet them. As he himself put it, "There are times when we want help in resolving a problem. There are others when we just want to be listened to. Then there are those moments when we need some time to ourselves, in order to be able to deal with a situation."

Self-knowledge and authenticity are key to recognizing what is best for us and seeking understanding, someone to talk to, or help from those around us.

Hope and Expectation

French gymnast Samir Aït Saïd competed in his first Olympics in Rio in 2016. For him, it was a magical moment, and he was proud to represent his country. However, when he jumped from the pommel horse, he noticed all the spectators were in shock at his landing—some held their hands over their mouths, and others were crying in the stands. Samir had fallen badly, suffering a double open fracture in his left leg. Those watching thought they were witnessing the early end to a young and talented sporting career.

But that never crossed Samir's mind. While still in hospital, unable to put his feet on the ground, he declared confidently, "Believe me, the Tokyo adventure is still on the radar," referring to the Olympics four years on.[9]

Once he was able to walk again, using a walker, he began his mental preparation, even though people told him it was impossible. To fulfill his dream, he would need to be prepared in much less than four years and compete in the Olympic trials.

Having recovered from his injury, with just two months of training behind him, he returned to compete in the London heats of the gymnastics World Cup, from which he qualified for the World Cup finals in Montreal in 2019. There he prepared for his specialty, the rings, needing to finish in the top three to secure his place in Tokyo. If he finished fourth, it would be over. With an almost perfect display in the final set of exercises, he fought his way into third place. He said, "Fate delivers all of us some knocks, and I had my share. But I had to fight!" It was hope, which never deserted him, that drove him on.

American psychologist Rick Snyder was a prominent scholar in the field of positive psychology and was known for his pioneering work in the study of hope. His theory posits that people are more likely to change their future when they have both willpower and *way power*—knowing how to get it done. The union of thoughts such as *I am determined to do it* with *I know what to do to get there, even if the path is arduous* generates a sense of hope, as with French gymnast Saïd.

Optimistic people are often happier and more successful. They tend to feel less anxious and stressed and deal better with the challenges and obstacles in their path. A key aspect to this is the way most optimistic people interpret their emotions. Faced with adversity, we can consider suffering as permanent and pervasive or as temporary and specific. For example, if players are frustrated by their own performance in a game, they might have thoughts like *I'm frustrated, and this is not going to pass* (permanent) or *I'm very frustrated. My life is horrible* (pervasive). This way of thinking leads us to conclude the situation is hopeless.

However, if the thoughts are instead *I'm frustrated right now, but I know this feeling will pass, and I'll feel good again* (temporary) or *I'm upset now, but I've already identified what I need to improve and how to practice this new skill* (specific), the person will tend to perceive the situation as manageable.

Optimistic individuals tend to interpret emotions as temporary and specific, which allows them to see themselves as active agents rather than passive victims of the situation. Consequently, they are more likely to engage in attitudes that bring them closer to achieving their goals.

Hope can also manifest itself in the expectations we set for future events, which then have the power to influence the behavior of both ourselves and others. Expectations can even affect the body's physiological response.

In medicine, it is called the placebo effect—health improves simply from the psychological effects derived from believing in the supposed medication received.

For more than forty years, Herbert Benson, professor of mind-body medicine at Harvard Medical School, has been an advocate of studying this effect, which to date has not been fully understood. He has said, "The placebo effect probably starts long before the patient takes the pill. It is associated with the relationship he establishes with the doctor, the way he views his symptoms and his expectations and beliefs regarding the treatment."[10]

When my father told me about his experiences in the Olympics, I dreamed of doing something similar, but women's water polo was not yet recognized by the International Olympic Committee. I had high hopes that the situation could be changed, and my enthusiasm rubbed off on my family. We gathered other athletes, family, and members of the sports community who all shared the same dream. From this developed a great collective expectation, which certainly influenced achievements with respect to the courage to act, as described in chapter 7.

Hope is essential for us to achieve our goals, which, in turn, will guide our journey to happiness. It is important to look around ourselves and identify the elements, both external and internal, that will be needed along this journey and that will lead to a happy and successful life.

- Studies from positive psychology have shown that people who find happiness along life's journey have better relationships; live longer; and are more creative, productive, and successful at work.

- High performance cannot be sustained if it is not associated with a journey of happiness.

- Our sense of fulfillment does not come simply from meeting our goals but from the process of achieving something meaningful to us.

- Happiness should be pursued indirectly, by working on the spiritual, physical, intellectual, relational, and emotional dimensions of our inner journey.

- Our level of well-being depends on what we choose to focus on and how we interpret the events that take place in our lives.

- When we appreciate the good and the beauty around us, life itself appreciates in value, becoming even more special than it already is.

- Expressing gratitude consistently and meaningfully changes our perspective on life events and encourages us to live in the present and develop the habit of focusing on positive experiences.

- Employees who work for companies that invest in their well-being are more creative, more engaged, and more effective at working in teams.

- The key to a fulfilled life lies in the genius of the *and*, when we combine the grit and determination to reach our goals with strategic pit stops for reflection and, occasionally, charting a new course.

- There are times in life when we should strive to be faster, higher, and stronger, while at other times, we need to go slower, deeper, and kinder. We need both approaches in order to thrive.

- Optimistic people tend to be happier and more successful while also feeling less anxious and stressed.

Powerful Questions to Reflect Upon

- What is happiness to you?
- How are the spiritual, physical, intellectual, relational, and emotional aspects of your life? Which element is in greatest need of your attention right now?
- What aspects of your journey have you focused your attention on?
- Can you name three things you are grateful for today?
- What are your expectations for tomorrow? What is about to happen that makes you excited?
- Have you applied the genius of the *and* in your life? Reflect on practical examples in your daily life.
- Have you allowed moments of inner silence and creative intensity throughout your day?

CONCLUSIONS FROM DIMENSION 4:
MEANING AND CHOICES

———

In this fourth dimension of the book, I have discussed the factors that guide our choices and give meaning to our journey toward high performance and well-being.

On this journey, in sport or in any aspect of life, self-knowledge is a key concept. It allows us to identify our deepest values that we live by throughout our lives.

To realize our potential, we need to develop a sense of purpose that sets our goals, guides our choices, and allows us to pursue the path toward our dreams.

Happiness is not a consequence of success but an essential factor in achieving it. Nurturing happiness and well-being has positive effects on our physical and mental health and is essential to sustaining performance.

The focus of my work is on developing a process for building self-knowledge, identifying a sense of purpose, and applying the elements we explore in the science of happiness studies. The things on which we focus our attention comprise our reality. When we focus on whatever it is we choose to transform—and act consistently and intentionally—we find excellence.

CONCLUSION

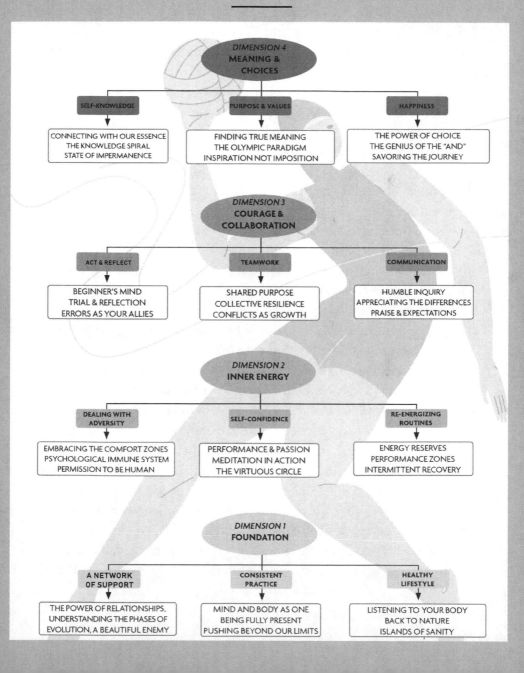

DIMENSION 4
MEANING & CHOICES

SELF-KNOWLEDGE	PURPOSE & VALUES	HAPPINESS
CONNECTING WITH OUR ESSENCE THE KNOWLEDGE SPIRAL STATE OF IMPERMANENCE	FINDING TRUE MEANING THE OLYMPIC PARADIGM INSPIRATION NOT IMPOSITION	THE POWER OF CHOICE THE GENIUS OF THE "AND" SAVORING THE JOURNEY

DIMENSION 3
COURAGE & COLLABORATION

ACT & REFLECT	TEAMWORK	COMMUNICATION
BEGINNER'S MIND TRIAL & REFLECTION ERRORS AS YOUR ALLIES	SHARED PURPOSE COLLECTIVE RESILIENCE CONFLICTS AS GROWTH	HUMBLE INQUIRY APPRECIATING THE DIFFERENCES PRAISE & EXPECTATIONS

DIMENSION 2
INNER ENERGY

DEALING WITH ADVERSITY	SELF-CONFIDENCE	RE-ENERGIZING ROUTINES
EMBRACING THE COMFORT ZONES PSYCHOLOGICAL IMMUNE SYSTEM PERMISSION TO BE HUMAN	PERFORMANCE & PASSION MEDITATION IN ACTION THE VIRTUOUS CIRCLE	ENERGY RESERVES PERFORMANCE ZONES INTERMITTENT RECOVERY

DIMENSION 1
FOUNDATION

A NETWORK OF SUPPORT	CONSISTENT PRACTICE	HEALTHY LIFESTYLE
THE POWER OF RELATIONSHIPS, UNDERSTANDING THE PHASES OF EVOLUTION, A BEAUTIFUL ENEMY	MIND AND BODY AS ONE BEING FULLY PRESENT PUSHING BEYOND OUR LIMITS	LISTENING TO YOUR BODY BACK TO NATURE ISLANDS OF SANITY

The 1981 Oscar-winning movie *Chariots of Fire* made a great impression on me as a child. I remember watching it with my parents and brothers and getting emotional. Based on a true story, it centers on two young British Olympians. Eric Liddell is a devout Christian who believes that his athletic abilities are a gift from God and that exploiting his gift to the maximum is the perfect way to give back. Harold Abrahams, meanwhile, is a Jewish student at Cambridge who dreams of proving to his anti-Semitic colleagues, and to the world, that Jews are not inferior in any way. Liddell and Abrahams took gold in the four hundred meters and hundred meters, respectively, at the 1924 Paris Olympics.

More than on their achievements, the movie focuses on the inspiring journeys of the two athletes. Both have a strong sense of purpose and are committed to fulfilling their dreams, overcoming the many obstacles that life places in their paths. The film extols the idea that the journey to the podium is the greatest reward for all their efforts. The final scene, with the runners on the beach, accompanied by Vangelis's soundtrack, still sends chills through me and reminds me of my own experiences when, as a child, I was introduced to sport on the beach with my father.

The melody has become an anthem for marathon runners the world over, and for me, it represents the power of approaching the finish line with the certainty that the maximum effort was applied to get there. While humming this song, I welcome you, once again, through these final pages. I hope your journey so far has been rewarding, with plenty of useful ideas to consider for your own life.

My mission with this book is to inspire and to offer the tools—through the WeTeam method—for you to discover the best version of yourself for this present moment in time and to realize your full potential on a journey of excellence and happiness. The great inspiration in developing the method was the maxim that gives the book its name: that sport is a stage for life. My experience in water polo has taken me on different journeys of discovery, both within and outside myself. The learning process has been a step in my journey of one thousand miles and has been beyond my imagination. It is indescribable how much I have learned, not only in the sports arena but also about the essence of human nature, the integration of our mind and body, how to surpass our limits, and the power of a purpose.

Playing sport has brought me closer to my family, helped me identify solutions and navigate through corporate life, and assisted me in managing the challenges of being a present mother to my family. I have gained the strength that comes from having purpose and cultivating dreams and the courage to act and experiment. I have glimpsed the power of relationships, of visualization, and of meditation and how to access the flow state, our peak performance, when we combine our passion and skills.

The power of sport—a laboratory that prepares us for life and allows us to apply these lessons to any other activity—was also evident in the life stories of the athletes who shared their experiences with my father and me as we went about writing these pages. It was gratifying to see, in their stories, the same passion and sense of purpose in playing sport that we share in our family.

In the WeTeam method, I have crystalized these lessons, having substantiated them scientifically and packaged them didactically to translate the knowledge into actions that can be more easily absorbed and applied. The four dimensions are interconnected and make up part of the same system, so when you work on one, the others are also positively impacted. It all comes down to the choices we make in seeking to transform our lives. We are creatures who have good habits and other habits we would like to improve. The key to introducing a good new habit is to focus on reality.

The WeTeam Method

In dimension 1, we talked about the importance of having a good foundation that enables us to have freedom of choice, with emphasis on three key aspects: a support network; investment of time, presence, and dedication in honing our skills; and a healthy lifestyle.

Having a support network is important not only in childhood but throughout our journey. It can be made up of family, friends, educators, managers, and teammates and also includes support from our community, organizations, and the government.

The time we spend with the people we care about and who care about us is the biggest contributor to happiness. Cultivating quality relationships with those with whom we can celebrate achievements and share our vulnerabilities garners us the support we need to develop our potential.

Achieving mastery and dominion over any competency requires continual practice and engagement in deep learning. Training should be treated as a competition, wherein we apply ourselves with total focus on the present moment, seeking to go one step further each day and generate incremental improvements. Consistent repetition and reminders lead to new habits that automate our actions and behaviors, thus freeing us to act more strategically.

Our body and mind are interconnected. Therefore, taking care of our bodies is key to making a difference in the quest for excellence in any activity. Healthy living requires us to respect our own nature and to understand the need to stay physically active, eat properly, rest well, and allow ourselves human touch. For example, an authentic hug emits much positive energy yet is often missing these days as we increasingly switch to virtual interactions.

For dimension 2, we discussed how to connect with our inner strength to deal with challenges and obstacles in our path, whether in striving for high performance or in facing the ups and downs that naturally come our way in life. The essential elements are how we learn from adversity and how we develop self-confidence and energizing routines in our lives.

According to the Kaiser Family Foundation, in recent years, there has been an increase in the recorded number of people diagnosed with anxiety, loneliness, and depression in several countries around the world, a trend that has been exacerbated by the COVID pandemic. Not only has the number of people diagnosed increased, but also, their average age is falling, as the problem is affecting increasing numbers of the young.[1] This is a concern that impacts parents, educators, managers, and the rest of us. With the coronavirus pandemic, it has become clear that we need not only to develop antibodies to the disease but also to build our psychological immune system. That is not to say that we will not get sick anymore but rather that we will become less so, and when we do, we will recover more quickly. So how do we develop this psychological immunity?

One of the most powerful lessons from competitive sport is that it is possible to exercise and improve our mental vigor. Not everything that happens in life is for the best, but we can always choose to make the best of what happens. When handling adversity, no matter how complex it may be, in sport or elsewhere, we strengthen our psychological muscles, which allows us to learn how to manage such situations, build self-confidence, and grow. Like physical and technical skills, psychological skills need time, practice, repetition, and patience for performance to improve and more consistent results to be obtained.

All emotions are legitimate, and it is important to give ourselves permission to be human and to accept painful feelings and allow them to flow through us. We should also allow ourselves to be happy and celebrate our achievements. Happiness is contagious. It increases our self-confidence and positively impacts those around us.

To cultivate self-confidence, we should focus not only on how we feel or think about ourselves but also on how we behave. By acting confidently and self-assuredly, we feel more confident and self-assured. We should seek to identify and develop our strengths, which are things that give us pleasure when we do them and things we do well. On the other hand, it is important to identify our potential limiters, so we can work on improving them and thus reduce errors and enhance our strengths.

For us to remain in the high-performance zone, it is necessary to combine periods when we push our limits with periods of recovery and energy renewal. Recovery routines should be applied at the macro, medium, and micro levels—such as taking annual vacations, ensuring quality sleep, and scheduling small breaks throughout the day to engage in breathing and meditation.

In dimension 3, we discussed how to cultivate a willingness to experiment and develop a spirit of collaboration. The key components are courage to act, teamwork, and communication.

Curiosity relates to our desire to learn, with an openness to experiment and make things happen. Combined, these attitudes lead us to understand what we can achieve. It is important to continually focus on action and reflection in order to access what has been learned. Mistakes and failures are a great opportunity for growth. Thus, fear of failure is the number-one enemy to our development.

A team creates a whole that is greater than the sum of its parts. To create a real team—in sport, the family, or the corporate world—it is necessary to invest quality time in different environments, to be willing and determined to survive times of conflict, and to learn from those times. We need to cultivate a healthy relationship with ourselves first and then expand this attitude to embrace others.

Effective communication contributes to developing trust, connection, and the forging of relationships. Throughout this process, it is essential to know ourselves, to listen, to show empathy for others, and to be genuinely curious and interested in getting to know them.

In dimension 4, we talked about finding greater purpose in our lives on a journey toward excellence and fulfillment. The three aspects related to this are self-knowledge, purpose and values, and happiness.

Self-knowledge and continuous learning are vital concepts that span all the dimensions of the WeTeam method. The process of getting to know ourselves flows like a spiral, in which the deeper we delve into our learning, the more we elevate our wisdom and understanding. Self-knowledge requires effort, dedication, and some introspection in reflecting on the experiences of the day.

In our daily lives, in order to make the best choices and chart a course of action, we should alternate our perspective between moments when we live intensely in the here and now (zoom in) and moments when we step back and look at the bigger picture (zoom out).

Identifying values, purpose, and meaning is crucial to following a path to excellence and happiness. When we find meaning in what we do or experience, we gain the strength to overcome the obstacles and challenges we face along the way. When we set long-term goals, we gain a sense of direction, which allows us to fully enjoy the journey and experience the present moment intensely.

Contrary to what we might think, happiness is not a consequence of success but an essential ingredient to achieving it. Cultivating happiness has positive effects on our physical and mental well-being and on our creativity and productivity, enabling us to be more engaged in achieving our goals. In order to be healthy and fulfilled, we need to work on the spiritual, physical, intellectual, relational, and emotional dimensions of our lives. All are interconnected, and at certain times, we will need to focus more on one aspect than another.

It is also important to strengthen the positivity muscle by learning to show a greater appreciation for events each day. We exercise this by looking out for the positive aspects in our journey with both hope and gratitude, because our well-being derives from what we choose to focus on and how we interpret events around us.

For me, happiness is associated with the choices we make. As a high-performance coach and mentor, I believe in the interconnectedness of all the elements in our lives. My role is to help everyone—from athletes, families, and managers to sports and corporate teams—identify the point of leverage at which interventions will promote a positive impact throughout the system as a whole.

Now It Is Up to You

I have prepared this book as a way of introducing the WeTeam method, every aspect of which is supported by a wide range of renowned writers, educators, philosophers, neuroscientists, psychologists, and researchers. It has also been my wish to share—in a way that is accessible but can truly impact your life—not only my story and that of my father but also the stories of many different athletes and coaches from different sports and countries.

As the great Greek philosopher Aristotle suggested, excellence is about what we do, not what we preach. Everything I have presented here only makes sense if it is put into practice and coupled with *mesearch*. Energy is generated from action—ideally with something we are passionate about. We often focus on things that do not make us happy, and that is why mesearch is so important. It is the act of experimenting and discovering new things that will enable us to fulfill our potential.

Even a small dose of energy allows us to begin an activity that will self-perpetuate—that is, one that leads us to produce more energy in an ascending spiral of fulfillment and well-being.

I want you to feel inspired, to reflect, and to identify what works for you at this present moment in your life. I invite you to carry out your own process of introspection and action.

Just as you need to cultivate your support network to sustain high performance and happiness, you are also part of someone else's support network, whether as a family member, educator, coach, manager, or team member. Everything discussed in this book can also be applied to encouraging those around you to fulfill their potential.

In supporting someone, we must keep in mind that the goal is to plant seeds that will germinate, grow, and flourish in their own time, which may not always be the time we are expecting. Never forget the power your expectations have on others. Setting the example as a role model is worth a thousand words. Be an example of what you want to see in others and in the wider world.

In 1675, the father of the theory of gravity, Isaac Newton, wrote in a letter to another English physicist, Robert Hooke, "If I have seen further, it is by standing on the shoulders of Giants."[2] This phrase is famous for demonstrating his humility in recognizing the scientists who preceded him as pivotal to his own contribution. Also embedded in this idea is that it is possible to create a positive spiral of evolution, wherein we each make increments based on what we learn from others.

I started this book by recounting a childhood memory in which I watched the beach while clinging to my father's shoulders as we celebrated pushing back the boundaries in swimming out farther than the surfers. I am immensely grateful to him for having always been this giant for me, allowing me to grow on the back of his teachings in sport and in life and to learn from all his experience and be inspired by his values and attitudes.

I believe in the power of sharing experiences; in interdependence; and in our ability to act as shoulders on which others can grow, evolve, and see further than we can and from other perspectives.

My most genuine wish is that as you read this book, you will superimpose your own knowledge and experiences over mine and, in so doing, excel. May you go as far as your potential can lead you!

MEMORIES

Pedro, with the old-style unprotected cap, at a
championship in Buenos Aires, Argentina, 1962.

Pedro at the World University Championship, known
as the Universiade, in Porto Alegre, Brazil, 1963.

Closing ceremony of the Tokyo Olympics, 1964. Pedro at the front.

Pedro waving at the closing ceremony of
the Mexico City Olympics, 1968.

Pedro with the Brazilian national team at the South American Championship (front row, in the middle), Arica, Chile, 1972.

Pedro receiving the gold medal at the South American Championship, Arica, Chile, 1972.

Cristiana, age three, in front of the pool Brazil, 1974.

Pedro and Cristiana at the World Aquatic Sports
Championships in Perth, Australia, 1991.

Cristiana celebrating qualification for the finals of the
Italian Championship with Visnova in Rome, 1991.

Filipe and Guilherme (brothers) watching Cristiana's
first game for Visnova in Velletri, Italy, 1991.

Celebrating the Champions Cup
(European interclub championship)
with the other Orizzonte Catania players,
Italy, 1993.

Receiving recognition as one of the best players
playing in the State of São Paulo, Brazil, 1994.

Cristiana inducted to the world-star team after being elected one of the seven best players in the world and second-highest scorer in the championship, Perth, Australia, 1998.

Receiving the award for outstanding achievement in Brazilian sport from the hands of Pelé in Brasília, Brazil, 1998.

Cristiana setting off with her parents for the Pan American Games in Winnipeg, Canada, 1999.

Olga, Cristiana's mother and director of Brazilian women's water polo, at the opening ceremony of the Pan American Games in Winnipeg shortly after the women's game was approved as an Olympic sport, 1999.

Cristiana with the Brazilian national water polo
team in Winnipeg, Canada, 1991.

Cristiana (with arm raised) celebrating
victory in Winnipeg, Canada, 1999.

Winning the bronze medal at the Pan American Games in
Winnipeg, Canada. Cristiana is holding the Brazilian flag,
and her mother, Olga, is at her side, in the pool, 1999.

With the bronze medal in Winnipeg, Canada, 1999.

Cristiana and yachtsman Robert Scheidt are received
by President Fernando Henrique Cardoso (center);
the minister for tourism and education, Rafael
Greca; and the president of the Brazilian Olympic
Committee, Carlos Nuzman, in Brasília, Brazil, 1999.

Olga and Cristiana with President Fernando Henrique
Cardoso at a lunch celebrating the achievements
of Brazilian sport in Brasília, Brazil, 1999.

Cristiana as an executive of Itaú Unibanco in São Paulo, Brazil, 2015.

Family moment celebrating the birth of the third daughter in São Paulo, Brazil, 2012.

Cristiana, Olga, and Pedro at the ceremony where Olga Pinciroli received the Paragon Award from the Swimming Hall of Fame, USA, 2015.

With the three daughters at the final of the Florida State Championship, USA, 2021.

Daughter Alissa is approved as a student
athlete at Stanford University, USA, 2021.

The Pinciroli and Pascual family, the support base, USA, 2021.

ABOUT THE AUTHORS

Cristiana Pinciroli

Born in São Paulo, I am a former professional water polo player and former executive with Brazilian bank Itaú Unibanco. Today I am a founding partner of WeTeam, a human development consultancy that works to mentor organizational teams in the field of high performance and positive psychology. I live, and am passionate about, high performance! During my forty-nine years, I have learned to be a professional athlete; an executive in the financial markets; an entrepreneur; and a wife and a mother to three girls.

The Athlete

My career began in professional sport. I was captain of the women's Brazilian water polo team for fifteen years, capturing a bronze medal at the Pan American Games in Winnipeg in 1999. I participated in three world championships, and at the last of the three, in Perth in 1998, I was the second-highest scorer and elected one of the seven best players in the world. I also represented the Italian national team and played professionally in Italy, winning both local championships and the European interclub championship.

The Executive

A former executive with Itaú Unibanco, I can call on twenty-five years of business experience. I was global chief human resources officer for

Itaú US and Bahamas and was the company's ombudsman and quality-excellence head for Itaú Brazil. I also worked with strategic management and sales. During my tenure, I developed strategies for human resources, performance and talent management, and leadership coaching. I also delivered business-transformation projects that promoted better people services, diversity, equal opportunities in the workplace, and engagement.

WeTeam

In 2019, I launched WeTeam, a company founded on uniting my personal, sporting, and professional experiences with the fruits of studying positive psychology and the science of happiness. WeTeam is a consulting and mentoring company specialized in the development of human potential, high performance, and happiness. I believe that the secret to living life to the fullest is in identifying our purpose and finding our essence. My job is to guide people through this process and to help those looking to develop their seed of greatness to flourish.[15]

The Book

These pages are the realization of a personal goal to write a book with my father, Pedro Pinciroli Júnior, recounting our experiences both in sport and in developing the potential, abilities, and knowledge of others.

Social Action

I also act as an education curator for a Brazilian social start-up called AkiPosso+ (akipossomais.org), with a view to identifying partners and relevant content for promoting social inclusion and transformation in the lives of people in vulnerable situations.

---

[15] For more information, visit weteam.today.

Pedro Pinciroli Júnior

Born in São Paulo on December 16, 1943, Pedro is a former Olympic water polo player who later worked as a media executive. Currently, he is president of iFob Group—Innovative Family Office—developing business opportunities in the financial and real estate sectors.

The Executive

Pedro worked in media as general manager and member of the senior board of Grupo Folha, the conglomerate that owns and publishes Brazilian newspaper *Folha de São Paulo*.

In 1991–1992, he presided over the ANJ—the National Association of Newspapers—whose goal is to defend free expression, promoting the newspaper as a bulwark for citizenship. He was responsible for launching the Jornal na Educação program in Brazil, an initiative that took newspapers into the classroom.

Pedro was also the creative mind behind Universo Online (UOL), one of Brazil's earliest web portals, acting as chairman of the board of directors from 1996 to 1999. Today this portal is the largest provider of Portuguese-language content in the world and of internet access in Brazil.

He also conceived of *Valor Econômico*, an economics, finance, and business newspaper, which launched in 2000, arising from a partnership between the groups Folha and Globo. He participated in the founding of CONAR in 1980, the National Advertising Self-Regulation Council, acting as an adviser for seven years.

Internationally

From 1997 to 1999, he served as a member of the executive committee of the Inter-American Press Society, an organization dedicated to defending freedom of expression and the press in the Americas.

In 1997, he was president of the Second International Conference of Newspapers in Education at the Memorial da América Latina in São Paulo, promoted by WAN (the World Association of Newspapers), a global press organization that represents more than eighteen thousand publications in more than 120 countries.

He received special recognition from UNESCO Director General Federico Mayor Zaragoza for leading a team in drafting the media declaration for the consolidation of a culture of peace. The year 2000 was declared the International Year for the Culture of Peace.

The Athlete

Pedro competed as a water polo player in two Olympic Games (Tokyo in 1964 and Mexico City in 1968), which made a lasting impression on both his mind and his body, helping to form a frame of reference that guides his thoughts and actions.

At the 1968 Olympic Games in Mexico, he finished among the top five scorers and was named one of the standout water polo players of the Olympics. He was runner-up and top scorer at the Pan American Championship in Winnipeg in 1967 and captain of the Brazilian team from 1968 to 1974. In 1965, he was recognized by the International Amateur Swimming Federation (FINA) as the standout player in the Americas and was nominated by the World Water Polo Coaches Association (WWPCoach) as a player who could play on any team in the world.

In 1967, he was recognized by sports critics in Brazilian publisher Universo's annual yearbook as one of the ten best water polo players in the world.

In 1971, he was recognized by North American magazine *Water Polo Scoreboard* and Italian newspaper *La Gazzetta dello Sport* as a world-class player in the sport.

The Strategist: Social Contribution to the Sport

Pedro conceptualized and led the process for adopting the Piva Law, approved by President Fernando Henrique Cardoso on July 16, 2001. According to this law, 2 percent of the gross revenue from all federal lotteries will be transferred to the Brazilian Olympic and Paralympic Committees, the COB and CPB.

INTERVIEWEES

My thanks to all who kindly agreed to be interviewed, contributing their time and sharing their stories and insights, which have greatly enriched the content of this book.

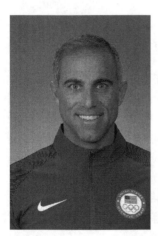

Adam Krikorian

Adam Krikorian coached the US women's national water polo team to three consecutive Olympic gold medals: in London in 2012, the US team's first ever Olympic gold medal; Rio in 2016; and Tokyo in 2020. Since his arrival in 2009, Team USA has competed in twenty-two major FINA championships and come away with the gold medal in nineteen of them. After the 2016 Olympic Games, Krikorian was named Coach of the Games by the USOC at the Team USA Awards. In early 2017, he was also honored by the Los Angeles Sports Council and the LA Sports Awards, receiving the first ever Extraordinary Achievement in Olympic Sport award. Krikorian won fifteen NCAA national championships as a player, assistant coach, and head coach at UCLA. He was awarded the 2004 national men's water polo Coach of the Year and the 2001, 2005, 2006, and 2007 national women's water polo Coach of the Year. Krikorian himself was an elite water polo player and swimmer. He was inducted into the UCLA Athletics Hall of Fame in 2016.

Aníbal Sánchez

Professional right-handed pitcher Aníbal Sánchez has played in Major League Baseball (MLB) since 2006. Born in 1984 in Maracay, Venezuela, he fell in love with the sport at the age of seven. In 2004, Sánchez completed a no-hitter,[16] the fourth in the history of the Florida Marlins. He was the nineteenth rookie pitcher since 1900 to complete the feat. He has played with the Detroit Tigers, Atlanta Braves, and Washington Nationals—the team with which he won the 2019 World Series.

Photo: Paul Kim at MLB.

Brenda Villa

Brenda Villa is the most decorated water polo player of all time. She was a four-time Olympic medalist—in Sydney in 2000, Athens in 2004, Beijing in 2008, and London in 2012. She was named Women's Water Polo Player of the Decade by FINA in the 2000s. Villa played for the US women's team for sixteen years. She now serves as director of equity and diversity at the Castilleja School in California, where she is also a water polo coach. She is cochair of the USA Water Polo Racial Equity Task Force and cofounder of a nonprofit organization, the Brenda Villa Foundation, which provides access to water sports to young people from under-resourced communities in the United States.

---

[16] When the opposing team fails to register a hit during the entire nine innings.

Bruno Schmidt

Born in Brasília, Bruno is a Brazilian beach volleyball player who won the gold medal at the 2016 Rio Olympics. In 2014, he formed a winning partnership with Alison Cerutti, "the Mammoth." In 2015, they were crowned champions at the World Championship, World Circuit, and World Tour Finals, thus winning the three main titles of the season. Schmidt also competed in the 2020 Tokyo Olympics, partnering with Evandro Oliveira and reaching the round of sixteen.

Felipe Perrone

Born in Rio de Janeiro in 1986, naturalized Spaniard Felipe Perrone plays for CAN Barceloneta and is the current captain of the Spanish national team. He has competed in four Olympic Games: Beijing in 2008, London in 2012 (representing Spain), Rio in 2016 (as captain of the Brazilian national team), and Tokyo in 2020 (as captain of the Spanish team). Perrone has played for clubs in Spain, Italy, and Croatia and is a three-time champion of the European Champions League. He was voted the best player in the world in 2018 and one of the top-ten best players of the century by *Total Water Polo* magazine. Away from the pool, he was founder of and ambassador for the social project Polo do Futuro and director and organizer of the An Olympic Dream campus in 2011 and 2013.

Frank Steel

A graduate of the University of Yale, with an MA from the University of Pennsylvania, Frank Steel spent twelve years as principal of Springside Chestnut Hill Academy, Philadelphia's largest independent private school. Since 2014, he has been head of school at Gulliver Preparatory School, one of the most highly regarded schools in Florida.

Kahena Kunze

Yachtswoman Kahena Kunze was born in São Paulo in 1991 and is a two-time Olympic gold medalist, in Rio in 2016 and Tokyo in 2020, in the 49er FX class. Partnering with helmswoman Martine Grael, she won the world championship in Santander, Spain, in 2014. The following year, the Brazilian Olympic Committee awarded her the Brazilian Olympic Athlete of the Year award. She was named the best yachtswoman in the world in 2014. At the 2015 Pan American Games in Toronto, she took silver. At the 2019 Pan American Games, she was the flag bearer of the Brazilian delegation at the opening ceremony in Lima, where she won yet another gold medal.

Leandro Guilheiro

Brazilian judoka Leandro Guilheiro was born in 1983 in São Paulo. At twenty-one, he won the bronze medal at the 2004 Olympic Games in Athens, and he took bronze again four years later in Beijing in 2008. Guilheiro took silver at the Tokyo World Championships in a different category—under eighty-one kilograms—in 2010 and bronze at the Paris World Championship in 2011. In 2009, 2011, and 2012, he was the Pan American judo champion. He was a medalist at the Pan American Games in Rio in 2007 (silver) and Guadalajara in 2011 (gold).

Lewis Senior

Briton Lewis Senior is a world-renowned leadership and high-performance coach and cofounder of Equilibria, a consulting company specializing in improving interpersonal and organizational communication skills. Senior began his career in the oil industry, and from that experience, he developed his methodology, which has been applied by companies, educational systems, and sports and nonprofit organizations around the world. He coauthored, with his daughter Laura Senior Garcia, an award-winning memoir entitled *At the End of the Day: How One Man Learned to Live like He Was Dying.*

Marcelinho Huertas

Born in São Paulo in 1983, Marcelinho Huertas is a former NBA player, two-time Olympian, and four-time world championship athlete who captains the Brazilian national basketball team. He has won the Copa America twice, in 2005 and 2009, and participated in four World Cups, in Japan in 2006, Turkey in 2010, Spain in 2014, and China in 2019. He is a three-time champion of the Spanish league, where he was voted the best point guard by Liga ABC, Spain's main basketball league, in 2008, 2011, and 2012. In 2015, he was hired to play in the NBA with the LA Lakers, alongside Kobe Bryant. Today he plays for Lenovo Tenerife, where in a single season, he completed 185 assists, the most in the club's history.

Marco Túlio de Mello

A graduate of physical education—specializing in physical education for people with disabilities—from the Federal University of Uberlandia, Marco Túlio de Mello completed his doctorate and postdoctorate at the Federal University of São Paulo. He is a professor on the faculty of physical education, physiotherapy, and occupational therapy at the Federal University of Minas Gerais. A researcher on the effects of sleep on physical exercise, he advised the Brazilian Paralympic Committee between 2010 and 2017. He also worked with the Brazilian Olympic Committee at the 2016 Rio Olympics on a groundbreaking project to help athletes adapt their sleep to perform better at the Olympic Games.

Maria Eugênia Risueño Anjos

A scholar and researcher of yoga for more than thirty-five years, Maria Eugênia Risueño Anjos works with the harmonization of cell-vibration frequencies, meditation, and specialized breathing techniques. She has a degree in the anatomy of movement from the Faculty of Medicine at Santa Casa de São Paulo, psychology, business, languages, and physiotherapy. She is also a master of Reiki and a Deeksha giver, focusing on circular dance. She holds a postgraduate degree in integrative medicine from the Faculty of Albert Einstein Hospital, São Paulo. She coordinates the ARHKA Respiration and Therapeutic Hands Project at the Children's Institute at Hospital das Clinicas in São Paulo.

Martine Grael

Born in Rio de Janeiro in 1991, Grael is a two-time Olympic gold medalist—in Rio in 2016 and Tokyo in 2020—in the 49er FX class. She has won her main tournaments with longtime companion Kahena Kunze. She was the flag bearer of the Brazilian delegation at the opening ceremony for the Pan American Games in Lima in 2019, where she won another gold medal. She was voted Brazilian Olympic Athlete of the Year by the Brazilian Olympic Committee in 2014. That same year, she was voted the best yachtswoman in the world. Grael and Kunze are currently ranked number one in the world in the 49er FX class by the International Sailing Federation. She was the only Brazilian woman to participate in the Volvo Ocean Race, the most challenging ocean-sailing race there is.

Raí Oliveira

Photo: Jairo Goldflus.

Raí Oliveira began his career as a professional soccer player by playing at youth levels for Botafogo Futebol Clube. In 1987, he was transferred to São Paulo Futebol Clube, where he won a Brazilian Championship (1991), two Libertadores da America Cups (1992 and 1993), and one Interclub World Cup (1992). In 1993, he signed for Paris Saint-Germain (PSG), where he won the French championship (1994), four national cups, and the European Cup (1996). In 2020, as part of PSG's fiftieth anniversary, Raí was elected the greatest player in the club's history. He captained the Brazilian national side for three years, winning the World Cup in the United States in 1994. In 1998, Raí founded the Gol de Letra foundation, an organization that serves 4,500 children, adolescents, and young people facing situations of social vulnerability. In 2012, Raí received the Laureus Award in the "Sports for Good" category, which recognizes the use of sport as a means for improving society. For his public service and achievements as an athlete, in 2013, he received the Chevalier de l'Ordre de la Légion d'Honneur from French president François Hollande.

Ratko Rudić

Born in 1948 in then Yugoslavia, Ratko Rudić is considered one of the most successful water polo coaches in the history of the sport. He has won five Olympic medals, including four gold medals (three consecutively), with three different national teams: with Yugoslavia at Moscow in 1980, Los Angeles in 1984, and Seoul in 1988; with Italy at Barcelona in 1992; and with Croatia at London in 2012. In 2007, he was inducted to the International Swimming Hall of Fame, described as "one of the best, if not the best, water polo coach." He received the Order of Duke Branimir in Croatia in 2012 and the Palma al Merito Técnico from the Italian National Olympic Committee in 2018. Ratko was invited to coach the Brazilian men's team for the 2016 Rio Games. In 2018, he became coach of Italian club Pro Recco, until he announced his retirement from water polo once again in 2020.

Robert Scheidt

Born in São Paulo in 1973, Brazilian yachtsman Robert Scheidt has competed in seven Olympics: Atlanta in 1996 (gold), Sydney in 2000 (silver), Athens in 2004 (gold), Beijing in 2008 (silver), London in 2012 (bronze), Rio in 2016, and Tokyo in 2020. At age eleven, he learned to enjoy sailing in challenging conditions and strong winds, a hallmark of his performances in future successes. He took three consecutive golds at the Pan American Games, in 1995, 1999, and 2003. Scheidt later migrated to the Star class, where he paired up with Bruno Prada, and went on to ascend the Olympic podium twice more, at Beijing in 2008 and London in 2012. At Rio in 2016, he returned to the Laser class, where he finished fourth overall. In 2021, at age forty-six, he took part in his seventh Olympics, a Brazilian record, reaching the final.

Rodrigo Koxa

Photo: Aline Cacozzi.

Born in 1979 in Brazil, Rodrigo Koxa holds the Guinness World Record for surfing the biggest wave ever recorded, a giant measuring 24.38 meters, at Nazaré do Oeste in central Portugal. He started surfing at the age of eight, and at fifteen, he decided to accept the challenge of the big waves. In a quest to gain the necessary expertise to become a big rider, he lived in Mexico, Indonesia, Hawaii, and Tahiti. In August 2010, in Chile, Koxa set his first record, surfing the biggest wave ever recorded in South America, with an estimated face height of more than sixty feet.

In 2018, he won the biggest prize of his career: champion of the WSL Big Wave Awards, the Oscars of the surfing world.

Sandy Nitta

Born in California, Sandy Nitta began her career as a swimmer and was part of the team who participated in the 1964 Tokyo Olympics when she was just fifteen years old. After the Olympics, Sandy was team captain for the City of Commerce Swim Team, winning the national championship in 1965. In 1968, she began her coaching career. After two years, she was given the assignment of coaching the US Amateur Athletic Association (AAU) swim team, and she trained many junior Olympic medalists. Between 1980 and 1997, Sandy coached the US women's water polo team, and from 1982 to 1991, they won medals at every world championship they participated in. Sandy Nitta's impact on water sports, especially women's water polo, was recognized with her nomination for the USA Water Polo Hall of Fame. Between 1999 and 2002, she coached the Brazilian women's water polo team, winning a bronze medal at the 1999 Pan American Games in Winnipeg. She now serves as a water polo official at the Mountain Pacific Sports Federation.

Tal Ben-Shahar

Born in Israel, Tal Ben-Shahar is an expert in positive psychology, having founded the HSA, the Happiness Science Academy. He graduated with degrees in philosophy and psychology from Harvard University, where he also completed a PhD in organizational behavior. He taught two of the most popular courses in Harvard history: Positive Psychology and Leadership Psychology. In 2011, he cofounded Potentialife, a company that offers leadership programs based on the science of behavioral change. He is the author of several international best sellers, including *Be Happier: Learn to See Joy in Small Things for Permanent Satisfaction* and *Choose the Life You Want: The Mindful Way to Happiness*, which have been translated into twenty-five languages. Ben-Shahar is a husband and a father of three children. He is also my teacher and mentor and has inspired me greatly.

FEATURED ATHLETES

———

In the pages of this book, I have mentioned the success stories, and tales of overcoming the odds, of a number of elite athletes, to whom I dedicate my sincere appreciation.

Adam Kreek

Canadian Adam Kreek won the gold medal at the world rowing championships in 2002, 2003, and 2007 in the men's eight with coxswain (M8+) category. He qualified for the 2004 Athens Olympics, where he finished fifth, and he won gold at the 2008 Beijing Olympics. Since his sporting career, Kreek's work has focused on executive leadership and performance. In 2019, he published his first book: *The Responsibility Ethic: 12 Strategies Exceptional People Use to Do Work and Make Success Happen*. He is a member of the Canadian Olympic Hall of Fame.

Allyson Felix

North American athlete who competed in the hundred-meter, two-hundred-meter, and four-hundred-meter sprints. She won twenty-five medals total in Olympic Games and World Athletics Championships, eighteen of which are gold. Felix has received the prestigious Jesse Owens Award, the highest award in American athletics, three times—in 2005, 2007, and 2010. She has achieved and advocates for greater gender equality in the salaries and conditions for female athletes. At the 2020 Tokyo Olympics, at age thirty-five, she won the bronze medal in the four hundred meters and gold in the 4×400-meter relay, her eleventh Olympic medal, becoming the most decorated American Olympian in track and field of all time.

Benita Willis

Australian long-distance runner Benita Willis was champion of the World Cross Country Championships, which is considered the most difficult race in the world, in 2004. In addition, she won bronze at the World Half Marathon Championships in 2003 in Portugal and at the World Cross Country Championships in 2006 in Japan. She participated in four Olympics: in Sydney in 2000 (five thousand meters), in Athens in 2004 (ten thousand meters), and in Beijing in 2008 and London in 2012 (marathon). After retiring, she went on to coach Queensland Athletics and the Brisbane Girls Grammar School running program, both in Australia.

Dana Hee

American martial arts athlete Dana Hee won a gold medal in tae kwon do at the 1988 Seoul Olympics. She also took a bronze medal at the 1986 Universiade and silver at the US National Championships in 1988. She was inducted into the Taekwondo Hall of Fame in 2013. Following a career transition, Dana Hee began in the film industry as a stunt double for actresses such as Jennifer Garner, Kristanna Loken, Talisa Soto, and Nicole Kidman, among others. Her TV debut as a stuntwoman was in 1989, in the series *SOS Malibu*. She also works as a sports commentator.

Danny Crates

A former British sprinter, Danny Crates began his career as a rugby player, but following a car accident in which his right arm was amputated, he joined the British Paralympic athletics team. He took the bronze medal in the four hundred meters at the 2000 Sydney Paralympics and gold in the eight hundred meters at Athens in 2004. He was a standard-bearer at the opening ceremony for the 2008 Beijing Paralympics. Crates called time on his sports career in 2009, and since, he has worked as a motivational speaker and high-performance coach. He worked for British TV network Channel 4 as a commentator for the Paralympics at London in 2012 and Rio de Janeiro in 2016.

David Boudia

Diver David Boudia represented the USA at the 2012 London Olympics, winning the gold medal for the men's ten-meter platform event and then, with partner Thomas Finchum, the bronze for the ten-meter platform synchronized event. His current partner in synchronized diving is Nick McCrory, with whom he won the silver medal in the ten-meter synchronized platform at the 2016 Rio Olympics.

Derek Clayton

Born in England, Derek Clayton moved to Australia at the age of twenty-one, where he began his career as a marathon runner. He was twice the world marathon record holder. The first time was at the 1967 Fukuoka Marathon, where he won with a time of 2:09:37. It was the first time anyone had run that distance in less than 2:10:00. Two years later, in Antwerp, Belgium, he lowered his own record to 2:08:34, which was surpassed only twelve years later. He retired from racing in 1974. He was elected to the Sport Australia Hall of Fame in 1999.

Dotsie Bausch

Dotsie Bausch is an American cyclist who, at age thirty-nine, won the silver medal in the team chase at the 2012 London Olympics with Sarah Hammer, Jennie Reed, and Lauren Tamayo. She attributes her longevity in high-performance sports to a plant-based diet. Bausch was featured in the 2015 documentary *Personal Gold: An Underdog Story* and the 2017 documentary *The Game Changers*.

Edwin Moses

Former American athlete Edwin Moses is a two-time Olympic four-hundred-meter hurdles champion: Montreal in 1976 and Los Angeles in 1984. The biggest name in the history of this competition, he won 122 races—107 consecutively—over a period of ten years, breaking the world record four times. Moses became a spokesman among athletes and a key player in a campaign with the International Olympic Committee (IOC) for a change in the rules regarding the requirement for athletes to be amateurs. His dedication led to the creation of an investment fund for athletes, which allowed governments and companies to finance athletes' training. The project was approved by the IOC in 1981, signaling the dawn of the professional era of the Olympic Games.

Iván Fernández

Iván Fernández is a Spanish long-distance runner, competing mainly in cross country and marathons. A video of Fernández guiding his opponent Abel Mutai toward the finish line rather than overtaking him during the Burlada Cross Country race went viral in January 2013. He was praised by the international press for his sportsmanship. His best time in the five-kilometer race was achieved at the Ibero-American Championships held in São Paulo, where he placed third.

Jack Nicklaus

Considered one of the best golfers of all time, American Jack Nicklaus holds the record for winning the most major golf tournaments, with eighteen wins. He was renowned for his physical prowess coupled with great mental and psychological strength. In 1990, at age fifty, he began playing on the senior circuit, where he continued to rack up victories. After retiring from the game, he devoted himself to designing golf courses, and in 1993, he was named US Golf Course Design Architect of the Year.

João Gonçalves

Brazilian swimmer, water polo player, and judo coach João Gonçalves participated in seven Olympic Games: five as an athlete (as a swimmer in Helsinki in 1952 and Melbourne in 1956 and as a water polo player in Rome in 1960, Tokyo in 1964, and Mexico City in 1968) and two as a judo coach (Barcelona in 1992 and Atlanta in 1996). At the Pan American Games, he won silver medals in 1951 and 1967, a bronze in 1959, and a gold 1963. He was the flag bearer of the Brazilian delegation at the 1968 Mexico City Olympics. Away from the pool, he became a judo coach, working with several Olympic medalists. He was honored by the Brazilian Olympic Committee in 2002 with the Adhemar Ferreira da Silva Trophy. He passed away in 2010.

John McEnroe

Former American tennis player John McEnroe, known for his strong temper, reached number one in the ATP world rankings, becoming famous for his epic matches against Björn Borg, Jimmy Connors, and Ivan Lendl. He holds the record for the greatest number of tournament wins held simultaneously in singles and doubles: twenty-nine. He also holds the record for most doubles matches won in a single season: seventy-eight in 1979. In the 1990s, he started a rock band. He is currently a television commentator for tennis. McEnroe has been a member of the International Tennis Hall of Fame since 1999.

Joshua Waitzkin

American chess player Joshua Waitzkin started playing chess at age six, became a national master at thirteen, and became an international master at sixteen. Currently, Waitzkin is dedicated to the practice of martial arts: tai chi and Brazilian jujitsu. Waitzkin is the author of best seller *The Art of Learning: An Inner Journey to Optimal Performance*, which is about personal development, in which he recounts his personal experiences and learning methods. The 1993 movie *Searching for Bobby Fischer* was based on his life and love of chess.

Kobe Bryant

A former NBA basketball player, Kobe Bryant played his entire career as a point guard for the Los Angeles Lakers. He is considered one of the greatest players of all time. He led the Lakers to three consecutive NBA championships between 2000 and 2002 and was the league's top scorer for two consecutive seasons. In 2009 and 2010, he carried the Lakers to two more NBA titles. He won Olympic gold medals at Beijing in 2008 and London in 2012. In 2018, Bryant won the Oscar for best animated short film for *Dear Basketball*. In the same year, he released the book *The*

Mamba Mentality: How I Play. Bryant died in a helicopter crash on January 26, 2020, at age forty-one.

Maya Gabeira

Brazilian professional surfer Maya Gabeira is a big rider who suffered a serious accident in Nazaré, Portugal, in 2013. After a number of surgeries, she returned to practicing the sport, and in 2020, she broke the women's world record by surfing a 22.4-meter wave in Nazaré—the same city where she almost lost her life. The record was made official following an online petition to persuade the World Surf League (WSL) and Guinness World Records (GWR) to establish a women's category for the biggest wave surfed. The petition garnered more than eighteen thousand signatures.

Natalie du Toit

South African swimmer Natalie du Toit was pursuing a promising sports career with Olympic aspirations, when she was involved in a car accident at age seventeen, following which she had one leg amputated. Her love for the sport was so great that three months later, before she started walking again, she was back in the pool with the intention of competing in the 2002 Commonwealth Games. She won a total of twelve gold medals at parasport championships and thirteen Paralympic gold medals: five at Athens in 2004, five at Beijing in 2008, and three at London in 2012. She competed in the 2008 Beijing Olympics, becoming the first female Paralympian to qualify for the ten-kilometer long-distance swimming event, in which she placed sixteenth.

Du Toit was the first athlete from her country to carry the flag at both the Olympics and the Paralympics in the same year.

Roger Bannister

At the Olympics in Helsinki in 1952, Englishman Roger Bannister broke the British record for the 1,500 meters, finishing the race in fourth place. This achievement strengthened his determination to become the first athlete to complete one mile in less than four minutes. He accomplished this feat on May 6, 1954, on Oxford's Iffley Road track, recording a time of

3 minutes and 59.4 seconds. Bannister subsequently became a neurologist and professor at Pembroke College, Oxford.

Ryosuke Irie

Ryosuke Irie is a Japanese swimmer who competes in backstroke events. At the 2012 London Olympics, he won a silver medal in the two-hundred-meter backstroke, a bronze in the hundred-meter backstroke, and another silver in the men's 4×100-meter medley with the Japanese team. During the coronavirus pandemic, he continued his training and achieved his goal of taking part in the Olympics in his home country, in Tokyo in 2020, where he reached the final of the men's two-hundred-meter backstroke.

Samir Aït Saïd

Samir Aït Saïd is a French gymnast and member of the national team. He competed at the 2015 World Artistic Gymnastics Championships in Glasgow and the 2016 Olympics in Rio. At the latter, during qualifications for the vaulting event, Aït Saïd broke his left leg. Recovering in record time, he managed to qualify for the Olympics in Tokyo in 2020 in his specialty, the rings, in which he finished fourth.

Shannon Miller

One of the most successful gymnasts in US history, Shannon Miller is a two-time all-around world champion and a world champion at balance beam, uneven bars, and floor. At the 1996 Atlanta Olympics, she won gold medals on the balance beam and team exercises. She is in the International Gymnastics Hall of Fame. She now hosts a TV show and writes for newspapers and magazines, such as *Sports Illustrated*.

Simidele Adeagbo

Nigerian athlete Simidele Adeagbo competed in the skeleton at the 2018 Winter Olympic Games in Pyeongchang. She is the first female athlete in the sport from Africa and the first black woman to compete in the sport at an Olympics. Previously, Adeagbo was a triple-jump athlete. She actively promotes the transformation of the global image of black women and of the African continent as a whole. She continues to train for the next Winter Olympics.

Tom Brady

NFL quarterback Tom Brady, who won his record-breaking seventh Super Bowl title at the age of forty-three, is considered by many to be the best quarterback in NFL history. In 2017, he launched the book *The TB12 Method: How to Achieve a Lifetime of Sustained Peak Performance*, in which he talks about his diet as well as hydration rules, muscle-flexibility exercises, and guidelines for full-body rest.

Yusra Mardini

Syrian swimmer Yusra Mardini helped to save twenty refugees from a dinghy that was cut adrift in the Mediterranean Sea. At just eighteen years old, Yusra Mardini participated in her first Olympic Games at Rio in 2016, under the flag of the Refugee Olympic Athletes. She competed again four years later at Tokyo in 2020. Mardini is an ambassador for the UN agency for refugees (UNHCR). In 2018, she launched her first book, *Butterfly: From Refugee to Olympian, My Story of Rescue, Hope, and Triumph*.

REFERENCES

Introduction

1   Chris Siddell, "What Is the Toughest Sport in the World?," Bleacher Report, September 14, 2011, https://bleacherreport.com/articles/832927-what-is-the-worlds-toughest-sport.

2   S. Ribeiro, V. Fernandes, N. B. Mota, G. Brockington, S. Pompeia, R. Ekuni, et al., "Ideas for a School of the Future," in *Neurotechnology: Methods, Advances and Application*, ed. Victor Hugo de Albuquerque, Alkinoos Athanasiou, and Sidarta Ribeiro, vol. 1 (Stevenage, UK: Institution of Engineering and Technology [IET] Digital Library, 2020), 247–79.

3   Aristotle, *Nicomachean Ethics*, trans. W. D. Ross, with an introduction by R. W. Browne (n.p.: Neeland Media, 2016).

4   Wholebeing Institute (website), accessed February 3, 2022, https://wholebeinginstitute.com.

5   V. E. Frankl, *Man's Search for Meaning* (Boston: Beacon Press, 2014).

Chapter 1

1   Victoria J. Rideout, Ulla G. Foehr, and Donald F. Roberts, *Generation M²: Media in the Lives of 8- to 18-Year-Olds* (Menlo Park, CA: Kaiser Family Foundation, January 2010), https://www.kff.org/wp-content/uploads/2013/04/8010.pdf. This survey by the Kaiser Family Foundation (a nonprofit organization that acts as an objective source of facts, analyses, and journalism for policy formers, with a focus on questions related to national health) was carried out with over two thousand children and adolescents (aged between eight and eighteen) in the USA and focused on the use of media for entertainment.

2   J. Côté, "The Influence of the Family in the Development of Talent in Sport," *Sport Psychologist* 13, no. 4 (1999): 395–417. Note: In the research they name the first stage "sampling," referring to having first contact with different sports. I have opted to use the term experimentation, as I consider it applies more generally to other contexts.

3   A. J. Visek, S. M. Achrati, H. Mannix, K. McDonnell, B. S. Harris, and L. DiPietro, "The Fun Integration Theory: Toward Sustaining Children and Adolescents Sport Participation," *Journal of Physical Activity & Health*, 12, no. 3 (2015): 424–33.

4   Carol Dweck, "The Perils and Promises of Praise," *Educational Leadership* 65, no. 2 (October 2007): 34–39. Available at http://www.ascd.org.

5   J. Côté and David J. Hancock, "Evidence-Based Policies for Youth Sport Programs," *International Journal of Sport Policy and Politics* 8, no. 1 (2016): 51–65.

6   M. A. Kanters, J. Bocarro, and J. M. Casper, "Supported or Pressured? An Examination of Agreement among Parents and Children on Parent's Role in Youth Sports," *Journal of Sport Behavior* 31, no. 1 (2008): 64–80.

7   "The Truth about Sports Parents...," Ilovetowatchyouplay.com, June 10, 2016, YouTube video, 4:30, https://www.youtube.com/watch?v=u2LR4c3JsmU.

8   Ribeiro et al., "Ideas for a School of the Future."

9   H. Gardner, *Frames of Mind: The Theory of Multiple Intelligences* (New York: Basic Books, 1993).

10   Rita Pierson, "Every Kid Needs a Champion," TED, May 2013, https://www.ted.com/talks/rita_pierson_every_kid_needs_a_champion.

11   *The Complete Essays and Other Writings of Ralph Waldo Emerson*, ed. Brooks Atkinson (New York: Modern Library, 1950).

12   Rafael Nadal, *Rafa: My Story*, with John Carlin (New York: Sphere, 2011).

Chapter 2

1   Daniel T. Willingham, "Ask the Cognitive Scientist: Practice Makes Perfect—but Only If You Practice beyond the Point of Perfection," American Federation of Teachers, Spring 2004, https://www.aft.org/periodical/american-educator/spring-2004/ask-cognitive-scientist-practice-makes-perfect.

2   Rob Clark, *Manchester United's Greatest Games* (n.p.: Pitch Publishing, 2014).

3   Charles Duhigg, *The Power of Habit: Why We Do What We Do in Life and Business* (New York: Random House, 2012).

4   Duhigg, *The Power of Habit*, 78.

5   Ellen Langer, "Counterclockwise: The Power of Possibility" (talk, Happiness & Its Causes, 2012), https://www.youtube.com/watch?v=fZffBAefwUM.

6   T. Eriksson and J. Ortega, "The Adoption of Job Rotation: Testing the Theories," *ILR Review* 59, no. 4 (2006): 653–66.

7   R. J. Harmison, "Peak Performance in Sport: Identifying Ideal Performance States and Developing Athletes Psychological Skills," *Research and Practice* 37, no. 3 (2006): 233–43.

8 Joshua Robinson, Joshua *and* Cohen, Ben, The World's Greatest Coach Is Not Who You Think, Wall Street Journal, May 19, 2020, https://www.wsj.com/articles/the-worlds-greatest-coach-is-not-who-you-think-11589882400

9 James A. Afremow, *The Champion's Mind: How Great Athletes Think, Train, and Thrive* (Emmaus, PA: Rodale Books, 2013).

10 Lesley Jones and Gretchen Stuth, "The Uses of Mental Imagery in Athletics: Overview," *Applied and Preventive Psychology* 6, no. 2 (1997): 101–15.

Chapter 3

1 A. Maslow, *The Farther Reaches of Human Nature* (New York: Viking Press, 1971), 7.

2 Dan Buettner, *The Blue Zones*: *9 Lessons for Living Longer from the People Who've Lived the Longest*, 2nd ed. (Washington, DC: National Geographic, 2008).

3 A. M. Herskind, M. McGue, N. V. Holm, T. I. Sørensen, B. Harvald, and J. W. Vaupel, "The Heritability of Human Longevity: A Population-Based Study of 2872 Danish Twin Pairs Born 1870–1900," *Human Genetics* 97, no. 3 (March 1996): 319–23, https://doi.org/10.1007/BF02185763.

4 René Stauffer, *Roger Federer: The Biography* (n.p.: Polaris Publishing, 2021).

5 Peter H. Diamandis, "Longevity & Vitality—a Renaissance of Drugs and Genomics," June 21, 2020, https://www.diamandis.com/blog/longevity-drugs-and-genomics.

6 Ilima Loomis, "The Transformation of Olympian Dotsie Bausch," *OMD Blog*, October 16, 2019, https://omdfortheplanet.com/blog/olympic-cycling-athlete-plant-based-journey/.

7 Paul Kita and Temi Adebowale, "Here's What Tom Brady Eats Every Day, and on Game Day," Men's Health, January 22, 2021, https://www.menshealth.com/nutrition/a19535249/tom-brady-reveals-insane-diet-in-new-book/.

8 Runner's Tribe and Len Johnson, *Australian Marathon Stars: Interviews and Training Insights from the Top 10 All-Time Male and Female Aussie Marathoners* (n.p.: Runner's Tribe Books, 2017), Kindle.

9 John Underwood and Keara White, "Sleep and Recovery," Life of an Athlete, accessed February 3, 2022, https://www.wm.edu/offices/sportsmedicine/_documents/sleep-manual.

10 Sourya C., "Roger Federer Sleeps 12 Hours a Day, Which Is Helping His Longevity," last modified May 18, 2020, Sportskeeda, https://www.sportskeeda.com/tennis/news-roger-federer-sleeps-12-hours-a-day-which-is-helping-his-longevity.

11 Megan Michelson, "The Sleeping Habits of 5 Olympic Athletes—and How They Use Rest to Gain an Edge," Insider, February 6, 2016, https://www.businessinsider.com/the-sleeping-habits-of-olympic-athletes-2016-2.

12 Jeanie Lerche Davis, "Meditation Balances the Body's Systems," WebMD, reviewed March 1, 2006, https://www.webmd.com/balance/features/transcendental-meditation#1.

13 A compilation of articles published from this study can be found at "Publications," Harvard Second Generation Study, https://www.adultdevelopmentstudy.org/publications.

14 Robert Waldinger, "What Makes a Good Life? Lessons from the Longest Study on Happiness," TED, November 2015, https://www.ted.com/talks/robert_waldinger_what_makes_a_good_life_lessons_from_the_longest_study_on_happiness.

15 Lauren F. Friedman, "A Psychologist Reveals the Biggest Predictor of Happiness—and It's Not Money," Insider, September 6, 2015, https://www.businessinsider.com/how-to-know-you-are-happy-psychology-2015-9.

16 E. Berscheid, "The Human's Greatest Strength: Other Humans," in *A Psychology of Human Strengths: Fundamental Questions and Future Directions for a Positive Psychology*, ed. L. G. Aspinwall and U. M. Staudinger (n.p.: American Psychological Association, 2003), 37–47, https://doi.org/10.1037/10566-003.

17 N. A. Christakis and J. H. Fowler, "The Spread of Obesity in a Large Social Network over 32 Years," *New England Journal of Medicine* 357 (July 26, 2007): 370–79.

18 Brittany K. Jakubiak and Brooke C. Feeney, "Affectionate Touch to Promote Relational, Psychological, and Physical Well-Being in Adulthood: A Theoretical Model and Review of the Research," *Personality and Social Psychology Review* 21, no. 3 (2017): 228–52.

19 Tiffany M. Field, "The Magic of Your Touch," BottomLineInc, April 29, 2008, https://bottomlineinc.com/health/wellness/magic-touch.

Chapter 4

1 Tal Ben-Shahar, "Post-Traumatic Growth Lecture," Happiness Studies Academy, uploaded January 14, 2021, https://vimeo.com/500365913?mc_cid=c8b054cdc1&mc_eid=0841526f7c.

2 A. Keller, K. Litzelman, L. E. Wisk, T. Maddox, E. R. Cheng, P. D. Creswell, and W. P. Witt, "Does the Perception That Stress Affects Health Matter? The Association with Health and Mortality," *Health Psychology* 31, no. 5 (2012): 677–84, https://doi.org/10.1037/a0026743.

3 J. P. Jamieson, M. K. Nock, and W. B. Mendes, "Mind Over Matter: Reappraising Arousal Improves Cardiovascular and Cognitive Responses to Stress," *Journal of Experimental Psychology: General* 141, no. 3 (2012): 417–22, https://doi.org/10.1037/a0025719.

4 Kelly McGonigal, "How to Make Stress Your Friend," TED, June 2013, https://www.ted.com/talks/kelly_mcgonigal_how_to_make_stress_your_friend.

5 Jim Afremow, "Think and Live like a Gold Medalist," Psychology Today, January 3, 2012, https://www.psychologytoday.com/us/ blog/trust-the-talent/201201/think-and-live-gold-medalist.

6 Brené Brown, "The Power of Vulnerability," TED, June 2010, https://www.ted.com/talks/brene_brown_the_power_of_vulnerability/.

7 Kristin Neff, *Self-Compassion: The Proven Power of Being Kind to Yourself*, *William Morrow Paperbacks, New York,* 2011

8 "Natalie Du Toit," International Paralympic Committee, accessed February 3, 2022, https://www.paralympic.org/natalie-du-toit.

9 C. Conversano, A. Rotondo, E. Lensi, O. Della Vista, F. Arpone, and M. A. Reda, "Optimism and Its Impact on Mental and Physical Well-Being," *Clinical Practice and Epidemiology in Mental Health* 6 (May 14, 2010): 25–29.

10 Hayley Phelan, "What's All This About Journaling?," *New York Times*, October 25, 2018, https://www.nytimes.com/2018/10/25/style/journaling-benefits.html.

11 S. Lyubomirsky, L. Sousa, and R. Dickerhoof, "The Costs and Benefits of Writing, Talking, and Thinking about Life's Triumphs and Defeats," *Journal of Personality and Social Psychology* 90, no. 4 (April 2006): 692–708.

12 Chad M. Burton and Laura A. King, "The Health Benefits of Writing about Positive Experiences: The Role of Broadened Cognition," *Psychology & Health* 24, no. 8 (2009): 867–79.

13 "Simone Biles: From Teen Phenom to Best Gymnast in the World," *USA Today*, October 30, 2018, https://www.usatoday.com/picture-gallery/ sports/olympics/2018/10/26/simone-biles-teen-phenom-worlds-best-gymnast/1732916002/.

14 James H. Hull, Mike Loosemore, and Martin Schwellnus, "Respiratory Health in Athletes: Facing the COVID-19 Challenge," *Lancet Respiratory Medicine* 8, no. 6 (2020): 557–58, https://www.thelancet.com/pdfs/journals/lanres/PIIS2213-2600(20)30175-2.pdf.

15 Retta Race, "30-Year-Old Ryosuke Irie Eyes Paris 2024 If Tokyo Olympics Don't Happen," SwimSwam, August 30, 2020, https://swimswam.com/30-year-old-ryosuke-irie-eyes-paris-2024-if-tokyo-olympics-dont-happe/.

16 Lindsay Shoop, "Olympic Athlete: Five Tips to Keep You Physically, Mentally Sane during Isolation," *USA Today*, April 21, 2020, https://www.usatoday.com/story/opinion/voices/2020/04/21/olympic-athlete-five-tips-keep-you-physically-mentally-fit-isolation-column/5145369002/.

Chapter 5

1   Amy Cuddy, "Your Body Language May Shape Who You Are," TED, June 2012, https://www.ted.com/talks/amy_cuddy_your_body_language_may_shape_who_you_are.

2   Edwin Moses and Anne McElvoy, "How Do You Become a World-Class Athlete?," July 30, 2020, in *The Economist Asks*, podcast, 29:52, https://www.economist.com/podcasts/2020/07/30/how-do-you-become-a-world-class-athlete.

3   Nathaniel Branden, *The Six Pillars of Self-Esteem* (self-pub., 2011), Kindle.

4   B. L. Fredrickson, "The Role of Positive Emotions in Positive Psychology: The Broaden-and-Build Theory of Positive Emotions," *American Psychologist* 56, no. 3 (2001):218–26, https://doi.org/10.1037//0003-066x.56.3.218.

5   "Overcoming Hardship with Yusra Mardini," Airbnb, accessed February 3, 2022, https://www.airbnb.com.br/d/yusramardini.

Chapter 6

1   Jim Collins, "Genius of the And," accessed February 3, 2022, https://www.jimcollins.com/concepts/genius-of-the-and.html.

2   "The Science behind the Wim Hof Method," Wim Hof Method, accessed February 3, 2022, https://www.wimhofmethod.com/science.

3   "João Gonçalves—Forte e Poderoso," uploaded August 9, 2017, https://vimeo.com/229017215.

4   David Lain, "Getting Your Mental Picture," Putting It on the Line, July 25, 2019, http://puttingitontheline.com/archery/getting-your-mental-picture/.

5   J. A. Bargh, M. Chen, and L. Burrows, "Automaticity of Social Behavior: Direct Effects of Trait Construct and Stereotype Activation on Action," *Journal of Personality and Social Psychology* 71, no. 2 (1996): 230–44.

6   Langer, "Counterclockwise."

Chapter 7

1   Todd B. Kashdan, David J. Disabato, Fallon R. Goodman, and Patrick E. McKnight, "The Five-Dimensional Curiosity Scale Revised (5DCR): Briefer Subscales While Separating Overt and Covert Social Curiosity," *Personality and Individual Differences* 157 (2020), https://doi.org/10.1016/j.paid.2020.109836.

2   "Walter Isaacson: Leonardo da Vinci," Chicago Humanities Festival, accessed February 3, 2022, https://www.chicagohumanities.org/media/walter-isaacson-leonardo-da-vinci/.

3   Fernando Duarte, "Maya Gabeira: The Extreme Surfer Who Went Back to Tame a Monstrous Wave," BBC, September 24, 2020, https://www.bbc.com/sport/54283775.

4   Brené Brown, *Daring Greatly: How the Courage to Be Vulnerable Transforms the Way We Live, Love, Parent, and Lead* (New York: Avery, 2015).

5   "Strong Inside and Out with Allyson Felix," Airbnb, accessed February 3, 2022, https://www.airbnb.com.br/d/allysonfelix2.

6   "Sarah Thomas: Inspiring the Next Generation," NFL on ESPN, accessed February 3, 2022, https://www.facebook.com/watch/?v=246799550235119.

Chapter 8

1   Pelé, Facebook post, December 2, 2020, https://www.facebook.com/permalink.php?story_fbid=4063492610336494&id=372164252802700.

2   Hannah Schulze, "Loneliness: An Epidemic?," *Science in the News* (blog), Harvard University, April 16, 2018, https://sitn.hms.harvard.edu/flash/2018/loneliness-an-epidemic/.

3   J. Holt-Lunstad, T. F. Robles, and D. A. Sbarra, "Advancing Social Connection as a Public Health Priority in the United States," *American Psychologist* 72, no. 6 (September 2017): 517–30.

4   Selby Frame, "Julianne Holt-Lunstad Probes Loneliness, Social Connections," American Psychological Association, October 18, 2017, https://www.apa.org/members/content/holt-lunstad-loneliness-social-connections.

5   "QS World University Rankings by Subject 2021: Sports-Related Subjects," QS Top Universities, accessed February 3, 2022, https://www.topuniversities.com/university-rankings/university-subject-rankings/2021/sports-related-subjects.

6   Paul B. C. Morgan, David Fletcher, and Mustafa Sarkar, "Understanding Team Resilience in the World's Best Athletes: A Case Study of a Rugby Union World Cup Winning Team," *Psychology of Sport and Exercise* 16, no. 1 (2015): 91–100.

7   Beatriz Jiménez, "Casillas, sobre 'los Galácticos': 'No teníamos un equipo,'" Diario Madridista, December 12, 2020, https://okdiario.com/diariomadridista/real-madrid/casillas-sobre-galacticos-no-teniamos-equipo-84658/amp.

Chapter 9

1   Amy Edmondson, "Building a Psychologically Safe Workplace," TEDx Talks, May 5, 2014, https://www.youtube.com/watch?v=LhoLuui9gX8.

2   Maurice DeCastro, "7 Takeaways from Barack Obama's Latest Speech That Will Make You a Better Presenter," Business 2 Community, September 22, 2018, https://www.business2community.com/communications/7-takeaways-from-barack-obamas-latest-speech-that-will-make-you-a-better-presenter-02120238.

3   Equilibria (website), accessed February 3, 20202, https://www.equilibria.com/.

4   "GulliverNamedOverallBestSportsProgram(5A-1A)for19[th]Time," GulliverPrep, May 24, 2019, https://www.gulliverprep.org/gulliver-named-overall-best-sports-program-5a-1a-for-19th-time/

5   Carol Dweck, "Carol Dweck Revisits the 'Growth Mindset,'" EducationWeek, September 22, 2015, https://www.edweek.org/leadership/opinion-carol-dweck-revisits-the-growth-mindset/2015/09.

6   R. Rosenthal and L. Jacobson, "Pygmalion in the Classroom," *Urban Review* 3 (1968): 16–20.

Chapter 10

1   "Relive Four Olympic Games with Allyson Felix," Airbnb, accessed February 3, 2022, https://www.airbnb.com.br/d/allysonfelix.

2   Polly LaBarre and Alan M. Webber, "Fast Talk: The Innovation Conversation," Fast Company, June 30, 2001, https://www.fastcompany.com/43221/fast-talk-innovation-conversation.

3   John Gottman and Daniel Goleman, *Raising an Emotionally Intelligent Child* (New York: Simon & Schuster, 2011), Kindle.

4   Runner's Tribe and Len Johnson, *Australian Marathon Stars.*

Chapter 11

1   Douglas R. Conant, "The Power of Idealistic-Realism: How Great Leaders Inspire and Transform," *Harvard Business Review,* January 12, 2012, https://hbr.org/2012/01/the-power-of-idealistic-realis.

2   "Item 8: My Company's Mission or Purpose," Gallup, May 10, 1999, https://www.gallup.com/workplace/237554/item-company-mission-purpose.aspx.

3   A. Alimujiang, A. Wiensch, J. Boss, et al., "Association between Life Purpose and Mortality among US Adults Older Than 50 Years," *JAMA Network Open* 2, no. 5 (2019): e194270.

4   Buettner, *The Blue Zones.*

5   Tom Brady, "The Only Way Is Through," Players' Tribune, April 6, 2020, https://www.theplayerstribune.com/articles/tom-brady-the-only-way-is-through.

6   Tal Ben-Shahar, *Being Happy: You Don't Have to Be Perfect to Lead a Richer, Happier Life* (n.p.: Academia, 2018), Kindle.

7   Simidele Adeagbo, "Shifting the Narrative, Talks at Google, April 1, 2019, https://www.youtube.com/watch?v=ITZlWQzOJPQ.

8   "Our Story," Brenda Villa Foundation, accessed February 3, 2022, https://www.bvfdn.org/our-story.

9   "Metade dos jogadores no Brasil ganha só um salário mínimo: E isso não deve mudar," iG Esporte, September 11, 2019, https://esporte.ig.com.br/futebol/2019-09-11/metade-dos-jogadores-no-brasil-ganha-so-um-salario-minimo-e-isso-nao-deve-mudar.html.

Chapter 12

1   Online Etymology Dictionary, s.v. "patience," accessed February 3, 2022, https://www.etymonline.com/word/patience.

2   S. Lyubomirsky, L. King, and E. Diener, "The Benefits of Frequent Positive Affect: Does Happiness Lead to Success?," *Psychological Bulletin* 131, no. 6 (November 2005): 803–55.

3   "David Boudia: Valuing the Journey," *What Moves Me*, International Olympic Committee, accessed February 3, 2022, https://olympics.com/en/original-series/episode/david-boudia-valuing-the-journey.

4   Helen Keller, "Three Days to See," *Atlantic Monthly*, January 1933, https://www.afb.org/about-afb/history/helen-keller/books-essays-speeches/senses/three-days-see-published-atlantic.

5   R. A. Emmons and M. E. McCullough, "Counting Blessings versus Burdens: An Experimental Investigation of Gratitude and Subjective Well-Being in Daily Life," *Journal of Personality and Social Psychology* 84, no. 2 (2003): 377–89.

6   Hadassah Littman-Ovadia and Dina Nir, "Looking Forward to Tomorrow: The Buffering Effect of a Daily Optimism Intervention," *Journal of Positive Psychology* 9, no. 2 (2014): 122–36, https://doi.org/10.1080/17439760.2013.853202.

7   "The 100 Best Companies to Work For," *Fortune*, accessed February 3, 2022, https://fortune.com/best-companies/2017/google.

8   Sophia Breene and Shana Lebowitz, "Why Are Google Employees So Damn Happy?," Greatist, May 28, 2013, https://greatist.com/happiness/healthy-companies-google#1.

9   "Samir Ait Said: Finding Strength in Pain," *What Moves Me*, International Olympic Committee, accessed February 3, 2022, https://olympics.com/en/original-series/episode/samir-ait-said-finding-strength-in-pain.

10   H. Benson and M. D. Epstein, "The Placebo Effect: A Neglected Asset in the Care of Patients," *JAMA* 232, no. 12 (1975): 1225–27, https://doi.org/10.1001/jama.1975.03250120013012.

Conclusion

1   Nirmita Panchal, Rabah Kamal, Cynthia Cox, and Rachel Garfield, "The Implications of COVID-19 for Mental Health and Substance Use," KFF, February 10, 2021, https://www.kff.org/coronavirus-covid-19/issue-brief/the-implications-of-covid-19-for-mental-health-and-substance-use/.

2   Chaomei Chen, "On the Shoulders of Giants," in *Mapping Scientific Frontiers: The Quest for Knowledge Visualization* (London: Springer, 2003), 135–66, https://link.springer.com/chapter/10.1007/978-1-4471-0051-5_5.

INDEX

F

failure, learning to fail or failing to learn, 160–163
fair play, 261
family life, focus on, 62
fear, listening to, 237
Federazione Nazionale di Nuoto, 18
Federer, Roger, 47, 48, 57, 122, 123
feedback, 12–13, 24, 74, 101, 105, 108, 134, 186, 216
Feeney, Brooke, 62
Felix, Allyson, 157–159, 229–231, 333
Fernández, Iván, 261, 336
Field, Tiffany, 62, 63
fight-or-flight mode, 122
Figo, Luis, 187
Filho, João Gonçalves, 70
Fiske, Susan, 100
fixed mindset, 5, 214
Flamingo (Rio de Janeiro), xxiv
flow, use of term, 107
focus
    leader's types of, 210–211
    where to focus our gaze, 280–282
foundation
    conclusions about, 66
    as dimension of WeTeam method, xxxiii, 1–21, 293
    elements of, xxxv. *See also* consistent practice; healthy lifestyle; network of support
Frankl, Viktor, xxx–xxxi, 69, 245
Fredrickson, Barbara, 110–111
freedom, to make most of here and now, 256–258
friendships, as forged from sport, 174–177
Froch, Carl, 43
fulfilling life, aspects of, 275–277, 278, 283

G

Gabeira, Maya, 156–157, 338
Gable, Shelly, 217–218
Gallup Organization, research on best place to work, 250–251
Gallwey, Timothy, 26
The Game Changers (film), 50
Gandhi, Mahatma, 228
Gardner, Howard, 8–9
generosity, benefits of, 280
George Washington University, research on young athletes' motivation, 4
Gibran, Khalil, 180
Gloster, Hugh, 108
goals, universal goals, 273
Gol de Letra foundation, 261–262, 267
Goleman, Daniel, 210–211
Gómez, Jesús Vidorreta, 13
Gonçalves, João, 130, 131, 211, 336–337
"good" hormones, 8
Google, organizational culture of, 283
Gottman, John, 183, 237
Grael, Lars, 249
Grael, Martine, 77, 78, 104–105, 125–126, 128–129, 135, 187, 200, 249–250, 327
Grael, Torben, 249
gratitude, effects of, 281–282
Greca, Rafael, **312**
Greenleaf, Robert, 280
grief, facing of, 81–82
growth mentality, 5–6
Guilheiro, Leandro, 79, 123, 131–132, 150, 153, 211, 240, 256, 325
Gulliver Schools
    awards of, 212–213
    sport competitions at, 5

H

habit, power of, 27

haka, 98

Hamilton, Lewis, 50

Happier: Learn the Secrets of Daily Joy and Lasting Fulfillment (Ben-Shahar), 256

happiness
  as contagious, 297
  described, xxx
  as element of meaning and choices, xxxv, 271–291, 293
  and interdependence, 181
  meaning of, 273–274
  paradox in search of, 275–277
  permission to be happy, 110–111
  science of, 279–280

Happiness Studies Academy, xxx, xxxi, 25

Harrison, Robert J., 34

Harvard University
  research on people's views of stress, 74–75
  study of adulthood, 61

healthy eating, secrets of, 49–51

healthy lifestyle, as element of foundation, xxxv, 43–65, 293

Hee, Dana, 37, 334

Heifetz, Ronald, 238

here and now, freedom to make most of, 256–258

High Flyers: Developing the Next Generation of Leaders (McCall), 240

The High Impact Leader: Moments Matter in Accelerating Authentic Leadership Development (Avolio and Luthans), 217

Hof, Wim (Iceman), 128, 232

Holt-Lunstad, Julianne, 179

Hooke, Robert, 300

hope, and expectation, 287–289

hormones, "good" ones, 8

How Full Is Your Bucket? Positive Strategies for Life and Work (Clifton and Rath), 283

Howard, Jane, 1

Hubbart, Elber, 143

Huertas, Marcelinho, 4, 13, 14–15, 24, 48, 50, 85, 124, 206, 214, 326

Human Performance Institute, 121

Human Performance Project, 55

humanistic psychology, 45, 121

The Human's Greatest Strength: Other Humans (Berscheid), 61

humble inquiry, art of, 200–203

Humble Inquiry: The Gentle Art of Asking Instead of Telling (Schein), 201

Hydra, 72

I

il Settebello, 2

Ilovetowatchyouplay.com, 7

improvement, hunger to keep improving, 163–165

individual, as level of knowledge, 45

individual truth, defined, 45

injury, recovery from, 77–79

inner energy
  conclusions about, 140
  as dimension of WeTeam method, xxxiii, xxxiv, 67–140, 293
  elements of, xxxv, 293. *See also* adversity, dealing with; re-energizing routines; self-confidence

inner focus, 210–211

Inner Game series of books, 26

intelligence
  emotional intelligence, 200, 210–211, 237
  types of, 8–9

9781663233677